The Voice of the Trobairitz

UNIVERSITY OF PENNSYLVANIA PRESS
MIDDLE AGES SERIES
Edited by EDWARD PETERS
Henry Charles Lea Professor of Medieval History
University of Pennsylvania
A complete listing of the books in this series appears at the back of this volume

The Voice of the Trobairitz

Perspectives on the Women Troubadours

Edited by WILLIAM D. PADEN

upp

UNIVERSITY OF PENNSYLVANIA PRESS
Philadelphia

PC
3308
.V65
1989

Printed in the United States of America

Library of Congress Cataloging-in-Publication Data

The Voice of the trobairitz : perspectives on the women troubadours /
    edited by William D. Paden.
      p.   cm. — (University of Pennsylvania Press Middle Ages
    series)
    Bibliography: p.
    Includes index.
    ISBN 0-8122-8167-5
    1. Provençal poetry—Women authors—History and criticism.
2. Women and literature—France, Southern—History.   3. Troubadours.
I. Paden, William D. (William Doremus), 1941–   . II. Series.
PC3308.V65   1989
849'.1009'9287—dc20
                                                        89-4920
                                                           CIP

Design: Adrianne Onderdonk Dudden

Contents

Introduction

> *But what I find deplorable, I continued, looking about the book-shelves again, is that nothing is known about women before the eighteenth century. I have no model in my mind to turn this way and that. . . .*
>
> Virginia Woolf, 1929

Since Virginia Woolf wrote *A Room of One's Own,* we have learned a great deal about women in the Middle Ages. We know more about their legal status, about their situation in the family, about their writings. We know that in the twelfth and thirteenth centuries women did not have a room of their own, but then neither did men; although the castles of the nobility were spacious, not even the lords enjoyed privacy, and the scriptoria in nunneries and monasteries were public like all other inhabited spaces. We have learned most about women in areas that are well documented and consequently well studied, areas such as England, northern France, and Italy. Although we know less about southern France, we have learned that this region differed from adjacent ones in significant respects, such as feudalism and urbanization. The real life of medieval women in the south of France remains difficult for us to recapture, but we have made a start with a number of soundly based regional studies. Our growing historical knowledge sheds light on the society which produced the poetry of the trobairitz.

Did women have a Renaissance? The question bears directly on medieval women because the concept of the Middle Ages was invented by men during the Renaissance and the Reformation. Men of the Renaissance rediscovered the inspiration of classical antiquity; men of the Reformation rediscovered the truth of Christ; both movements discovered the period intervening between their present time and their newly appreciated sources—the *medium aevum,* which was consequently destined to neglect and low esteem by its inventors.[1] The traditional doctrine that Renaissance women enjoyed greater individual freedom than their medieval predecessors, a doctrine expressed by Jacob Burckhardt in his classic *Civilization of the Renaissance in Italy*,[2] merely transcribes the self-esteem of the Renaissance thinkers who invented the Middle Ages. Accordingly, the doctrine must be questioned by historians whose view of the Renaissance has become more detached. If we should conclude that women did not have a Renaissance, then they cannot have had a Middle Age in anything like the usual meaning of the term. A case can be made that the tripartite structure of Antiquity, the Middle Ages, and the Renaissance, undoubtedly based upon male experience, does not correspond to the historical experience of women.

Joan Kelly, who first raised the question, answered it in the negative. Basing her study on the contrast between medieval France in the twelfth and thirteenth centuries and Renaissance Italy in the fourteenth through sixteenth centuries, she argued that "women as a group, especially among the classes that dominated Italian urban life, experienced a contraction of social and personal options," "a new repression of the noblewoman's affective experience" (20, 22). Focusing on courtly love as expressed in Occitan lyric, in the Latin treatise *De Amore* by Andreas Capellanus, and in the French romances, Kelly stressed that the metaphorical vassalage of the lover signified service and fidelity, not domination, and that the lady entered a relation of mutuality, not subordination. Kelly pointed out the partial harmony between courtly love and Christianity, which elevated passionate love by purging it of sexuality, although she did not take seriously the claim that courtly love was asexual as well. She further argued that courtly love supported the male-dominated social order of feudalism, despite the conflict between sexual liberation in courtly love and the patriarchal demand for female chastity, because it benefited men as courtly lovers while enabling them to inherit fiefs through their wives. In Renaissance Italy, on the other hand, women were placed under the male cultural authority of tutors who espoused "classical culture, with all its patriarchal and misogynous bias" (35). The courtly lover became a poet-scholar who worshiped the memory of a beloved preferably long dead, as Dante mourned for Beatrice, Petrarch for Laura, and Vittoria Colonna for her husband. If a living woman loved, she must love her husband and him alone.

In a response to Kelly, David Herlihy expanded the discussion to embrace history from the early Middle Ages through the Renaissance.

> By many social indicators—access to property, power or knowledge—the
> position of women deteriorated across the long centuries of the Middle Ages.

Women in fact fared better in barbarian Europe of the sixth or seventh centuries than they did in the cultured Europe of the fifteenth or sixteenth. (1)

Herlihy supports this view with a study of Christian saints from the earliest times to 1500. Of the more than three thousand saints, the greatest number lived during the earliest periods; but there was a resurgence that began around the millennium, peaked during the "long thirteenth century" (A. D. 1151–1347), and declined to a new low after that. Overall, the ratio of male saints to female is about five to one. This ratio peaked in an era of startling patriarchy among the blessed, 1000–1150, when there were more than twelve male saints to one female saint; then it dipped precipitously to less than four in 1151–1347, and continued down to less than three in 1348–1500. Furthermore, Herlihy's calculation of what he calls "density," or the number of saints divided by the number of years in the period, shows that women were more likely to become saints during the "long thirteenth century" than later, and that they were about three times more likely to be canonized than they had been in preceding periods since 750. Although Herlihy does not himself emphasize this high point in the feminine achievement of beatitude, we may observe in anticipation of our later discussion that it corresponds to the period of the trobairitz.

Turning to women and the family, Herlihy points out that the high frequency of female saints in the early middle ages corresponds to a privileged status in earthly society. From around the millennium on, this status suffered by the introduction of a new patrilineal kinship system. The noble family was newly understood as a descent group constituted of fathers and sons, and "daughters lost their traditional claim to an equal share with their brothers in their parents' property" (13). At the same time the Gregorian reform imposed stricter ethical standards on the nobility, and "monogamy became established as the unquestioned rule of western marriage" (14). "By most social indicators, women, especially elite women, were losing status, power, and visibility as the Middle Ages progressed" (15). Herlihy finds one area of exception to this generality in what he calls "the charismatic sector." He concludes his argument as follows:

Catherine of Siena, Joan of Arc, and many other charismatic women of the epoch were individualists in the full meaning of the word, trusting in their interior voices, critical of the male-dominated establishment and the manner it was leading society. Charismatic women appear with extraordinary frequency in the late-medieval world. In at least one sector of social and cultural life, women had a Renaissance. (16)

Despite their numbers, however, if charismatics were the only women who had a Renaissance, the traditional periodization of Western culture seems in need of further reconsideration.

The time of immediate concern in this book, the twelfth and thirteenth centuries, was one of social and economic expansion throughout western Europe. The demographic surge that provided the impetus for this expansion was never observed directly, but chroniclers recorded such side effects as more drastic famines, heavier traffic on roadways, and renewed construction of churches, many of which stand today. The growth in population was possible because of improved nutrition, which resulted from better techniques of cultivation, especially cultivation of legumes such as the humble field pea (White 76). Perhaps it reflected cyclical changes in the climate, which was relatively cold after the fall of Rome but grew warmer from the eighth through the thirteenth centuries before cooling in the fourteenth century, warming once more around 1400–1550, and then plunging into the "little ice age" which lasted from about 1550 to 1850 (Alexandre, Brochier). Around 1200, Languedoc was as densely populated as the region of Paris or Flanders; the countryside of Languedoc, especially in comparison with that of Gascony to the west, threatened to pass the threshold of rural overpopulation (Higounet).

The situation of women during this period was influenced by conflicting ideologies. In the eyes of the church, women were equal to men with respect to grace and salvation, but unequal in the stories of creation and original sin (Shahar 22). Eve had been created from Adam's rib; as Peter Lombard explained, "God did not make woman from Adam's head, for she was not intended to be his ruler, nor from his feet, for she was not intended to be his slave, but from his side, for she was intended to be his companion and his friend" (Power 34). Eve's role in the Fall caused the sorrow of mankind, but salvation was achieved through Mary. The fall of *Eva* was reversed in the "*Ave,*" the "Hail, Mary" of the Annunciation. In the vivid language of the misogynous tradition, woman was called, among other unflattering epithets, a sack of dung, but a more generous spirit such as Saint Bernard of Clairvaux, who felt the necessity for a principle of nonviolence to compensate for the daily cruelty of the world, exalted femininity in worship of the Virgin. In an encounter with Eleanor of Aquitaine in 1144, Bernard of Clairvaux promised that after seven years of childless union the queen would bear a child by her husband, Louis VII of France, if she would exert her wifely influence upon the king in favor of peace. Louis learned of this exchange, and peace was achieved. When Louis demanded that Bernard make good his promise, the abbot repeated his words. Within the year Eleanor gave birth to a daughter, and immediately sent to thank the man of God (Leclercq 65–67). The esteem for women expressed by Saint Bernard in various writings remained exceptional among his general concerns, which he naturally defined, monk that he was, in a male perspective. As the Benedictine scholar and admirer of Saint Bernard, Jean Leclercq puts it (22), when Bernard addressed the monks of Clairvaux as their abbot he was no more misogynous than the Lord.

With the gradual entry of vernacular languages into cultural discourse, secular society began to express a view of life which showed considerable independence of church teaching. The role of women in vernacular poetry has been the focus of discussion of "courtly love," a term and concept created by Gaston Paris in 1883. In a study of a French romance by Chrétien de Troyes, *Le Chevalier de la Charrette*, Paris adapted the expression *amour courtois* from scattered medieval occurrences and launched it on its prestigious twentieth-century career (see Boase). According to this view, the lady loved by the troubadour was the wife of the troubadour's lord, who, in the absence of her husband on campaign or crusade, attracted a swarm of admirers to her castle. The passion that she inspired in them is often said to have been platonic. The supposed invention of courtly love in the twelfth century has been considered an epoch-making event in the history of civilization, an event that formed a watershed between uncourtly Antiquity and modern times.[3]

The courtly thesis dominated discussion for many years, but it eventually provoked an antithesis in the form of revisionist doubts about specific elements of the doctrine. The weakest point was the claim that courtly passion was intrinsically chaste. This claim has been criticized in elaborate detail by Moshé Lazar, who distinguished among the *fin'amors* of the troubadours, passionate love as in the romance of Tristan and Isolde, courtly love within marriage as in romances by Chrétien de Troyes other than *Le Chevalier de la Charrette*, and the more general notion of courtliness or *cortezia*. While it is true that the eroticism of troubadour expression rarely becomes explicit since the troubadours wove their sensuality into artful ambiguities (Paden, "*Utrum copularentur*"), we no longer feel able to disregard its pervasive overtones. A second point of contention is the social standing of the troubadour's lady, which becomes explicit in very few of the texts (Paden et al., "The Troubadour's Lady"). If we bring to the texts the assumption that medieval women were compelled to choose between marriage and the nunnery—an assumption that can be questioned on the basis of a study such as the one by Verdon (see below)—it still remains possible that the troubadours sang of women who were not yet married, or of marriageable widows. It is not implausible that the troubadours sang of an ideal type, a poetic fiction that could be personified as a woman of flesh and bone whether she was married or not. But the texts of the troubadours do not identify the lady, just as they rarely make explicit the nature of the troubadour's feeling toward her. The songs make a spectacle of the speaker, not of his beloved. Finally, Peter Dronke has argued that courtly love, far from an invention of the twelfth century, is a universal tendency, a *secteur du coeur humain* that has found expression independently in literatures as widely scattered as those of ancient Egypt and medieval Georgia as well as in medieval Latin and the vernaculars (*Medieval Latin*). Like the language of the church, troubadour discourse tells us less than has sometimes been supposed about the condition of real medieval women.

Marriage was regarded by neither church nor nobility as an end in itself, much less as a means for the fulfillment of romantic love. For Saint Paul, marriage was better than fornication but less worthy than virginity; it became institutionalized within the church as a sacrament as late as the eighth century, and the role of the church in solemnizing union gained general acceptance as late as the twelfth century (Duby). For the nobility, marriage was a means by which great houses strengthened their social and political alliances. The church insisted, against the wishes of authoritarian noble fathers, that marriage required the consent of bride and groom (*consensus facit nuptias,* Shahar 83), but in reality this principle was often strained because young women were dependent upon their families for their dowry.

Within marriage, sexuality was never recognized by the church as an end in itself but as a means to procreation; to make love for the sake of pleasure with one's spouse was considered as sinful as it would have been to make love with someone else. Various means of contraception were known from antiquity, at least to the celibate authors of medical treatises, but seem to have been little practiced by married couples before the early fourteenth century; at that time, however, authors in England, Normandy, Savoy, and Spain complained of increased usage of *coitus interrup-*

tus, the sin of Onan—a complaint which was perhaps echoed by Dante in *Paradiso.*[4] Nor was abortion frequently employed. Partly for these reasons, the rate of illegitimate birth was high. Although useful instructions for midwives circulated in the thirteenth century, "including much about manual rectification of incorrect presentation of the foetus" (Biller 14), the circumstances of childbirth must have frequently been such as to strike a modern parent with horror. The mortality rate of newborn children has been estimated as "something perhaps in the order of one or even two in three" (McLaughlin 111); it may have been the loss of so many infants that caused the surprising lack of maternal or paternal tenderness toward children in the few sources where, with our twentieth-century outlook, we might expect to find it. Some noble families became quite large. Eleanor of Aquitaine, after having two daughters in fifteen years of marriage to Louis VII of France, presented her second husband, Henry Plantagenet (Henry II of England), with eight children in fourteen years, five boys and three girls. When Eleanor died at about the age of eighty-two (the year of her birth is uncertain), she had outlived both her husbands, four of her five sons, and four of her five daughters. Her experience of repeated bereavement must not have been extraordinary.

Our most direct access to the experience of medieval women lies in their own writings. They wrote more and were better educated than has sometimes been thought. Among the nobility, male literacy was largely restricted to the eldest son of the king, who could be expected to inherit the divine office of his father, and younger sons of kings or of other noblemen who were destined for the clergy. Eldest sons who became squires and then knights remained largely illiterate. The daughters of the nobility, on the other hand, were trained to read the psalter in Latin, and enjoyed a higher level of literacy than their brothers (Grundmann). Women were educated at home by private tutors, in nunneries, or in schools run by parish priests; in the thirteenth century, when the development of universities (which women did not attend) required a relatively organized preparation for boys, the education of women suffered (Shahar 157–59). Dronke and Wilson recently surveyed the writings of medieval women from early times to late, and found much to ponder. Dronke characterized the women's writings he analyzed as follows:

> The women's motivation for writing at all . . . seems rarely to be predominantly literary; it is often more urgently serious than is common among men writers; it is a response springing from inner needs, more than from an

artistic, or didactic, inclination. There is, more often than in men's writing, a lack of apriorism, of predetermined postures: again and again we encounter attempts to cope with human problems in their singularity—not imposing rules or categories from without, but seeking solutions that are apt and truthful existentially. Hence the women whose texts are treated here show excellingly a quality (literary, but also "metaliterary") of immediacy: they look at themselves more concretely and more searchingly than many of the highly accomplished men writers who were their contemporaries. This immediacy can lend women's writing qualities beside which all technical flawlessness is pallid.[5]

This assessment is echoed in Perkal-Balinsky's study of the trobairitz' poems in dialogue with troubadours: she finds a more personal quality in the women, a quality which she explains as a result of their "willingness to deviate from accepted social behavior, or perhaps the rules of the game, in an effort to attain the intimate pleasures in a love relationship" (46).

To conclude this survey of recent work on the general situation of medieval women, we may turn to a study by Sharon Farmer. She accepts the consensus that the status of women evolved from privilege to dependency:

> The decline in the status of women was largely due to the emergence, towards the middle of the eleventh century, of the system of primogeniture, which served to protect the power and wealth of the nobility by consolidating landed property. Daughters and younger sons were excluded from patrimonial inheritances, and the dowry, formerly the woman's to dispose of as she wished, fell increasingly under the husband's control. Moreover, noble marriage was a matter of strategy, in which women served as pawns—or, as anthropologists would say, media of exchange—in the negotiation of alliances between lineage groups. In normal circumstances, men dominated women. Only widows, or wives whose husbands were away on crusade, retained a measure of independence and influence.[6]

Despite this overall decline, however, Farmer claims that "the position of women was more complex" than historians have realized (520). She studies a countercurrent among scholastic and monastic authors who "began to recognize the moral and spiritual potential of women's persuasion" exercised upon their husbands. We have seen an early example of such wifely persuasion in the exchange between Eleanor of Aquitaine and Saint Bernard. The authors studied by Farmer "called attention to the fact that wives could now take certain independent economic actions which benefited both their husbands and the church" (521).

> Emphasis on the spiritual influence of wives seems to have reemerged in scholastic circles during the course of the twelfth century, and it intensified in the final years of that century. It was accompanied, moreover, by portrayals of women who exercised independent economic influence rather than acting through their husbands. (526)

The chronology of this development returns us once more to the trobairitz.

In the south of France women could inherit fiefs, as Eleanor inherited Aquitaine. Ermengarde of Narbonne ruled the lands she inherited from her father for more than half a century. Marie of Montpellier inherited the city of her birth—in the absence of a male heir, that is, an heir of the better sex (*melior sexus*), as it had been identified in an earlier declaration of law by Louis VII. Marie's father died in 1204, when she was about twenty-two years old, and she was recognized for several years as lord of the city. In principle, however, a husband controlled the inheritance of his wife, so that Pedro of Aragon, Marie's third husband, was able to compel her against her will to assign her own fief as her daughter's dowry, as Marie attested under duress (Switten).

Mundy's study of testaments and marriage contracts in Toulouse between 1150 and the 1280s sheds light on the lives of women in all social classes. Mundy shows that women often married older men, and outlived their husbands in a ratio of five cases out of six. Men bequeathed real estate to their sons, but almost always money to their daughters because a woman was excluded from inheritance of real property once she had been provided with a dowry. This proviso of customary law stimulated men to endow their daughters in order to preserve the patrimony intact. The marriage contract required two sums of money, the bride's dowry, or *dos,* and the groom's brideprice, or *dotalicium,* usually about one-third as large. Despite the principle of canon law that consent makes marriage, women were sometimes forced to accept men they did not wish to marry in order to satisfy their family and to gain a dowry; likewise, young men could be forced to satisfy their fathers in order to get the *dotalicium*—but for them the price was not as high. Upon the death of either spouse the survivor received both *dos* and *dotalicium.* The system was designed to protect widows, and in fact enabled those in the elite to live independently; but one-third to one-half of the widows in the documents were obliged to eke out their income by working or by depending on their children. Many women sought to become the heirs or the co-heirs of their husbands, despite the general pattern of real inheritance in the male line. Some husbands made special provision for their wives in their wills; two husbands made arrangements against the eventuality that their widows might remarry and wish to free themselves of their children.

Verdon studied a cartulary, a collection of legal acts, that was compiled by the bishopric of Limoges during the thirteenth century. He found forty acts by women acting alone or with their children. Thirteen are acts of homage or other business by individual women who are positively identified as unmarried, or whom Verdon presumes to have been unmarried because there is no mention of a husband. Despite their small number, these acts suggest that women could play an economic role before marriage, if they married at all. Such evidence contradicts the assumption voiced by other scholars that women of the nobility faced the sole alternatives of marriage or life as a nun. The unmarried women who are mentioned range in social class from the viscountess of Comborn, who does homage to the bishop for the castle and the castellany of Comborn with its dependencies, to La Guibort (in French Guibourc), who does homage for four *setiers* (48 bushels) of rye, presumably an annual income. Since, in principle, husbands administered the property of their wives, it is surprising that three married women executed deeds of homage without their husbands. Eight widows acted without their children, showing that they had in fact inherited real property after having received their dowries, perhaps because there were no surviving male heirs. In addition to their dowries, women might receive donations from their husbands at the time of marriage or later, donations that were called *oscla* (in classical Latin *oscula*, "kisses"). Women also had the right to bequeath fiefs to their sons. Wives had sufficient independence within marriage to appear in acts together with their kinsmen, usually their brothers, more often than with their husbands. On the other hand, they appeared with their husbands to do homage for fiefs inherited by the women. Husbands often did homage for goods inherited by their wives.

Verdon shows clearly that males sought to marry above their social status. (For Europe in general this was possible because fathers sought to marry off all their daughters but only their eldest sons; hence the marriageable sons had their pick of the daughters, and the unlucky daughters were destined for the nunnery.) In Limoges it was exceptional for the daughter of a knight (*dominus*) to marry a knight, according to the acts of the cartulary. Rather, the daughters of knights often married squires (*domicelli*); occasionally the daughters of squires did the same. Several clerics are identified as married (*clerici uxorati*), one of them to the daughter of a squire.

These synchronic analyses are supplemented by diachronic studies. The increasing subjection of women to men has been documented for Languedoc in general by Duhamel-Amado and for Béziers in particular by Gramain-Derruau. Most impressive is Aurell i Cardona's study of the deterioration in the status of aristocratic women in Provence from the tenth century to the thirteenth. As he shows, a long process led the aristocratic woman from an originally privileged situation to the legal status of a minor. At the beginning, the high aristocracy counted some twenty families, a vast clan clustered around the count, who would strengthen his alliances with other families by marrying his daughters to their sons. In this system of hypergamy (that is, in which the wife was superior to her husband), women participated in the legal commitments of their husbands by adding their seals immediately after the men's. The strong position of women deteriorated somewhat during the period from 1030 to 1180 as the clan structure yielded to the patrilinear system. The dowries granted daughters became less valuable than they had been, and were consistently smaller than the inheritances of sons.

The period from 1180 to 1230 witnessed a renaissance in the situation of women, who briefly regained the rights they had enjoyed in the tenth century. Cartularies from the city of Arles, in particular, provide documentation on this "parenthèse dorée," or golden interlude, as Aurell i Cardona calls it. He illustrates this development with the case of Guilhema Garcin, the daughter and wife of wealthy townsmen. When her husband made out his last will in 1172 it was she who received most of his property—not merely in usufruct (to enjoy during her lifetime) but to dispose of as she chose. Guilhema also inherited lands in the Camargue from her father. As a widow she administered her fortune in complete liberty. Nor is her case exceptional: among twelfth-century acts in one cartulary from Arles, 146 were executed by men acting alone, and 33 by women acting alone. Around 1200, women acted as guardians of their descendants, received and gave homage for their fiefs, were named executrices of wills, and received inheritances equal to those of their brothers. In their wills they disposed of their goods as they wished. Some women left property to their husbands in usufruct, as husbands usually did to their wives, specifying what would become of the legacy upon the death of the first beneficiary.

From 1230 on, noblewomen in Provence lost all the prerogatives they had enjoyed a few decades earlier. Under the impact of Roman law they lost all judicial function, and they lost economic power through the disappearance of the brideprice formerly paid by the husband or his family, the exclusion of women from inheritance once they received their dowry, and their loss of any power of decision over the goods of the married couple. The husband gained the powers of the Roman *pater-familias*. At Marseilles, the minority of children lasted until the age of twenty-five, and daughters of whatever age were treated as though they were minors. Their consent was not required for marriage, despite the consensual principle of canon law. Women no longer served as witnesses to legal acts. The adoption of Roman law served the interests of the count, who was able to strengthen his rights at the expense of the no-bility, while incidentally restricting the rights of women. At the same time, marriages were increasingly contracted in a relation of hypogamy, that is, one in which the woman was the social inferior of the man; her access to a higher rank was made possible by the dowry paid by her family. Aurell i Cardona regards the shift from hypergamy to hypogamy as the fundamental explanation for the deterioration in the status of aris-tocratic women.

The subject of women's names in the Midi has been discussed by several of these scholars. Aurell i Cardona observed that as a corollary to the establishment of patrilineal kin structure, patronyms replaced moth-er's names in the identification of individuals. He explains the earlier use of matronyms, which was typical of acts of the tenth century, as a means to disambiguate among males with the same name, observing that the variety of women's names far surpassed that of men's: "Here as else-where, the world of women shows more imagination, even fantasy, in the choice of names" (15). (Aurell i Cardona does not discuss who chose the names of daughters—perhaps their mothers?—or the names of sons.) Verdon studied the first names of noblewomen in the cartulary of Limoges in contrast with those of women whose social status is not men-tioned, and concluded that the names of the noblewomen show greater diversity. One name which he found frequently among both noble-women and others is Almos or Almuos, which is a form of the name of the trobairitz Almuc de Castelnou. In his study of charters from Tou-louse, Mundy found that women took the last name of their husbands, or, if the husband did not have a last name (as the convention of last names was still in the process of development), the name of his craft or business. The first names of women were more varied than those of men: among the married couples mentioned in Mundy's sources there are twenty-five different first names of men, and fifty-eight of women. The women's first names are more colorful, evoking distant countries, rank, or personal qualities. Among the trobairitz, Mundy's remark applies to Castelloza, whose name is quite rare, and suggests a meaning such as "Castle Lady" (see Paden et al., "The Poems of the *Trobairitz* Na Castelloza," 158–59).

The term "trobairitz" has not hitherto been naturalized in English. It combines the root of *trobar,* "to compose," with the suffix *-airitz,* expressing a feminine agent in contrast to masculine *-ador.* Thus *trobairitz* means "a woman who composes." *Trobairitz* and *trobador* correspond, as do other Occitan words such as *emperairitz* and *emperador* (from Latin *imperatrīcem* and *imperatōrem ,* "empress" and "emperor").[7] *Trobairitz* is very rare in medieval Occitan. It does not occur in lyric poetry, in the grammatical treatises, or in the biographies of the trobairitz or troubadours; it seems to be found only once, in the thirteenth-century romance *Flamenca.* The heroine of the romance becomes involved in a clandestine exchange of two-syllable messages with the knight who will become her lover; at one point, when her maid thinks of the perfect response, she congratulates her as a *bona trobairis,* a "good trobairitz."[8] (As the exchange continues to develop, it will eventually reproduce a passage from a *canso* by a twelfth-century troubadour.)[9] Despite the rarity of the term, however—which surpasses the rarity of the trobairitz—it fulfills a logical and useful function in contrast with the word "troubadour." English has assimilated "troubadour" in the literal sense since the early eighteenth century and in the figurative sense since the early nineteenth ("one who composes or sings verses or ballads . . . ").[10] Today's interest in women poets of all ages has created a need for "trobairitz" in English, a need which is felt particularly by the scholars who have contributed to this book. The word will be treated here as a naturalized English term.[11]

Among the trobairitz are three countesses: the Comtessa de Dia, perhaps named Beatritz; Garsenda, comtessa de Proensa; and Maria de Ventadorn, wife of Count Eble V. The first of these seems to have enjoyed her title by inheritance from her father (Monier); the other two, by marriage. Both of the trobairitz who have left more than a single song apiece, the Comtessa de Dia and Castelloza, refer in their songs to their husbands, and we have historical traces of the husbands of Almuc de Castelnou and Gaudairenca. On the other hand, since Alais and Iselda ask Carenza whether they should marry or become nuns, they must have been unmarried; and since the *vida* of Tibors makes no mention of a husband, she may have been unmarried as well. Shahar (166) assumes that any women who wrote during this period must *ipso facto* have been noble; Jeanroy (*Poésie lyrique* 1:314–15) arrived at the same conclusion regarding the trobairitz, reasoning that since they commanded the respect of the authors of the *vidas* and *razos,* they cannot have been *joglaresas,* female entertainers like the disreputable male *joglars.* The trobairitz we know represent the east and the center of the Midi, but not, for whatever reason, the regions lying to the west.[12]

The chronology of the trobairitz phenomenon is not easily grasped. It is uncertain whether a number of trobairitz are real or fictional; it is difficult to assign dates to several whose names we know; it is all the more difficult to date compositions that are anonymous. One may, however, generalize that the trobairitz seem to have been active from around 1170 to around 1260. We have no evidence of trobairitz during what may be called the first and second generations of the troubadour period (from 1100 on), or during the last generation (to 1300). In the Appendix to this Introduction the reader will find an argument, based on statistical evidence, that the chronology of the trobairitz is not merely a reflection of the chronology of the troubadours. There must be some reason or reasons why the trobairitz appeared in history later than their male counterparts and disappeared sooner.

We may speculate, then, as to what caused the trobairitz to enter the scene and to exit as they did. We have seen several historical movements that correspond more or less closely: the frequency of women saints during the "long thirteenth century" according to Herlihy; the emergence of the doctrine of wifely persuasion among male clerical writers late in the twelfth century according to Farmer; the "golden interlude" in Provence around 1180 to 1230 according to Aurell i Cardona. Aurell i Cardona alludes to the songs of the troubadours, "which reverse the relations of fidelity in favor of the lady," and which "reached their peak of popularity in the courts of the county" at this time. Geneviève Brunel-Lobrichon extends the conclusions of Aurell i Cardona to the trobairitz, reasoning that "for this brief period, the privileged status of the aristocratic woman in Provence must have been marked by *fin'amors* . . . , which allowed the magnificent and singular blossoming of trobairitz songs in which the superiority of the woman is expressed in another manner" (in this volume, 220). The applicability of Aurell i Cardona's conclusions to the trobairitz is limited, however, by the fact that only the Comtessa de Proensa and Tibors are known to have had associations with Provence.

Interestingly enough, several Occitan *albas*, or dawn-songs, present female protagonists who are passionately expressive.[13] Although some of these texts are difficult to date, Poe observed in a recent study that all the *albas* that can be dated were composed "from the late twelfth through mid-thirteenth centuries,"[14] that is, precisely during the period of trobairitz activity. Although the number of *albas* is too small to permit statistically meaningful conclusions, it is difficult to resist connecting the *albas* and the trobairitz as two contemporary aspects of an underlying, enhanced female expressiveness.

The history of the *pastorela,* or pastourelle (in French), in which the speaker narrates his encounter with a shepherdess and his attempt to seduce her, provides indirect support for this view. The prototype of the genre was composed by Marcabru (fl. 1130–49), and was imitated by Gui d'Ussel (fl. 1195–96) and Gavaudan (fl. 1195–1211); but production in Occitan was then interrupted until the series of *pastorelas* by Guiraut Riquier, written in 1260–82, and other late texts.[15] That is, we have no *pastorelas* from 1220 to 1260, which we have called Period IV (see the Appendix to this Introduction). After an initial overlap in the production of *pastorelas* and the activity of trobairitz during Periods II and III, the *pastorelas* cease to appear while the trobairitz continue; then in Period V the trobairitz apparently cease to write, and the *pastorelas* begin again. Although the historical process is more complicated than a simple alternation between composition of *pastorelas* and composition by trobairitz, one may speculate that there may have been a degree of tension between these two. Perhaps the feminist view of the French pastourelle recently proposed by Gravdal provides the key to understanding the role of the *pastorela* in this process.[16] The classical form of the genre is predicated upon the assumption that a man who happens to meet a shepherdess in a rustic setting will naturally attempt to seduce her, an assumption that may have seemed objectionable to women then as now, whether the seducer succeeds or fails. It is not implausible to relate the hiatus in production of Occitan *pastorelas* to persuasive disapproval by women. Perhaps the historical relation of the *pastorela* and the *alba* is essentially one of alternation, as the position of women in Occitan culture evolved through the golden interlude (corresponding to the *alba* and the tro-bairitz) between periods of deepening subjection (corresponding roughly to the *pastorela*).

If it is true that sociocultural changes as sweeping as those outlined here shook the Midi during the twelfth and thirteenth centuries, they can scarcely have left no trace at all in the poetry of the troubadours—even though any such traces have been obscured by the longstanding sup-position that for two centuries troubadour poetry remained essentially static. I shall conclude these speculations by sketching some such possible traces.

The degradation of women was amply expressed by Guilhem de Peitieus in his "law of *con*" and his other bawdy songs, while he also formulated the subtler antifeminism of courtly love in a song such as "Ab la dolchor del temps novel." The latter strategy was refined by Bernart de Ventadorn to the point of placing the lady on a pedestal and worship-ping her in narcissistic devotion to his own perfection. With Bertran de Born, however, one may perhaps claim to detect in at least some songs a new interest, and even dignity, accorded to women.[17] Such is the case, I believe, in Bertran's song of youth and age, "Belh m'es quan vey camjar lo senhoratge."[18] Within a framework of an introductory stanza and a *tornada,* Bertran reflects in successive stanzas on the figures of an old lady, a young lady, a young man, and an old man. As he rings the changes on his theme in relation to men, most of the virtues of the young are simply negated in the vices of the old: a young man is poor and pawns his prop-erty, an old man is rich and pawns nothing; a young man is extravagant in hospitality, an old man is stingy with his friends; a young man likes to flirt, an old man does not. The preceding stanzas on women, which of course serve to introduce those on men, move in the more positive (and counter-naturalistic) direction from old to young. An old lady has ugly skin; she has either no lover or two lovers, sometimes a lover of unwor-thy standing (*avols hom*) or a lover within her castle—all to her discredit. She may dabble in magic and talk too much. In contrast:

> Jov'es domna que sap honrar paratge,
> et es joves per bos fagz—quan los fa.
> Joves se te quan a adreg coratge
> e vas bon pretz avol mestier non a;
> jove se te quan guarda son cors belh
> et es joves dona quan be·s capdelh.
> Jove se te quan no·y cal devinar,
> qu'ab belh jovent se guart de mal estar.

[Young is a lady who knows how to honor nobility, and she is young from good deeds, when she does any. She stays young when she has a nimble heart, and does not use base schemes to gain good repute; she stays young when she keeps her body beautiful, and a lady is young when she behaves properly. She stays young when she doesn't care to gossip, when she avoids being cross with beautiful youth.]

Bertran praises the young lady for qualities of nobility, goodness, character, and temperament—as well as personal appearance—which seem more diverse and more independent of simple economic considerations than the criteria he applies to the advantage or disadvantage of men. In this song the woman's life may be felt to seem more attractive and interesting than the man's.

There is a passage in Peire Cardenal that is perhaps suggestive of hypergamy. The satirist depicts *las amairitz*, "amorous" or "licentious women," as defending themselves against criticism of their escapades with every kind of sly excuse:

Las amairitz, qui encolpar las vòl
Si razonon a for d'en Isengri:
L'una fai drut quar esta'n grant aujòl,
L'autra lo fai quar paubreira l'auci;
L'una a vieil marit e es tozeta,
L'autra es granz e a pauc garsi;
L'una non a sobrecot de brunéta,
L'autra n'a dos e fai lo atressi.

[If someone criticizes licentious women, they defend themselves in Sir Isengrim's style. One takes a lover because she has a great inheritance, the other does it because poverty kills her; one has an old husband though she is a girl, the other is large and has a little boy; one has no mantle of dark cloth, the other has two and does it all the same.]

Prop a guerra qui l'a en mieg son sòl,
Mas plus prop l'a qui l'a a son coissi.
Can lo maritz a la moiller fai dòl,
So es guerra peior que de vezi,
Qu'ieu en sai tal que, s'era part Toleta,
Non a moiller ni paren ni cozi
Que ja disses: que Dieu sai lo trameta.
Mas, can s'en vai, lo plus iratz s'en ri.[19]

[He has war close who has it on his land, but he has it closer yet who has it on his pillow. When a husband displeases his wife, that is war worse than with a neighbor; for I know a man who, if he were beyond Toledo, has no wife or kinsman or cousin who ever would say, "God send him here!" But when he leaves, the saddest one laughs.]

Peire is impartially critical of women in the first stanza and men in the second. Though only the *grant aujòl* ("a great inheritance") explicitly suggests higher standing on the part of the wife, it seems clear throughout the passage that these wives are under no husband's thumb—perhaps not only for generic reasons of satire, but because of evolving social reality.

With Guiraut Riquier the *pastorela* reenters Occitan, where it will also be cultivated by Cerveri de Girona, Paulet de Marseille, Guilhem d'Autpol, Gautier de Murs, Joan Esteve, and others. Between 1291 and 1295, there was written in Barcelona an *Ensenhamen de la donsela,* or "Instruction of a Young Girl," by the Catalan Amanieu de Sescars.[20] Amanieu says that once in the month of May a gracious maiden—who, as we learn later on, was no less than a marquise, *Na marqueza*[21]—begged him to advise her how to lead a good life, since she lacked good judgment ("no soy senada si cum mestier m'auria," vv. 82–83). Protesting that she was ten times wiser than he, the poet nevertheless produced an exact and detailed regimen. She must be an early riser, wash her face and hands, clean her nails, and brush her teeth. She must attend her lady as soon as she rises, but not before the head of the household (the *capdel*) is up, if he has slept with his wife.[22] In church she must not let her glance wander, if she can help it ("si gandir y podetz," v. 209), or make too much noise. After church she may have fun with her friends:

E si voletz bastir
solatz de iocx partitz,
no·ls fassatz descauzitz,
mas plazens e cortes. (vv. 230–33)

[And if you want to amuse yourself with *jocs partitz,* don't make them coarse, but pleasant and courteous.]

The *joc partit* is an Occitan genre, often synonymous with the *partimen,* in which two speakers take sides in a discussion of a point of amorous casuistry. It appears, then, that in the world of Amanieu de Sescars young women might be encouraged to become trobairitz, which makes it all the more puzzling that we have no record that any of them did so in this late period. Amanieu continues with advice on how a girl should talk to her admirers, and suggests topics suitable for *jocs partitz*. If she wishes to have an admirer, an *entendedor* (v. 345), she must not choose him for rank or wealth but for *pretz* and *dreg paratie* (merit and true nobility, vv. 349, 353). In closing, Amanieu sends his composition to his lord, the King of

Aragon, and to the noblemen of the court, asking them who, in their opinions, are the best *donas* and *donzelas,* so that his student may learn from their example.

Can we learn from the *ensenhamen* any reason why in its time the trobairitz had ceased to write? We could cite the authoritarian tone of the male preceptor (somewhat more authoritarian than the tone Amanieu takes in another *ensenhamen* to a squire), reinforced as it is by the family authority of the *capdel* and the political authority of the king. If *Na marqueza* and others like her did amuse themselves with *jocs partitz,* perhaps their poems were judged unworthy of parchment; or possibly Amanieu's advice was old-fashioned, and the *joc partit* was a parlor game no longer enjoyed by women. If we can, indeed, take this text of Catalan provenance as evidence for Occitan culture at all, then we can easily imagine how the oppressive structure of hypogamy may have stilled the voice of the trobairitz.

In the essays that follow, twelve American and European scholars view the trobairitz in perspectives ranging from philological to Bakhtinian, Derridean to feminist. Four of the essays have been translated for this volume. All of them are published here for the first time.

The first two essays survey the corpus that may be attributed to the trobairitz. François Zufferey finds forty-three texts, including all the poems in dialogue between a man and a woman, even those who may have been fictitious. He does not, however, include the *canso* attributed to Beatritz de Romans because for him it seems to speak with the voice of a man. Zufferey's census includes eleven *cansos,* three *sirventes,* sixteen *tensos,* three *partimens,* seven exchanges of *coblas,* two *baladas,* and one letter.

Frank M. Chambers focuses on the genres in dialogue, attempting to distinguish fictional trobairitz from real ones. In his case-by-case analysis, he finds circumstantial reasons to doubt the reality of the female speaker in fifteen of the poems discussed by Zufferey and in one which Zufferey does not mention (Chambers's no. 13). On the other hand, Chambers grants the reality of trobairitz identified by name in the text of the poem (his nos. 1 through 6) or in the rubric of a manuscript (no. 7). Combining Chambers's conclusions with Zufferey's, then, we have twenty-seven poems by trobairitz; or if we add Beatritz de Romans, as Angelica Rieger advocates, twenty-eight. As for the imaginary ladies, Chambers concludes that all except two of them "stay well within the code of courtly behavior." It also emerges from his remarks that their principal function (with the exceptions of Chambers's nos. 11, 16, and 17) may be seen as providing encouragement for their male Pygmalions, within the bounds of modesty or beyond them.

Joan M. Ferrante asks whether there is a female rhetoric in the poetry of the trobairitz and answers with a tentative yes. Comparing the trobairitz *cansos* with those of a group of near-contemporary troubadours, she finds that the trobairitz make much greater use of direct address, especially for the lover, while the troubadours address other men more often than their ladies. The women use negative words more frequently and consistently. Relative to "verbs of current reality" (in the present), the women use more "contrary-to-fact verbs" (in the subjunctive or the conditional) and more verbs in the past tenses. Their rhyme schemes tend to be simple, although Castelloza and the Comtessa de Dia produce more elaborate structures. Lombarda plays on feminine forms of names as a means of asserting her distinctive voice. Overt remarks on the role of women occur in Castelloza, and in several *tensos* the trobairitz are critical of the artificial rhetoric of the troubadours.

Angelica Rieger confronts a view that has been expressed casually by several scholars: that the *canso* of Beatritz de Romans expresses lesbian desire. If this were true, she points out, the poem would be unique in Old Occitan. A new edition of the poem provides the basis for three hypotheses: either it is lesbian, or corrupt passages in the text require emendations that remove all lesbian suggestion, or, rather than lesbian, it expresses affection—tender rather than erotic—in a manner that was conventional between women at the time. In support of the third hypothesis, Rieger marshalls evidence from a variety of sources to show "that Bieiris adopts an entirely normal, even conventional, colloquial tone which was proper between women of equal social position." The poet refers discreetly to the admirer of Maria, the lady to whom she speaks, so discreetly that the role played by this man in the relation between the two women remains indecipherable. But Rieger concludes that the interpretation of the poem as lesbian springs from later evolution in the tone of affection considered normal between women, and not from medieval evidence.

Amelia E. Van Vleck studies the implications of composition in the poetry of Castelloza. She finds that Castelloza prompts her addressee to respond, and thus to assume the usual role of the troubadour and to restore the powerless trobairitz to the powerful, but speechless, role of the adored *domna*. Her songs are a "complex of speeches" involving "several alternate discourses," including possible reproaches from a third party, responses from her lover, her own inarticulate utterances, and pleas for love by knights and ladies. Van Vleck interprets Castelloza's line, "Tost me trobaretz fenida," as a double-entendre meaning both "Soon you will find me dead" and "Soon you will compose for me a *tornada*," or indeed an entire song. She finds evidence that the addressee of a poem might indeed compose a response to it, and suggests that this would be especially plausible if—as seems to have been the case—Castelloza's intended audience were a broad one including trobairitz and troubadours.

H. Jay Siskin and Julie A. Storme take a different view of Castelloza, relating her unhappiness to the complexity of her language. She expresses the compulsive nature of her masochism through a preponderance of negatives, and does so on the syntactic level by progressing from an established condition to a contradictory result. Similarly, the familiar metaphor of love as feudal service would logically lead, under conditions such as Castelloza describes, to renunciation of allegiance—but Castelloza never renounces her lover. In her negative universe, the principle of reversal leaves no alternative to suffering; she reverses her actions and her emotions, negating joy and hope. She undermines the syntactic distinction between hypothesis and reality and creates a poetic world in which reality eludes the reader. The lover is passive, and the only central figure is Castelloza herself. In her reversed order, "suffering and self-effacement become positive expressions of the self . . . ; she thus transforms her negative world into a positive self-image," and self-denigration becomes "an expression of self-esteem."

Katharina Städtler provides a translation of the *sirventes* by Gormonda de Montpellier, which reverses the polemical thrust of Guilhem Figueira's attack on Rome within an identical metrical form. Gormonda's "reevaluating method" puts Guilhem's rhyme-words into contexts antithetical to his. Invoking both secular and religious values, Gormonda opens with praise for Rome and blame for Rome's enemies; she refutes Guilhem's political incriminations, then attacks heresy on religious grounds, and finally looks briefly to the future. Städtler elucidates Gormonda's arguments with detailed historical analysis and concludes with a suggestion that the trobairitz may have written for an audience of Dominicans.

Sarah Kay studies derived rhyme, in which two or more rhyme forms are derived from the same root. After outlining the effects of which this technique is capable, she reviews the scattered references made to it in grammatical treatises and in troubadour verse, concluding that it is uncertain to what degree the technique was employed self-consciously. Two trobairitz used derived rhyme, the Comtessa de Dia and Lombarda. Kay proposes a new stanza-order for the Comtessa's "Ab joi et ab joven m'apais," and interpets the song as "self-undermining in that it licenses the expression of individual desire and self-determination only at the moment when the individual becomes indistinguishable from society at large," that is, from a society dominated by men. In Lombarda's exchange of *coblas* with Bernart Arnaut d'Armagnac, the trobairitz penetrates the troubadour's technical display with the "simple language . . . of female rhetoric," and "insists on knowing if Bernart loves her."

Tilde Sankovitch sees "Lombarda's Reluctant Mirror" in the perspective of feminist psychoanalysis. For her, Lombarda withdraws from the typical function of the *domna* as passive mirror of the troubadour's quest for his own perfection, in this case the quest of her interlocutor Bernart Arnaut. Through a technique of "subversive imitation," she first undermines the ploy by which Bernart pretends to name himself Lombard in subjection to her, and then "fracture[s] the mirror [which he offers . . .] to recuperate, from the shards, her name." Thus she deconstructs the model of identity in troubadour songs, accepting neither the role of *domna* nor that of the male speaker but asserting her own presence and self-perception.

Two essays look beyond the trobairitz at their counterparts in Italy and at the memory of them that lingered in early modern France. Paolo Cherchi traces the "troubled existence," the birth and difficult survival or demise, of three Italian women poets who may have lived during the thirteenth century—or at least who did so in the opinion of critics who wrote especially during the Romantic period. Gaia da Camino, mentioned in the *Divine Comedy,* surely lived, but she wrote no extant poetry. Nina Siciliana is now regarded as the apocryphal invention of a sixteenth-century anthologist. Only La Compiuta Donzella remains, with her three sonnets, two religious and one secular. Cherchi's investigation sheds light on the problematic distinction between real and fictional trobairitz studied by Zufferey and by Chambers, and on the larger issue of the problematic perception of medieval women by modern scholars.

Geneviève Brunel-Lobrichon discusses a chansonnier from the late seventeenth or early eighteenth century, now held at Béziers, which is an abbreviated copy of troubadour manuscript *I*. It contains miniature portraits of three trobairitz: Castelloza, Azalais de Porcairagues, and the Comtessa de Dia *(see plates)*. The first depicts its subject as a figure of piety, the second as a prostitute, and the third as a feminine version of a Roman orator. These three faces of the trobairitz give us "a shattered image in which the three sides of the luminous and fascinating prism have fallen flat . . . , moving witnesses of a brilliant past."

Following the essays the reader will find a checklist of poems by the trobairitz, a bibliography, and an index.

Timothy Watson translated the articles by Rieger and Städtler from German, and Ann Williams translated those by Brunel-Lobrichon and Zufferey from French. I am grateful to Merritt R. Blakeslee, who provided valuable additions to the bibliography, and to Michael F. Dacey for his help in applying the chi-square test.

APPENDIX: *The Chronology of the Trobairitz*

Because the number of troubadours varied over time, first growing larger and then somewhat smaller, and because the number of trobairitz whose poems can be even vaguely dated is small, it is possible that the apparent restriction of their activity to the period of the greatest number of troubadours is merely a random effect of chance—that, in fact, about one Occitan poet in twenty tended to be a woman throughout the twelfth and thirteenth centuries. To test this view, which in statistics would be called the null hypothesis, we must specify both the number of troubadours and the number of trobairitz in appropriately defined periods. I suggest adopting periods of forty years and assigning individuals to given periods according to the midpoint of their known poetic careers.[23] The periods correspond to the activity of some of the best-known troubadours:

Period I (1100–1140): Guilhem de Peitieus

Period II (1140–1180): Bernart de Ventadorn

Period III (1180–1220): Bertran de Born

Period IV (1220–1260): Peire Cardenal

Period V (1260–1300): Guiraut Riquier

The number of troubadours active in each period may be determined from the "Liste biobibliographique" published by Jeanroy in his *Poésie*

TABLE 1   *Total Troubadours per Period*

Period	Number (percent)	
I	5	(2%)
II	24	(7%)
III	121	(37%)
IV	94	(29%)
V	80	(25%)
Total	324	(100%)

TABLE 2   *Chronology of Individual Trobairitz*

Period II

Azalais de Porcairagues, fl. c. 1173

Period III

Almuc de Castelnou, beginning of the 13th c.
Comtessa de Dia, attested in 1212
Comtessa de Proensa, married in 1193, widowed in 1209, entered a religious order in 1225
Gaudairenca, wife of Raimon de Miraval, who was active 1191–1229
Isabella, first third of the 13th c.
Iseut de Capio, exchanged *coblas* with Almuc de Castelnou
Lombarda, attested in a charter of 1206; exchanged *coblas* with Bernart Arnaut, Count of Armagnac 1219–26
Maria de Ventadorn, died shortly after 1225

Period IV

Azalais d'Altier, addressed in a *canso* by Uc de Saint-Circ, who was active c.1217–53
Castelloza, early 13th c.
Clara d'Anduza, perhaps contemporary of Uc de Saint-Circ; perhaps addressed by Azalais d'Altier
Gormonda de Montpellier, fl. c. 1229
Guilhelma de Rosers, participated in a *partimen* with Lanfranc Cigala, who was active c.1235–57
Domna H., fl. 1220–40
Tibors, first half of the 13th c.

lyrique (1:326–436), with corrections by Riquer in *Los trovadores*. The results are shown in Table 1.

As for the trobairitz, we must set aside those who cannot be dated at all (Alais and Iselda, Beatritz de Romans, Carenza) and those who are probably fictitious (see the essay by Chambers in this volume). Because of the latter consideration I shall omit Alamanda, but I shall include Domna H. with most scholars (*pace* Chambers). The datable trobairitz, according to the information marshalled in the Checklist, are listed in Table 2. The information in Table 2 yields the totals shown in Table 3.

TABLE 3   *Total Trobairitz per Period*

Period	Number (percent)
I	0
II	1 (6%)
III	8 (50%)
IV	7 (44%)
V	0
Total	16 (100%)

TABLE 4   *Trobairitz Observed and Expected, per Period*

Period	Observed	Expected
I	0	0.2
II	1	1.2
III	8	6.0
IV	7	4.6
V	0	4.0

TABLE 5   *Trobairitz Observed and Expected in Combined Periods*

Periods	Observed	Expected
I, II, V	1	5.4
III, IV	15	10.6

It is evident that there are relatively more trobairitz than troubadours in Periods III and IV, and fewer in Period V. (We may add that we know the names of 107 men who composed poetry in Occitan during the fourteenth and fifteenth centuries, but of no women at all.)[24] To assess the significance of this observation we may employ a statistical technique called the chi-square test.[25] To do so we must calculate how many trobairitz would have been active in each period by the null hypothesis, that is, how many we would expect if their numbers were proportional to those of the troubadours. For statistical purposes, Table 4 gives the expected figures to one decimal place. However, since the test requires that the expected number be at least five in all categories but one, we are obliged to combine Periods I, II, and V. It is then appropriate to combine Periods III and IV as well. We arrive at the array in Table 5. According to the chi-square test, differences this large will occur by chance 2 percent of the time. This statistical evidence supports the claim, at the 98 percent significance level, that the chronology of the trobairitz is not merely a reflection of the chronology of the troubadours.

Notes

1. See the study by Burrows, who argues that since its original meaning has become obsolete the term "Middle Ages" should be abandoned.

2. Burckhardt 292: "To understand the higher forms of social intercourse at this period, we must keep before our minds the fact that women stood on a footing of perfect equality with men."

3. For a discussion of "L'amour, cette invention du XIIe siècle," see Davenson 96–108.

4. See Biller, who refers to Genesis 38:9 and *Paradiso* 15.106–08.

5. Dronke, *Women Writers* x; cf. Wilson xix–xxi.

6. Farmer 518, referring, among others, to Duby, *Medieval Marriage* 6; Duby, *The Knight, the Lady and the Priest,* 99–106, 235; David Herlihy, "Land, Family and Women in Continental Europe," in Stuard, *Women in Medieval Society,* esp. 31–34. See also Bloch, chapter 2: "Kinship" (64–91).

7. The Latin accusative forms are the etyma of the Occitan words; the nominative forms are *imperator* and *imperatrix*. The etymon of *trobar* has been much discussed; recently, the case has been strengthened for Arabic *tarab* "song," pronounced *trob* in the Arabic vernacular of southern Spain (Menocal).

8. Flamenca says,
    Margarida, trop ben t'es pres
    e ja iest bona trobairis.
[Margarida, you have done very well, and already you are a good trobairitz.] Ed. Gschwind vv. 4576–77; Gschwind glosses *trobairis* as "femme qui sait trouver, imaginer." Bec observes that "le terme paraît bien lié à un effet de style" ("Trobairitz occitanes" 60).

9. Peire Rogier, "Ges non puesc en bon vers fallir" (P-C 356,4, ed. Nicholson no. 6), stanza 6. See Limentani 276.

10. See the *Oxford English Dictionary,* which also documents the forms "troubadourish, troubadourishly, troubadourism, troubadourist," but not "trobairitz."

11. The language of the trobairitz and troubadours is referred to in this book either as Occitan, by some contributors, or as Provençal, by others. The latter term has been used more widely by scholars since the nineteenth century, when modern study of the troubadours began, but has the disadvantage that it seems to refer to Provence, which is a specific region lying to the east of the Rhône, rather than to southern France in general. "Occitan" has no such deceptive connotation, and enjoys increasing acceptance despite its air of neologism. In fact both terms, and others as well ("Limousin," "Romance"), date from the thirteenth century (Gonfroy). "Occitan" relates to the distinction made by Dante, in his *De vulgari eloquentia,* between the *lingua d'oc* (Occitan, in which the word meaning "yes" is *oc*), the *lingua d'oïl* (modern French *oui*), and the *lingua di si* (Italian).

12. According to Jeanroy's "Liste par régions des troubadours dont la patrie est connue" (*Poésie lyrique* 1:321–25). Jeanroy lists trobairitz by regions as follows: Limousin, Marche (Maria de Ventadorn); Auvergne, Velay, Gévaudan,

Vivarais (Almuc de Castelnou, Castelloza, Iseut de Capio); Dauphiné, Viennois, Valentinois (Comtessa de Dia); Provence (Garsende de Forcalquier, comtesse de Provence; Tibors); Languedoc, comté de Foix (Azalais de Porcairagues, Clara d'Anduza, Gormonda de Monpeslier, Lombarda). He does not list trobairitz in the following areas where he lists troubadours: Poitou, Saintonge, Périgord; Quercy, Rouergue; Gascogne, Comminges, Agenais, Bordelais; Roussillon, Catalogne; Italy.

13. Anonymous, "En un vergier sotz fuella d'albespi" (P-C 461,113); Cadenet, "S'anc fui belha ni prezada" (P-C 106,14); Raimon de las Salas, "Dieus, aidatz" (P-C 409,2). These texts are conveniently assembled in Woledge 358–68.

14. "New Light" 148. In her study of the anonymous *alba* "Ab la gensor que sia" (P-C 461,3), however, Poe has suggested that this anomalous poem may be the work of the fourteenth-century scribe of manuscript *C* ("The Lighter Side" 88, 101–03).

15. Another Occitan *pastorela,* "Quant escavalcai l'autrer" (P-C 461,200), was apparently composed around 1218–20 in Italy. See Paden, *The Medieval Pastourelle.*

16. I have argued in a forthcoming study that Gravdal exaggerates the importance of rape in the pastourelle.

17. Compare Kay's skepticism concerning another poem by Bertran de Born, as expressed in her footnote 19.

18. Ed. Paden, Sankovitch, and Stäblein no. 24; ed. Gouiran no. 38.

19. P-C 335,30, ed. Lavaud no. 56, vv. 1–16. "Difficile à dater avec précision, la pièce doit appartenir à la première partie de sa carrière poétique" (Lavaud 365).

20. Riquer 3:1653–54. For the text (P-C 21a,II) see Sansone, *Testi didattico-cortesi* 229–90.

21. V. 485. Perhaps, however, we should read *Na Marqueza,* taking Marqueza as a proper name rather than a title; cf. the proper name Marquesia, cited by Mundy among other feminine first names suggestive of rank or wealth, names such as Castellana, Comtors, Riqua (120).

22. "No y devetz anar tro·l capdel s'er levatz," vv. 146–47. *Capdel:* "chef, commandant, seigneur; maître, patron; possesseur," *PD.*

23. I have used the same technique for discussing troubadour chronology in my study, "The Role of the Joglar." The figures given below for troubadours active in the various periods differ slightly from those in my earlier article because I here distinguish troubadours from trobairitz.

24. The apocryphal "Dona de Vilanova" is not an exception but a nineteenth-century hoax. See Zufferey, *Bibliographie* xxiii, 87.

25. See Muller 95–103, Siegel 42–47.

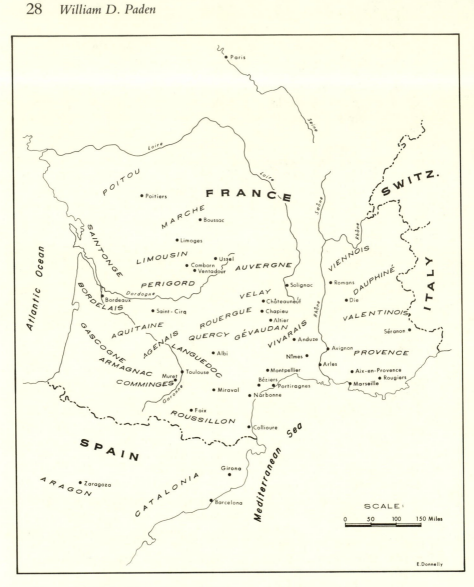

Places identified with various trobairitz

I Preliminary Considerations

1 Toward a Delimitation of the Trobairitz Corpus

The idea that we develop about the Provençal women poets of the twelfth and thirteenth centuries will vary depending upon the scope we attribute to their production. The corpus of their work may appear to have become permanently set, if we consider that Meg Bogin, in her edition of 1976, reproduced more or less exactly the collection published by Schultz-Gora in 1888.[1] In reality, however, Provençalists know that the outlines of this corpus remain imprecise in more than one place because of the uncertain status of some poems, most of which involve composition by anonymous ladies. These blurred areas are what I propose to examine by reviewing the various lyrical genres that were cultivated by the trobairitz.

«» I. *Cansos*

Only four names of the women who became famous through the *grand chant courtois* are attested to us with some certainty.

1. From the **Comtessa de Dia**, the most famous of all, four songs (P-C 46, 1–2 and 4–5) have come down to us. The first two, at least, must have had a certain amount of success, if we can judge by the number of manuscripts that transmit them.

2. **Castelloza**, a lady from Auvergne, ranks second with three songs (P-C 109, 1–3), but she is also probably the author of a fourth poem: "Per joi que d'amor m'avegna" (P-C 461,191), which immediately fol-

lows her anonymous corpus in chansonnier *N*. Whatever uncertainty may remain about its attribution, it is difficult to understand the hesitations concerning this song expressed by Schultz-Gora (4). The song should in any case be considered an integral part of the trobairitz corpus.[2]

3. As for **Azalais de Porcairagues**, she is represented by only one composition (P-C 43,1), which can be read in six chansonniers.

4. Last, **Clara d'Anduza** is known to us through only one song (P-C 115,1), preserved solely in manuscript *C*.

5. It could be tempting to add a fifth trobairitz to these four: **Beatritz de Romans**. Indeed, chansonnier *T* (Paris, Bibl. Nat., fr. 15211) contains on folio 208v the poem "Na Maria, pretz e fina valors" (P-C 93,1 = 16a,2),[3] which is attributed there to a certain *nabietris deroman*.[4]

Linguistically this rubric creates no problems. The form *Bietris* for *Beatritz* is well attested in Old Provençal (for example in chansonnier *R*),[5] and since the scribe of *T* writes *folcet*[*t*] *deroman* (fols.182v–183v), everything points toward the designation of a lady (*na*) named Béatrice de Romans.[6] As the poem is addressed to one Marie, we may have here the sole example in Old Provençal of a love poem sent by a woman to another woman.

It would be unfair to claim, with René Nelli, that "les philologues ont essayé, bien sûr, de réduire ce 'scandale'" (301). If Schultz-Gora, who had included the poem in his 1888 edition, took pains some years later to demonstrate that *Na Bieiris* could result from a deformation of *N'Alberis* (in which he sees Alberico da Romano), it is not because of the shocking nature of the song, but rather because nothing in the text confirms that the love at issue is lesbian.

From the codicological point of view, it may be observed that the poem in question is found in bad company, since it is followed on the same page and the next one by two compositions whose attribution is incorrect, in the section serving as a transition between the corpus of Gui d'Ussel and that of Peire Rogier.[7] In addition, it is likely that if the rubric which interests us here had been missing, no one would have thought of attributing the song to a woman: in all probability it would have been included in the corpus of Gui d'Ussel. And, in fact, upon reading the poem, we have the impression of hearing the Limousin troubadour sing the praises of Maria de Ventadorn, as in the poem "En tanta guisa·m men'Amors" (P-C 194,6).[8] Here are the links that can be established between the two compositions:[9]

Gui d'Ussel	*Na Bietris de Romans*
11 Bona dompna, pretz e valors,	1 Na Maria, pretç e fina valors . . .
12 E cortesi'ab gen parlar,	4 E·l gintç parlars e l'avinens solas . . .
13 Huoill rizen, amoros e clar . . .	6 E·l ducç esgart e l'amoros se[m]blan
15 Et agratz, don non avetz par . . .	7 Ce son e vos, don non avetç egansa . . .
(. . .)	(. . .)
23 Per qe . . . devetz . . .	19 Vos prec . . .
24 . . . fugir feignens prejadors.	20 Ce non ametç entendidor truan.

Even if such intertextual relationships are not conclusive concerning the attribution of the poem, it will be agreed that the discourse of Na Bietris has a frankly masculine resonance and that one must have quite a healthy imagination to see the prayer in lines 19–20 as that of "une féministe convaincue" who is attempting to turn Lady Maria away from "tout amant . . . de sexe masculin" (Nelli 305 n. 1). It therefore seems difficult to me to follow the copyist of *T* in his attribution of "Na Maria, pretz e fina valors," although I have no wish to deny the existence of a trobairitz by the name of Béatrice de Romans.

6. In addition to these five poetesses whose names we know, we must not forget that an **Anonymous Lady** composed the *canso:* "Quan vei les praz verdesir" (P-C 461,206), which is transmitted in a gallicized form by chansonnier *W*. This text brings the number of *cansos* to eleven (thanks to the fourth by Castelloza), if we agree to set aside the composition by Bietris.

«» II. *Sirventes*

Even though three varieties of *sirventes* by trobairitz have come down to us, unfortunately none has had the honor of entry in the anthologies dedicated to their work.[10]

1. The first is the *planh* of an **Anonymous Lady** on the death of her lover: "Ab lo cor trist environat d'esmay" (P-C 461,2). The slightly unusual codicological status of this complaint has given rise to the hypothesis of a Catalan origin. Indeed, the poem, which appeared on the flyleaf at the beginning of the chansonnier by Bernart Amoros,[11] may be read more completely on folio 6v of the Barcelona manuscript, Bibl. Centr., 1744 (formerly in the collection of Baldiri Carreras; Massó Torrents *G*). We may note in passing that the metrical scheme is the same as that of the controversial poem by Bietris de Romans (Frank number 407).

2. It was also an **Anonymous Lady** who must have written the second *sirventes:* "No posc mudar no diga mon vejaire" (P-C 404,5), even though it is attributed to the troubadour Raimon Jordan by chansonnier *C* and by two citations in the *Breviari d'Amor* of Matfre Ermengaud, who used a source close to the tradition of *C.* It was above all the last two lines:

> Car domna deu az autra far onransa,
> E per aisso ai n'eu dit ma semblansa;
>
> [For one lady must show respect for another,
> And for this reason I have given my opinion;]

which rightly suggested to Appel ("Zu Marcabru" 419, 421 n. 1) and then to Jeanroy (review of Kjellman 115) that this protest against the *antic trobador* of the school of Marcabru who spoke ill of women must be the work of a trobairitz.

3. The third *sirventes,* "Greu m'es a durar" (P-C 177,1), preserved by the Languedocian chansonniers *C* and *R,* is the answer by **Gormonda de Monpeslier** to Guilhem Figueira's violent diatribe against Rome. Although Schultz-Gora (16) omitted this poem because it had already appeared in the edition of Guilhem Figueira that we owe to Emil Levy, we must be careful not to forget that women like Gormonda did not hesitate to take pen in hand to express their moral (if not political) convictions.

« » III. *Genres in Dialogue*

A. *TENSOS*

Among the genres in dialogue, the *tenso* is by far the most problematic in regard to the actual participation of women. When these poetical jousting matches—which could be fictitious—bring ladies into play, the criteria which serve to determine whether or not the speaker is real are largely subjective. It will not be surprising, therefore, to see opinions diverging from one critic to another, and to find occasional contradictions in the work of a single philologist. This is notably the case of Alfred Jeanroy, who treats the *tenso* between Isabella and Elias Cairel as real at one point in *La poésie lyrique des troubadours:*

> Dans d'autres pièces . . . la participation de dames est sûrement attestée par les textes mêmes: . . . Elias Cairel [s'adresse] à une *domna Isabela* . . . (1:312)

and another time as fictitious:

> Voici quelques autres dialogues qui sont, selon toute apparence, purement fictifs. . . . Elias Cairel se fait demander compte de son inconstance par une dame Isabelle, qui l'accable de doux reproches ressemblant fort à des promesses . . . Assurément il n'y a là qu'un jeu. Mais, il a été parfois si bien joué que la critique s'y est trompée: sur la participation réelle de femmes aux pièces que je viens de mentionner, elle n'a pas fait, que je sache, les réserves qui s'imposaient. (2:257)

The criterion that guided Schultz-Gora in his choice was the presence or absence of the lady's name in the rubric.[12] Even though the German Provençalist did not uphold this principle rigorously, one cannot fail to emphasize the arbitrariness of discrimination founded on anonymity. Moreover, the existence of some trobairitz has sometimes been doubted by critics even though they are clearly named.[13] For this reason it seems obvious that other, more rigorous criteria must be defined to distinguish the fictitious *tensos* from real debates.

For my part, I shall merely give an inventory of the poems about which it would be appropriate to undertake a comparative study.[14] I shall group them in two categories, according to whether the person who is supposed to have proposed the *tenso* is a woman or a man.[15]

In four poems, a lady or maiden is presented as the initiator of the debate:

1. [P-C 46,3 = 389,6] Anonymous lady (the Comtessa de Dia?) and Raimbaut d'Orange:
   "Amics, en gran consirier";
2. [P-C 252,1 = 133,7] Isabella and Elias Cairel:
   "N'Elias Cairel, de l'amor";
3. [P-C 306,2] Anonymous lady and Montan:
   "Eu veing vas vos, seigner, fauda levada";
4. [P-C 461,56] Anonymous maiden and anonymous lady:
   "Bona domna, tan vos ai fin coratge."

In this category, only poem 3, which Nelli describes as "le poème le plus licencieux de toute la littérature occitane" (199), has not been included in editions of the trobairitz.

The number of *tensos* in which a troubadour initiates dialogue with a lady, usually to ask her for advice,[16] amounts to twelve:

5. [P-C 10, 23] Aimeric de Peguillan and an anonymous lady:
    "Domna, per vos estauc en greu tormen";

6. [P-C 15a,11] Albert de Saint Bonet and an anonymous lady:
    "Bela domna, si·us platz,"
    of which only the first line is preserved in the table of chansonnier *B*;

7. [P-C 87,1] Bertran del Pojet and an anonymous lady:
    "Bona domna, d'una re que·us deman";

8. [P-C 231,1] Guillem Rainol d'At and an anonymous lady:
    "Auzir cugei lo chant e·l crit e·l glat";

9. [P-C 231,4] Guillem Rainol d'At and an anonymous lady:
    "Quant aug chantar lo gal sus en l'erbos";

10. [P-C 242,69 = 12a,1] Guiraut de Borneill and Alamanda:
    "S'ie·us quier conseill, bel'amig'Alamanda";

11. [P-C 269,1] Joan de Pennas and an anonymous lady:
    "Un guerrier, per alegrar";

12. [P-C 296,1a = 16,10] Marques and an anonymous lady:
    "Domna, a vos me coman";

13. [P-C 372,4] Pistoleta and an anonymous lady:
    "Bona domna, un conseill vos deman";

14. [P-C 392,7] Raimbaut de Vaqueiras and a Genoese lady:
    "Bella, tant vos ai prejada";

15. [P-C 409,3] Raimon de las Salas and an anonymous lady:
    "Domna, quar conoissens' e sens";

16. [P-C 409,5] Raimon de las Salas and an anonymous lady:
    "Si·m fos grazitz mos chans, eu m'esforsera."

In this group only three poems, numbers 9,[17] 12 (see Véran 79–84), and 15,[18] have been included in the trobairitz anthologies.

B. *PARTIMENS*

The three *partimens* have been luckier, in that their authenticity has scarcely been challenged. It is a question of the following poems:

1. [P-C 249a,1 = 426,1] Domna H. and Rofin:
    "Rofin, digatz m'ades de cors";

2. [P-C 282,14 = 200,1] Lanfranc Cigala and Guillelma de Rosers:
    "Na Guillelma, maint cavalier aratge";
3. [P-C 295,1 = 194,9] Maria de Ventadorn and Gui d'Ussel:
    "Gui d'Uisel, be·m peza de vos."

All of these debates may be read in the editions dedicated to the
trobairitz.

C. EXCHANGES OF *COBLAS*

For the inventory of exchanges of *coblas* I shall use a codicological order,
beginning with chansonnier *H*. This manuscript (Rome, Bibl. Apost.
Vat., lat. 3207) contains on folios 43 through 57 a section presenting two
characteristics: on the one hand, the genres in dialogue dominate, and on
the other, women take up a preponderant amount of space and their
compositions have the honor of being preceded by miniatures.[19]

An exchange of *coblas* between Bernart Arnaut d'Armagnac and
Lombarda, a lady from Toulouse, appears at the beginning of this section. She answers her interlocutor in these terms:

1. [P-C 288,1] "Nom volgr' aver per Bernard Na Bernarda."

After a sequence of three *tensos* and one *partimen* broken up by two
lacunae, chansonnier *H* contains one half-leaf (fol. 45) of which there
remain only the first column recto and the last verso. At the top of the
first column is transcribed a stanza with an adjoining miniature which
indicates to us that it must be the work of a trobairitz.[20] Nonetheless,
since the lacuna preceding folio 45 deprives us of the *razo* which must
have introduced the stanza, we do not know whether it is a *cobla esparsa*
or an **Anonymous Lady**'s answer to a friend or lover in the framework
of an exchange of *coblas*. The codicological context seems, in any case,
to substantiate the latter solution. Given that the poem has not been included in the trobairitz anthologies and that it has only been edited once
in an unsatisfying manner (Kolsen "25" 289, 303–04), I will present it
here in its entirety along with a translation:

2. [P-C 461,81]

> Dieus sal la terra e·l pa[is]
> On *mos* <amics> es ni estai! (*ms.* uos es)

On q'eu sia, mos cors es lai,
4   Qe sai no n'es om poderos;
Aissi volgr'eu qe·l cor lai fos,
Qi qe sai s'en fezes parliers.
Mais n'am un joi qe fos entiers
8   Q'el qe s'en fai tan envejos.

[May God protect the land and the country where my friend is to be found!
Wherever I may be, my heart is there, for no one here possesses it; I wish
my body were there too, even if it were talked about here. I prefer a joy that
would be complete to the man who seems so jealous.][21]

Immediately after this *cobla,* still in the first column of folio 45, a
commentary presents the composition by **Tibors**, a lady from Provence:

3.   [P–C 440,1] "Bels dous amics, ben vos puosc en ver dir."

This poem, of which only the first eight lines and the beginning of the
ninth are readable (the rest appearing on the missing column), has generally been considered as a fragmentary *canso.* Only Frank (1:XX and
2:180) sees in it the beginning of a *salut d'amour* made up of decasyllables
in rhymed couplets. This analysis is obviously erroneous, since lines 5
and 6, with rhymes in *-es* (*veses*) and *-is* (*pentis*), can under no circumstances form a couplet. In addition, the *razo* clearly specifies: "e fetz aqestas coblas e mandet las al seu amador," which necessarily implies a
stanzaic structure. Supposing that each couplet[22] was composed of nine
lines, the metrical formula could be the following:

10a 10a 10b 10b 10c 10d 10e 10e [10d]

and would conform to rhyme-scheme number 187 in Frank. The number of stanzas remains to be seen, as does whether or not the lover answered Tibors. The available space in the two missing columns makes
the hypothesis of an exchange of two *coblas* likely, but this is only a
supposition.

After an anonymous poem[23] (no. 151 in the edition by Gauchat and
Kehrli), in the final column of folio 45 appears the request addressed by
Iseut de Capion to **Almois de Castelnou**, followed by the latter's
answer:

4.   [P–C 253,1] "Domna N'Almucs, si·us plagues";
[P–C 20,2] "Domna N'Iseutz, s'ieu saubes."

Another manuscript, chansonnier Q, preserves a conversation between several women. We find two sisters, **Alais** and **Iselda** (though
only one is supposed to speak), who ask advice from a lady named
Carenza:

5. [P-C 12,1] "Na Carenza al bel cors avinen";
    [P-C 108,1] "N'Alais e N'Iselda, ensenhamen."

Out of all the exchanges of *coblas,* only the one between the **Comtessa de Proensa**—who has been identified as Garsenda de Forcalquier—
and Gui de Cavaillon may be read in two chansonniers (*F* and *T*):

6. [P-C 187,1] "Vos que·m semblatz dels corals amadors."

Finally, I see no reason not to add to this list the dialogue, after a
separation, between an **Anonymous Lady** and Uc Catola (or Marcabru?). Chansonnier *D*[a] alone transmits this composition:

7. [P-C 451,2] "No·m pois mudar, bels amics, q'en chantanz."

This gives us a total of seven poems involving ten women, two of
whom are anonymous. Doubt remains as to the exact nature of two *coblas* (nos. 2 and 3) because of the incomplete state of chansonnier *H*.

«» IV. *Other Genres*

Along with the principal lyrical genres (*cansos, sirventes,* and genres in
dialogue), in order to do justice to the trobairitz we should mention that
the wife of the troubadour Raimon de Miraval, a certain **Gaudairenca**
(P-C 169), was also a poet when she chose, as we learn from a *razo* in
chansonnier *H* : "Bela era et avinens, e sabia ben trobar coblas e dansas"
[She was beautiful and attractive, and knew well how to compose *coblas*
and dances] (Boutière and Schutz 380). Unfortunately, none of these
dance songs has come down to us.

On the other hand, we have no *a priori* reason to deny that certain of
the anonymous *dansas* and *baladas,* a list of which was compiled by Frank
(2:70), were composed by poetesses. Once again, however, we must take
care not to confuse (to adopt Bec's formulation) "une féminité génétique
(avec un auteur dont on sait pertinemment qu'il est une femme), et une

féminité textuelle, à savoir une pièce, dans la très grande majorité des cas amoureuse, et dont le 'je' lyrique est une femme (l'auteur pouvant être assez fréquemment un homme)" ("'Trobairitz' et chansons de femme" 235–36). As for cases of "féminité textuelle," if we consider that an explicit reference in the poem to the act of composition carried out by the lyric "I" makes plausible the hypothesis of a female author, then two *baladas* transmitted in chansonnier Q could enrich the corpus of the trobairitz:

[P-C 461,69] "Condeta sui, si cum n'ai greu cossire,"

in which we note at verse 31: "En aqest son faz coindeta balada . . . ," and

[P-C 461,201] "Quant lo gilos er fora,"

in which we read at verses 4–6: "Balada cointa e gaia / faz. . . ."
Things are somewhat different in the ballad of the Queen of April:

[P-C 461,12] "A l'entrade del tens clar,"

where the "we" of the refrain, which includes not only the lady and her lover (*un legeir bachelar,* v. 27) but also the young people who have come to dance (*pucele ni bachelar,* v. 11), contrasts with the third person forms used by an author who holds himself deliberately on the exterior of his description.
It is the same for the famous dawn-song:

[P-C 461,113] "En un vergier sotz fuella d'albespi,"

where this time the "we" of the lovers in stanzas 3 and 4 is contained within stanzas spoken by the "I" of the lady (2 and 5), and the lady also seems to speak the refrain, while the poet, speaking in stanzas 1 and 6, observes the same distance in regard to the scene depicted. Nothing in this composition of nested Chinese boxes or in the preceding ballad suggests that the author was a woman.
To conclude and to return to firmer ground, in the epistolary genre we may cite the letter by **Azalais d'Altier** addressed to Clara (d'Anduza?). In so doing, we have reviewed all of the literary production by trobairitz, at least what has been preserved for us.[24]

What should we remember from this overview in relation to the collective editions dedicated to the trobairitz? The *cansos* remain the largest group, with eleven poems, since we should add the fourth composition by Castelloza and the one by the anonymous lady, and take away the poem attributed to Na Bietris de Romans, or at least relegate it to an appendix. Beside these texts, in the absence of the *dansas* by Gaudairenca, we may put a few *chansons de femme:* two *baladas* (perhaps three and an *alba*), and the letter of Azalais d'Altier. The three *sirventes,* despite their small number, nonetheless make up a non-negligible quantity (especially if we take into account the length of the one by Gormonda de Monpeslier—220 lines), and there is no reason to banish them from the corpus. As for the "genres inférieurs, n'exigeant qu'un médiocre effort (tenson, partimen, cobla)" according to Jeanroy (1:315), they make up an imprecise group of variable extension, except for the three *partimens.* The number of exchanges of *coblas*—including the fragment by Tibors—should be enlarged by two, and thus rise to seven (two of which are incomplete). It would seem rash to specify the exact number of *tensos* in which women really might have participated. In order to solve this problem, it will be necessary to take into particular consideration the place held by each of the sixteen poems in question in the chansonniers that dedicate a special section to the genres in dialogue. And I would like to add that a return to the manuscripts can only be helpful for assembling a new critical edition of the trobairitz.

Notes

1. The only item lacking is the final anonymous poem (P-C 461,204), which is not, in any case, the work of a woman but rather that of a troubadour. Schultz-Gora edited the text for the first time, since it alluded to the trobairitz Guilhelma de Rosers.

2. On the attribution of this piece to Castelloza, see D. Rieger, "Die *trobairitz* in Italien" 211–12; Paden et al., "Castelloza" 163–65; Bruckner 252n.

3. This poem is generally considered to be a *canso,* even though it is made up of only two *coblas* followed by two four-line *tornadas.* In line 22, the author designates the composition as *mas* (*mes* ms.) *coblas.*

4. One must, in fact, read *bietris* and not *bierris* (Diez 485, Mahn 3:331) or *bieiris,* as others have done. Bertoni (*I trovatori d'Italia,* 67) hesitated between *bieiris* and *bietris,* before opting for the first solution. However, to convince oneself that the correct reading is *-tr-*, it is sufficient to compare the *-ir-* sequence in the rubric *Peire rogier* on folio 209r. A horizontal stroke in front of the *r* distinguishes *t* from *i.*

5. The form *Bietris* presents two phonetic evolutions: the simplification of the affricate *-tz* to *-s* and the adjustment *e—a* > *i—a* > *i—e*. It is therefore unnecessary to bring into play a difference in treatment for the subject case and the object case (Schultz-Gora 16). On the other hand, I am unaware how Camproux explained to Bogin (177) "the linguistic process through which Beatrice might become Bieiris."

6. Perhaps referring to Romans-sur-Isère (dép. de la Drôme), but this is only a hypothesis.

7. They are poems P-C 96,10, attributed to Blacatz instead of Blacasset, and P-C 9,11, included in the section by Peire Rogier, although in all likelihood it belongs to Aimeric de Belenoi.

8. Which appears on folio 207 of chansonnier *T*.

9. For the poem of Gui d'Ussel, I follow the edition by Audiau 34–36, and for Na Bietris, that of Bertoni, *I trovatori d'Italia* 265.

10. With the exception of the *sirventes* by Gormonda, which Véran included in his collection (196–205).

11. Jacques Teissier transcribed it on page 166[4] of his copy, where he points out: "era scritto inanzi al principio del originale nelle carte che si soglion lasciar bianche per conservare i libri cosi imperfetto."

12. "Wir werden auch hier die Beteiligung von Frauen so lange zurückweisen müssen, als in den Ueberschriften keine Namen überliefert werden" (4).

13. For instance, Jeanroy, in regard to Alamanda: "Je n'hésite pas non plus à rayer de la liste des 'trobairitz,' en dépit de la jolie historiette racontée dans une razo, la *donzela* Alamanda, à qui Giraut de Borneil demande de plaider sa cause auprès de sa dame justement courroucée" (1:312).

14. Pierre Bec proposes to "revenir sur cette question dans un prochain travail" (*Cahiers de civilisation médiévale* 22 [1979]: 262, additional note 2). [Cf. Chambers's essay in Part 1 of this volume.—Editor's Note]

15. In each of these categories, I shall follow the order in which the poem appears in P-C.

16. Whence the term *conselh,* by which it is designated in the rubrics of certain chansonniers such as *L,* fols. 42r, 48v.

17. Even though Alamanda's existence was challenged by some critics, such as Jeanroy (see above, n. 13).

18. This poem is not exactly a *tenso,* since it is divided into two parts. The first three couplets, spoken by the poet, are answered by the last two stanzas, put in the mouth of the lady.

19. The section is quite incomplete, as the fourteen and one-half leaves that are preserved are supposed to be divided into four gatherings (VII to X) that should be quaternions, as may be seen from the first complete gatherings. Therefore, seventeen and one-half leaves are missing. Along with some *tensos* and *partimens,* we find mostly exchanges of *coblas,* possibly mixed with *coblas esparsas,* and accompanied sometimes by a commentary.

20. As the editors of the chansonnier, Gauchat and Kehrli, rightly saw (560).

21. That is to say, my husband. Kolsen adds a fair amount of complication to the end of the stanza; at line 8 he prints : "Qu'el que *sens* fai tan enueios," and

translates the last two lines: "lieber habe ich eine solche Liebe (Freude, Liebes-freude), die sich zu einer vollkommenen gestaltet, als die, welche der Verstand zu einer ganz widerlichen macht."

22. The copyist of *H* must have transcribed at least two of them, if we may judge by the plural "aqestas coblas."

23. Which does not concern the production of the trobairitz, at least in what we can read of it, but which could quite well be a troubadour's answer to a lady.

24. I leave aside the problem caused by the existence of a second Comtessa de Dia and by the legendary Blanchemain, referring the reader to the work of Thomas.

2   *Las trobairitz soiseubudas*

In his poem beginning "Dompna, puois de mi no·us cal" (P-C 80,12), Bertran de Born tells his lady that since she has dismissed him from her presence, if he cannot find another who is her equal in merit, he would rather have no *druda* at all. Naturally, no other could combine all the virtues of the one he loves; therefore, he has decided to go from one noble lady to another, begging each in turn to lend him some admirable quality in which she excels, and out of these contributions he will form a composite *domna soiseubuda* as close as possible to the perfection of his beloved. In a somewhat similar manner, a number of troubadours created as interlocutors for their *tensos* imaginary ladies whose opinions satisfied the poets' requirements. In the following pages, I shall examine briefly the whole field of fictitious opponents in poetic debates, and then narrow the discussion to those cases in which the opponent is a woman.

Three poets begin on the highest level and discuss their problems directly with God: the Monge de Montaudon in "Autra vetz fui al parlamen" (P-C 305,7) and "L'autrier fui en paradis" (P-C 305,12), Guilhem d'Autpol in "Seignors, aujatz, qu'avetz saber e sen" (P-C 206,4), and Rostanh in "Bels segner Dieus, s'ieu vos soi enojos" (P-C 461,43). Peirol takes a step downward and chooses Love for his interlocutor in "Quant Amors trobet partit" (P-C 366,29). Others descend lower still, to animals and objects not customarily thought of as endowed with speech: horses, in three poems, "Carn-et-ongla, de vos no·m voill partir" (P-C 184,2), by a Count of Provence, and two pieces by Bertran Carbonel, "Ronci, cen vetz m'avetz fag penedir" (P-C 82,13) and "Si anc nul temps fui ben encavalcatz" (P-C 82,14); and a cloak in "Mantel vil de croi fil" (P-C

192,3) by Gui de Cavaillon. Guilhem de Saint-Didier, on the contrary, introduces an invented partner in discussion who is presented as a human being in "En Guillem de Saint Deslier" (P-C 234,12), which consists of a dialogue between Guilhem and a man identified only as *Don* 'Sir.' *Don* comes to Guilhem and says that he has had a dream, which he would like to have explained. Guilhem interprets the details of the dream as allegorical allusions to various aspects of love. This poem, outwardly a *tenso* in arrangement and in the characters involved, is more like an *ensenhamen* in content. In a *tenso,* the participants voice conflicting views on the subject proposed for discussion, whereas here *Don* has no views at all, only questions. In addition, *Don* is a very shadowy figure, about whom all we know is that he has had a dream. Aimo Sakari mentions the efforts of Bertoni to identify this person, and comments, "Chercher l'interlocuteur de Guillem est de la peine perdue; la tenson est sûrement fictive" (128), an opinion with which I am in complete agreement.

The *domnas soiseubudas* who are the subject of this essay are, like the other fictitious characters we have mentioned, to be sought in genres made up of dialogue: *tensos, partimens,* and exchanges of *coblas.* It was taken for granted that these types of verse were composed by two individuals who addressed each other back and forth. We have seen, however, that this rule was sometimes violated and both sides of the argument were presented by one poet. Unfortunately, absolute certainty is difficult to obtain in such matters, and scholars disagree about the reality or fictitiousness of several female collaborators. Jean–Charles Huchet, in "Les femmes troubadours ou la voix critique," goes to the extreme of denying the existence of any trobairitz, not only in the *genres dialogués,* but in *cansos* and other forms as well. He says that the *vidas* where they are mentioned and the manuscripts in which their poems have come down to us were written much later than the time when the troubadours themselves lived, and therefore this testimony is not to be trusted. I am not convinced by his arguments to the point of rejecting all the trobairitz as male inventions, but some of them surely were. The remainder of this article will be devoted to a survey of all the poetic dialogues nominally including women, with an attempt to decide in every case, sometimes subjectively, whether the female interlocutor was real or invented, and to see if any generalizations can be made about the *trobairitz soiseubadas.*

It seems reasonable to assume that when the lady is identified by name in the poem itself her authorship is probably genuine, especially if she is a person known to history or is the author of other poems. This criterion validates the following compositions beyond any serious doubt, except to extremists like Huchet:

1. Maria de Ventadorn and Gui d'Ussel, "Gui d'Uisel, be·m peza de vos" (P-C 295,1), a *partimen*.
2. Isabella and Elias Cairel, "N'Elias Cairel, de l'amor" (P-C 252,1), a *tenso*.
3. Bernart Arnaut d'Armagnac, "Lombartz volgr' eu esser per na Lombarda" (P-C 54,1) and Lombarda, "Nom volgr' aver per Bernart na Bernarda" (P-C 288,1), an exchange of *coblas*.
4. Lanfranc Cigala and Guilhelma de Rosers, "Na Guilielma, maint cavalier arratge" (P-C 282,14), a *partimen*.
5. Iseut de Capio, "Domna n'Almucs, si·us plagues" (P-C 253,1), and Almuc de Castelnou, "Domna n'Iseutz, s'eu saubes" (P-C 20,2), an exchange of *coblas*.
6. Alaisina Yselda and Carenza, "Na Carenza al bel cors avinen" (P-C 12,1), a brief *tenso* consisting of one *cobla* by each participant and one *tornada* by each.

All the other dialogues with a woman as one of the speakers call for individual attention. In most of them, the woman is addressed simply as *Domna*.

7. Comtessa de Proensa, "Vos qe·m semblatz dels corals amadors" (P-C 187,1), and Gui de Cavaillon, "Bona dompna, vostr'onrada valors" (P-C 192,6), an exchange of *coblas*.

The authors are not named in the texts, but are identified by a heading in one of the two manuscripts (*F*) that preserve them. This identification could be due to the statement in Gui's *vida* that he was believed to have been the lover of Countess Garsenda, wife of the Count of Provence. The content of the *coblas* resembles that of other exchanges between a male troubadour and a lady (genuine or fictitious), and they might equally well have been ascribed to any man and any woman of gentle birth. Therefore, *F*'s attribution to Gui and the Comtessa is either a sheer invention of its compiler, or he had some external reason for making it—possibly the *vida;* but even so, why pick on this particular pair? Manuscript *F* does not contain any other poems by Gui de Cavaillon, and nothing in the poem would suggest him rather than some other troubadour. I agree with everyone who has discussed the authorship of these *coblas* that the identification of both partners is justified.

8. Guiraut de Bornelh and Alamanda, "S'ie·us quier conseill, bell' amig'Alamanda" (P-C 242,69), a *tenso*.

Guiraut requests advice and help from a *donzela* named Alamanda; her mistress, also Alamanda by name, has dismissed him from her sight because he had paid too much attention to another, and now he wants to get back into her good graces. Alamanda justifies her lady's conduct, but finally relents and agrees to help Guiraut if he promises to amend his behavior in the future. In spite of the fact that Alamanda is named in the poem itself as well as in the *vida* of Guiraut de Bornelh and by Bernart Arnaut in his exchange of *coblas* with Lombarda (no. 3 above, whose metrical pattern is modeled closely on this poem), and that she is accepted as legitimate by many scholars, her status has been questioned by a number of others. Appel puts the poem under the heading *fingierte Tenzone* (*Chrestomathie* 129–30); and Chaytor (144), Jeanroy (*PL* 1:312), Boutière-Schutz (45), and Riquer (1:506) are convinced that the entire poem was written by Guiraut. As Riquer says, "Es evidente que todo el debate es obra de Giraut de Bornelh, que lo ha redactado con gracia y con una leve ironía" [It is obvious that the entire debate is the work of Guiraut de Bornelh, who composed it with grace and delicate irony], and it must be placed among the best songs of this "master of the troubadours." For an amateur (and that is what Alamanda would have been) to write such flawless verses as these would demand extraordinary aptitude—and luck; I must agree, reluctantly, with the authorities just named, and place her among the *trobairitz soiseubudas*. At most, she could have discussed some such situation with Guiraut and perhaps inspired this graceful poem.

9. *Donzela* and *Domna,* the *tenso* beginning "Bona domna, tan vos ai fin coratge" (P-C 461,56).

The situation here has been compared with that which might have existed between the two Alamandas (no. 8); *Donzela* pleads with *Domna* to forgive a lover who, the lady says, "a son cor fol e leu e volatge," and "a fag vas me tal falhimen / don ges no·s pot escondir ni defendre"; but after some urging from *Donzela,* she eventually says that if he wishes to regain her favor, he must be cheerful and courteous and not hold grudges, to which the maid replies that she shall have him so, an ending that seems to satisfy the lady. It has been suggested that this *tenso* is actually the work of the two Alamandas; others have said that it was simply written under the influence of the Guiraut-Alamanda *tenso*. Perhaps not even this explanation is necessary; chance alone could account for the coincidence. At all events, I think the poem was probably composed by one person, possibly a man, since much emphasis is put on the lover's sufferings, and *Donzela* takes his side very enthusiastically.

10. Raimbaut d'Aurenga, "Amics, en greu consirier" (P-C 389,6), a *tenso* between *Amic* and *Dona,* appearing in the manuscripts under the heading Raimbaut d'Aurenga.

There is no indication that the Comtessa de Dia had any part in the authorship, although she was long considered to have composed the *Dona* stanzas. Two reasons that have been suggested for this attribution are the similarity of incipits between this poem and one of her unquestioned compositions, "Estat ai en greu consirier" (P-C 46,4), and the words in her *vida,* "Et enamoret se d'En Rambaut d'Aurenga, e fez de lui mantas bonas cansos" [And she fell in love with Sir Raimbaut d'Aurenga, and made about him many good *cansos*] (Boutière-Schutz 445). Pattison, in his edition of Raimbaut (157), and Riquer (2:791), along with most other recent scholars, are convinced that the *tenso* is the work of Raimbaut alone. The lady opens the discussion with the complaint that *Amic* is making her suffer all the pains of love; in later stanzas, his excuse is that he avoids seeing her because of *lausengiers,* who would ruin her reputation if they saw him near her. She replies that she herself has no such fears, and he is being unnecessarily solicitous of her honor; actually, instead of thinking of her reputation, he is staying away because he is fickle and has ceased to love her. He in turn blames *lausengiers* for giving her this opinion of him, and insists that he is no deceiver. In the *tornadas,* they reach the conclusion that she will believe him because she wants to think him loyal, and he pledges himself to have eyes for no other woman.

11. Raimon de las Salas, "Si·m fos graziz mos chanz eu m'esforcera" (P-C 409,5), three *coblas* by a man, and then two by a woman (neither addressed by name); it has been called a *canso* or two half-*cansos*.[1]

The rhyme-sounds are the same in all five stanzas. The first two complain of the lady's indifference to the man, and his sufferings as the result of her attitude; they refer to her in the third person. In the third stanza, he speaks directly to the lady and says how good it would be if she would show some kindness to him. In her reply (the last two *coblas*), she says that she belongs to him completely, although certain annoying and hateful persons make it necessary for her to be circumspect; even so, she will come to him if he tells her to. It seems highly likely that the lady was invented by Raimon to provide a novel conclusion to his *canso*.

12. Bertran del Pojet, "Bona domna, d'una re que·us deman" (P-C 87,1), a *partimen* between Bertran (who is named in the text), and the usual *Domna*.

Bertran asks the lady: If a true friend of yours loves you so much that he pays no attention to any other woman, will you love him or let him suffer? The lady asks in return who this person is, for she is afraid that Bertran is a false messenger, and she will not give him her answer until she knows whom he represents. Bertran only answers that he is sad for his friend, who loves her faithfully. The lady: If he were so much in love, he would show it by his behavior. Bertran: Lady, *I* am your true friend; accept me. Lady:

> Amic Bertran, ben es joc comunals
> q'eu am celui q'es mon amics corals;
> e l'amics, voil qe sia, sabez qals:
> fins e fezels, vertaders e non fals,
> ni trop parlers, ni janglos, ni gabaire. (Text of ms. *O*)

The expression *joc(s) comunals* is interesting: "It is fair play for me to love the man who loves me sincerely; and you know what (sort of person) I want my friend to be, loyal and faithful, true and not false, not too talkative, nor windy, nor boastful." This represents the male point of view; it suggests that it is Bertran who puts these words into her mouth, and that he alone composed this poem. Pillet-Carstens call it a "fingierte Tenzone," and it is so designated in Boutière-Schutz's note to Bertran's *vida* (514).

13. Lanfranc Cigala, "Entre mon cor e me e mon saber" (P-C 282,4), a *tenso* between the poet on the one hand and his heart and mind on the other, presented as a dream.

The poet says that lovers are responsible for their own sufferings, but his heart blames Love, and his mind says that ladies are to blame.

Lanfranc is not convinced by their arguments, and maintains once more that lovers are fickle, so that ladies, seeing their unfaithfulness, are slow in bestowing their favors in order to distinguish the sincere lover from the deceiver. At this point, the lady appears in the dream and thanks the poet for having spoken well of ladies; if all lovers were like him, none would be unhappy, but the wise man has his joy while the fool drinks his folly. Her words, spoken in a dream, are indisputably of Lanfranc's own composing. Shall we say in many other cases of women's intervention in troubadour poems not professedly representing dreams, "La vida es sueño, y los sueños sueños son?"

14. Raimon de las Salas, "Donna, qar conoissenza e senz" (P-C 409,3), a *tenso* between Raimon (identified in both text and heading) and a lady (not otherwise identified in the text, and not mentioned at all in the heading).

Raimon asks this lady for advice on a hackneyed subject: he loves a person of such nobility and merit that he does not dare to tell her of his pain; what shall he do? His interlocutor encourages him in the traditional manner not to be afraid, but to ask this lady for her love. Raimon is convinced that this is the proper course of action, and vows to follow it; the lady who has given him this counsel wishes him well. Kolsen (*Trobadorgedichte* 63), Pillet-Carstens, and Frank (2:170) agree in calling this a fictitious *tenso,* as I did in my edition (Chambers, "Raimon de las Salas" 37); we have already reached a similar conclusion for another poem by Raimon (no. 11 above).

15. Pistoleta, "Bona domna, un conseil vos deman" (P-C 372,4), a *tenso* between two persons identified in the text only as *Domna* and *Seingner,* although its attribution to Pistoleta is assured by the testimony of a majority of the manuscripts.

The basic situation is the same as in the preceding poem (no. 14), but the development is different. The man asks his interlocutor if he should tell his lady he loves her, or should he keep silent for fear of a brusque rejection? She replies that he should tell the lady about his love; she will not hit him, but will answer him courteously, even if she is not interested, and he will know where he stands. After some discussion back and forth, he says he will reveal his love to the person concerned, and begs his adviser to intercede for him. She asks, naturally enough, who the lady is, and he replies: "You are the lady I love; forgive me for speaking so boldly." There is general agreement among those who have dealt with this text that it is a fictitious *tenso;* Niestroy (13), Pillet-Carstens, Jeanroy (*Romania* 19:394, note), Frank (2:162), and others listed by Niestroy. This seems a very reasonable conclusion.

16. Marques, "Dona, a vos me coman" (P-C 296,la).

This poem was formerly ascribed to Albert Marquis of Malaspina (P-C 16,10), but this identification of Marques has been discredited by Bertoni (50, 159–60, 469), Pillet-Carstens, Jeanroy (*PL* 1:334). According to Pillet-Carstens, Márques here is a proper name, not a title (Marqués). The poem is anonymous in the only manuscript where it appears. It begins as a dialogue between *Dona* and *Amics,* but the last two stanzas have *Marques* instead of *Amics.* The distribution of the two roles is unusual: of the six verses in each stanza, the first two are addressed to *Dona,* 3 and 4 to *Amics* (or *Marques*), 5 to *Dona,* and 6 to *Amics* (*Marques*). As far as content is concerned, in the first five stanzas the two speakers are in complete agreement: they love each other dearly, and the woman promises to do whatever the man wishes; but the tone of the last two stanzas is quite different. Stanza 5 ends with these comforting words of *Dona:* "Amicx, ye'us retenc bayzan"; but here are *coblas* 6 and 7:

VI   —Dona, doncs a vos mi ren
        De mas jonchas humilmen.
        —Marques, en trop d'onramen
        Cujatz pujar veramen.
        —Dona, qu'ie·us am finamen.
        —Marques, e tu fas no-cen.

VII   —Domna, mot ay gran talan
        Qu'ie·us tengues a mon coman.
        —Marques, be·m n'iray gardan,
        E dizetz folia gran.
        —Dona, ja no·y agras dan.
        —Marques, no me·n plieu en tan!

[VI "Lady, therefore I surrender to you humbly with my hands joined in prayer." "Marques, you truly expect to rise to too much honor." "Lady, I love you truly." "Marques, then you are making nonsense."

VII "Lady, I have a great wish to have you at my command." "Marques, I shall protect myself from you, and you are saying great foolishness." "Lady, you would have no harm by it." "Marques, I don't promise myself that!"]

Notice that these are the only two stanzas in which the name *Marques* is used instead of *Amics,* and also that *tu* and the corresponding verb forms are used twice in these two *coblas:* "e *tu fas* no-cen" and "ja no·y *agras* dan." I have no explanation for these anomalies; was a stanza omitted that would have accounted for *Dona's* change of attitude? At any rate, it seems most unlikely that two persons could have collaborated on a poem with such elaborate and unusual stanzaic structure; *Amics* (or *Marques*) must have written the whole poem—or should we admit the possibility that *Dona* wrote it all?

17. Raimbaut de Vaqueiras, "Domna, tant vos ai preiada" (P-C 392,7), a *tenso* between a man who is addressed as *jujar* (i.e., *joglar*) and a woman who is addressed as *domna,* or *bella* or *bella domna.*

The authorship of Raimbaut de Vaqueiras (or Raimbaut and *la domna*) is indicated in the manuscript headings. Linskill, Raimbaut's editor, points out (104) the similarity between this poem and a *pastorela;* like the knight in that genre, the male speaker here tries to seduce a young woman, who resists his advances very successfully. He addresses her in courtly fashion, praising her beauty, her good breeding, and her "merit." She replies in her native Genoese and in a very different tone—familiar, coarse, appropriate for a member of a class lower than that of the lady the man describes. At the end, however, the man becomes more explicit in his request: "Allow me to show you how a Provençal does the deed, when he is mounted." The woman takes this metaphoric reference to horsemanship literally, not as the speaker had intended it, and replies, "Go to Lord Obizzo, who will perhaps give you a pack-horse, as you are a minstrel" (Linskill's translation, 102). It seems evident that this was Raimbaut's main purpose in writing; he needed a horse (a common gift to troubadours), and he asks for one in this indirect manner after having put Obizzo Malaspina in a good humor with the incongruous dialogue that led up to this conclusion. There can be no doubt that Raimbaut alone was responsible for the entire composition, which is one of his best pieces. One can picture him reciting it before the court, taking both roles himself, and doubtless being rewarded with much laughter and applause, and possibly a horse as well.

18. Rofin and Domna H., "Rofin, digatz m'ades de cors" (P-C 249a,1 = 426,1), a *partimen* between two people who are so identified in some manuscripts, although in the text of the poem the female participant is addressed only as *domna.*

Various suggestions have been made about the identity of *Domna H.*, but no one seems to doubt that she was a real person. Rofin himself is unknown; this may be only a *senhal,* inspired by *rofian* "pander," "pimp." *Domna H.* poses this question to Rofin: A lady has two suitors, both of whom she admits to her bed on condition that they swear to go no further than hugging and kissing; one disregards his oath and goes all the way, while the other keeps his promise; which one acted better? Rofin answers that the man who kept his promise did the right thing, and should be rewarded by the lady. *Domna H.,* following the rules of the game, has to defend the other alternative: the lady should reward the suitor who showed his love by enjoying it fully; the other man was a coward. Essentially the same alternatives are presented by Aimeric de Peguilhan in a *partimen* beginning "N'Elias, conseill vos deman" (P-C 10,37) but in this case the interlocutor is a man, Elias d'Uissel; Elias chooses the path of sensuality, and Aimeric is left to defend virtue. If the participants in the present poem had been called only Rofin and *domna,* the woman would in all likelihood have been considered fictitious; the H., however, seems to suggest a woman of some respectability who wishes to cloak her identity behind an initial. I would like to propose another possibility, remote though it may be: Rofin (whoever *he* was) chose this method of lending a certain piquancy to a poem entirely of his own making by having a "veiled lady" propose a risqué topic for a *partimen* and offer a strong defense of the more sensual of the alternatives involved.

19. Montan, "Eu veing vas vos, seingner, faoda levada" (P-C 306,2).

This is a *tenso* with still another *domna* who opens the discussion by saying she has heard that Montan is an expert at sexual games. She boasts of her own endowment and expertise along those lines, and challenges him to a joust to see which of them is really better equipped and more knowledgeable in such matters. Montan accepts the challenge with enthusiasm, and the remainder of the poem consists of further boasting on both sides. This *tenso* has been labeled fictitious by Pillet-Carstens and Frank (2:148), but Jeanroy called it simply a "tenson obscène" (*PL* 1:398). There can be little doubt that Montan was solely responsible for the scabrous little piece, which may have been presented with the collaboration of a *joglaresa* before a stag party like the *companhos* of William IX.

20. Aimeric de Peguilhan, "Domna, per vos estauc en greu turmen" (P-C 10,23).

Beginning as a *tenso* between *Senher* and *Domna,* this poem ends as a two-stanza argument between *Amic* and *Amor.* The distribution of roles is somewhat similar to that in "Dona, a vos me coman" (no. 16); both poems divide every stanza between the participants, though in a slightly different manner; according to Aimeric's system, each has a single line at a time. For three stanzas, *Senher* pleads with *Domna* to grant him the mercy that would ease his torment; but she refuses, like many a cruel lady in troubadour *cansos.* Then, under the new name *Amic, Senher* turns to Love for help, first upbraiding him for his indifference. Love replies that he led him to the worthiest of women, but hints that another lady might be more receptive. When the suitor rejects this suggestion, Love says that he might yet win his lady *sufren et ab servir.* The introduction of Love as a speaker, and the stichomythic format as well, justify the editors (Shepard-Chambers 135) in calling this *tenso,* or these two half-*tensos,* a fictitious discussion composed by a single author.

21. Joan de Pennas, "Un guerrier per alegrar" (P-C 269,1), a *tenso,* or "*guerrier*" ('combat') on the subject of love, as Joan announces in the opening stanza.

The participants, addressed as *Guerier* and *Guerieira,* express great admiration for each other: "I cannot find a man of greater intelligence or a finer lover;" "You are the flower of beauty, and I do not know . . . a more beautiful lady in Tarascon who strikes more effectively with the dart of love." All the same, *Guerieira* is reluctant to give concrete evidence of her love, for fear of the *lauzengador maldizen.* To this, *Guerier* replies that a lady who loves her honor should have no fear of slanderers. The localization of the lady at Tarascon may be a sign that she really existed and took part in the *tenso;* Jeanroy (*Poésie lyrique* 1:391) and Meyer (*Derniers troubadours* 95) seem to accept it as a genuine discussion between two people, but Pillet-Carstens call it a "fingierte Tenzone." I am inclined to agree with the latter opinion, largely because of the narrative introduction and the words "*I* wish to begin a *guerrier,*" which sound like the beginning of a *canso:*

> Un guerrier per alegrar
> vuelh comensar car m'agensa,

que non lo dey plus celar,
trop l'auray tengut en pensa;
e guerejaray d'amor
en domens que ma guerieira
a trobat guerejador
que guereja volontieira.

Whether the lady was a real trobairitz or not, the remarks ascribed to her here are the conventional ones expressed by male troubadours in many a *canso.*

22. Guilhem Rainol d'At, "Quant aug chantar lo gal sus en l'erbos" (P-C 231,4), a *tenso* between *Seingner* and *Domna.*

After evoking several bird-songs, most of them not noted for their beauty (the crowing of a rooster, the cries of a magpie, a jay, a blackbird), the poet continues:

Farai un vers ses prec e ses somos.
Ma domn'es tan bell'e cortes'e pros
que·m fai loirar plus que falco lanier.

This narrative introduction, like that of "Un guerrier per alegrar" (no. 21), and the declaration "I shall compose a *vers*" imply that what follows is not a joint venture of Guilhem with a lady, but, as Kolsen says (*Dichtungen* 61), "eine fingierte Kanzone," or, more accurately, "eine Kanzone in Gesprächsform." Frank (2:130) calls it a "romance parodique." This judgment is supported by a number of details that suggest a humorous parody of the genre—*Seingner:* "My lady makes me tamer than a hunting falcon;" *Domna:* "You are lucky; when I see a vain young man coming, I run to the barn and hide;" *Seingner:* "I have never taken part in a tournament since you ordered me not to; I prefer to eat cheesecake, and bread dunked in broth;" *Domna:* "Let's sell the striped pig and buy some fine clothes for Miquel the shepherd; people will take him for a knight" (I translate *so* twice as "the" here; see Smith-Bergin 83); *Seingner:* "I'd rather see Miquel hanged." The whole poem strongly suggests a domestic quarrel between husband and wife (Riquer 3:1240), on a barnyard level, in which the function of both *trobairitz soiseubuda* and her male opponent is to amuse the audience by feeding material for jokes back and forth to each other.

23. Guilhem Rainol d'At, "Auzir cugei lo chant e·l crit e·l glat" (P-C 231,1), a dialogue whose participants, like those of Guilhem Rainol's other poem (no. 22), are identified as *Seingner* and *Domna*.

Kolsen (*Trobadorgedichte* 37) calls the composition a "Kanzone (in Gesprächsform)," Frank (2:130) a "tenson (fictive?)," Jeanroy (*Poésie lyrique* 1:381) and Pillet-Carstens a *tenso* with a lady. There is little doubt that it is fictitious, although the text and the allusions are so uncertain that it is difficult to characterize the relation of the speakers to each other. The poem begins with a rumor implying that the man had lied about his lady (?), whereas he loves her "more than fish in rosemary." The lady wishes she had cut off the nose of the person who started such a rumor, and who (she says) has a "puta color de Sarrazin." *Seingner* reproaches her for speaking ill of a lady who is "ric' e de gran parentat," and also an accomplished spinner of thread. *Domna* is vexed to hear this woman's lineage and skill at spinning compared with her own, and counters, "I also have a good knight for a protector, and you are not so badly off in At: I covered you with a well-laundered sheet." *Seingner:* "You will be rewarded for not putting (men) in a sack full of holes. . . . If I were richer, you would have a mirror, elegant toilet articles, and a ribbon to tie up your hair."

> Pois disseran tuit li plus avezat:
> "Quals es aquist?" qant vos vengras d'orat,
> "ben, vos plevisc, bell, amest sobrefin!"

I do not understand this, or the following stanza, in which *Domna* tells how she climbed onto the rampart and fell down sick ("sick with love," swooned?) on a cushion. "I knew it was your fault," she says, "but I forgave you." He replies:

> Domna, ben fon saubat et azalbat
> lo luns mati com fes la caritat;
> quant portest guans e borsa de cendat,
> a las meillors aguest lor pretz baissat
> que tot un jorn n'esteron al latin.
> Si fossetz lai, on vos fon destinat,
> foratz al bois part Sancta-Trinitat,
> al port de Sorc, en terra de sanguin.

What deed of charity did *Domna* perform? Does *n'esteron al latin* mean "were bewildered by it" (French *perdre son latin*)? The allusions in the last three verses escape me completely. At all events, one can say that *Domna*'s remarks in this poem, as in the previous one, are on a far lower level than those of courtly ladies, of which they are clearly a parody.

In conclusion, I shall try to categorize the roles played by the imaginary *trobairitz* in the dialogues we have been examining. First of all, their reply to this question: If a man loves a woman, should he let her nobility and her merit intimidate him into suffering in silence, or should he pluck up courage and plead his case openly with her? The *domnas* of Raimon de las Salas (no. 14) and Pistoleta (no. 15) both declare that the lover should speak up without hesitation; he has nothing to lose but the torture of uncertainty, and he has the possibility of winning great happiness.

But how does the lady react when the man approaches her with his declaration? Bertran del Pojet's *domna* (no. 12), when asked if she will give her love to a man (unidentified) who loves her truly, begins by instituting some preliminary probing, which turns out to be satisfactory; the man in question is the one standing before her. Knowing this, she answers that it would be only fair for a lady to love one who loves her, if he is sincere, faithful, and circumspect; this ending seems a happy one for her as well as for him. The Genoese *domna* of Raimbaut de Vaqueiras (no. 17) gives a very different answer; but it is clear that the man who is flattering her with fine phrases is a very different kind of suitor. All he wants is to seduce her, and she, like a sensible shepherdess in a *pastorela*, gives him short shrift: "Go find yourself a horse somewhere else," she says.

Once the *drudaria* is established, its course is not always smooth. In four poems, one participant complains of the other's coldness and inaccessibility, a well-worn troubadour theme when the plaintiff is a man, as in Raimon de las Salas's "Si·m fos graziz" (no. 11), Aimeric de Peguilhan's "Domna, per vos" (no. 20), and Joan de Pennas's "Un guerrier" (no. 21); but in Raimbaut d'Aurenga's *tenso* (no. 10), it is the woman who makes this charge. All the sufferings of love, she says, are on her side; this is a new development in Old Provençal dialogue poems, but not unlike the woman's complaint in the Old French *chansons de toile*. Both the man and the woman blame the *lausengiers*, or tale-bearers, for the apparent coldness they see; these people would spread scandalous rumors against the lady if they saw her with her lover. An attempt is made in Lanfranc Cigala's dream-*tenso* (no. 13) to fix the responsibility elsewhere: the dreamer's heart and mind tell him that Love and ladies, respectively, are to blame. He stoutly rejects their arguments and maintains that the lovers themselves are at fault. They are notoriously fickle and untrustworthy, so it is no wonder that their ladies prudently hesitate to yield to their pleas for intimacy. The function of the lady in this piece, when she appears, is to applaud her champion for his defense of women. Another poem, Marques's "Dona, a vos me coman" (no. 16), poses something of a problem. At the outset, the two partners seem to share a reciprocal affection for each other; then suddenly, in the last two stanzas, *domna* upbraids the man for his presumption in daring to offer her the homage she has apparently encouraged up to that point. It would seem that an intermediate stanza, in which the man's aspirations become sensual to an unseemly degree, has been lost. And finally, in two poems (nos. 8 and 9), the intervention of a *donzela* is requested or actually used in an attempt to effect a reconciliation between a lover and his lady.

Only two of our poems involve what might be considered impropriety on the part of the lady. One is the *partimen* between Rofin and *Domna H.* (no. 18), which, as we have seen, is not generally accepted as fictitious, although the lack of a real name for the female participant (she is called only *Domna* in the text) makes it a possible candidate for inclusion in this study. Here, *Domna* defends a mildly scabrous position, namely, that a lover does well to disregard his promise to stop short of sexual intercourse when his lady exposes herself to the possibility of such behavior on his part. One might say that the rules of the *partimen* oblige her to take this alternative, since Rofin has chosen the other; but the fact remains that she herself brought the question up in the first place, knowing full well that this might happen. The only really obscene *tenso* involving a woman is that in which the male participant is Montan (no. 19), and this is one of the most pornographic poems in troubadour literature. Notice that here also, as in the case of *Domna H.,* it is the woman who broaches the matter for discussion. Montan's poem differs from that of Domna H. in that it is a coarse parody of the courtly *tenso,* in which the "love" involved is only raw sexuality. The two poems of Guilhem Rainol d'At, "Quant aug chantar" (no. 22) and "Auzir cugei" (no. 23) are also parodies, but of a very different kind. In them, the courtly style is brought down, not to the level of obscenity, but to that of bourgeois household matters, such as domestic animals, eating, dress, spinning, toilet articles, and the like—presented in a comic, very familiar style.

Taking all these considerations into account, one sees that the role of the *domna soiseubuda* is, with few exceptions, not strikingly different from what one might expect of courtly ladies in general. The Montan poem and those by Guilhem Rainol d'At are completely untypical of the others, and one might say that Domna H. somewhat exceeded the bounds of propriety as they existed in courtly society. The lady in Raimbaut d'Aurenga's poem who says that *she* is the one who suffers in love is probably a simple transposition by a male writer of the standard masculine cliché into a female context, but authentic trobairitz sometimes voice similar sentiments. All the other *domnas* stay well within the code of courtly behavior, whether this code was imposed by men or whether support for it came from women as well.

Note

1. [Or a *tenso*, by Zufferey in this volume—Editor's Note.]

II *The Voice of the Trobairitz*

3   Notes Toward the Study of a Female Rhetoric in the Trobairitz

Is there a female rhetoric in the poetry of the trobairitz? When I first considered this question, I expected the answer to be no. But when I went over the material I had collected in order to begin to answer the question, I discovered that the answer seemed to be yes, albeit a hesitant yes. One would have to make a far more extensive survey than I have done to be able to draw such a conclusion, and even then the available material is so sparse that such a conclusion would still be tentative. Nonetheless, I offer my findings here as one step in that direction.

There are various ways one might tackle the question: a study of the vocabulary of the trobairitz, compared with representative contemporary male poets; a study of the imagery; a comparison of the use of traditional conventions;[1] a study of style; the use of negatives; the use of the second person; the use of different tenses or moods of verbs; rhyme schemes; grammatical plays based on feminine forms; direct references to male and female patterns of behavior; a particular stance taken in relation to male rhetoric, to the game of courtly love. I have not attempted to cope here with the topics of vocabulary, imagery, or style, which are very important but too vast for this study. I will, however, say something about the others, bearing in mind that with such a small body of extant poetry, any statistics may be meaningless.[2]

I have attempted to compare certain aspects of the trobairitz poems with those of a small group of troubadours. My control group, so to speak, was chosen from poets writing at the same time as the women or just before, Bernart de Ventadorn and Peire d'Alvernhe from one generation, Arnaut Daniel from a second, Peire Cardenal and Sordello from a third, representative I think, but certainly not comprehensive.[3] I used only the love-poems (the *cansos*) of the poets, male and female, for my statistical study; I will say something about the women's *tensos* at the end, but à propos of rhyme and tone. I took the statistics several times and they varied each time, but since the variations were slight, I can vouch for their overall validity, if not for each specific number. That is why I have frequently resorted to fractions, which at least give the right proportions.

Probably the most rewarding area I looked into was the use of direct address, of the second person as compared to the first or third. In this there is a striking difference between the women and the men. The trobairitz use the second person, specifically addressing the lover as "amics," in all but one of their *cansos* (the Comtessa de Dia's "Fin joi me don'alegranssa"). They often do so more than once, the Comtessa in four of the five stanzas of "A chantar m'er de so q'ieu no volria," Clara in all four stanzas, and Castelloza frequently, in five of six stanzas in one poem, in four of seven in another, in five of five, and in three of five in the others. The women rarely use the second person for anyone but the lover; the Comtessa addresses the "gelos mal parlan" in one envoi and her messenger in another, Azalais a *joglar*, and Castelloza another woman.

Among the male poets, the use of the second person is far less frequent and by no means restricted to the object of the poet's love. Bernart addresses the lady directly in only one stanza in thirteen of his forty-one *cansos* (and five of those are in the envoi); he addresses her in more than one stanza in eleven poems (in two stanzas in eight of them, of which five are envois, in three stanzas twice, with a high of four stanzas in one poem, no. 24). He also uses the second person to address the audience in sixteen poems (two of which are directed to his enemies), as well as the song (twice) or the singer (thirteen times), not to say Love, *Amors,* in six poems, *Cortesia* in one, and *Orgolhs* in one. Whereas Bernart addresses the audience in fewer than two-thirds as many poems as those in which he addresses the lady (16/27), and the singer in half as many (13/27), these various other addressees figure in half again as many poems as does the lady (39/27).

Peire d'Alvernhe uses the second person once to another poet, once to Love, twice to the audience (three times in one poem), but never to a lady except through the voice of the nightingale, his bird messenger, and in four of his ten poems he does not use it at all. Arnaut, in the seventeen *cansos,* addresses the lady in four poems, three times in one, twice in another, Love three times, the song itself five times, and the audience six times, one of those to the *lauzengier*. Peire Cardenal, in ten love–poems (I exclude the brief dialogue, no. 8), most of them of only one *cobla*, addresses the lady once and the audience once. Sordello addresses the lady in eight of his twelve love poems, only once in five of those (four in the envoi); in the other three poems, the address to the lady dominates the poems. This is certainly a higher proportion of address to the love-object than in the other male poets' works, but still not comparable with the women's. It seems, therefore, not unreasonable to conclude that the women are more given to the direct approach. They address the object of their feelings, while the male poets are as likely to address their fellow men as their ladies.

The difference in the use of negative words is less striking, but still fairly suggestive. Most of the women use a higher number of negatives than the men, and there are few stanzas in their poetry in which at least one negative does not appear. By negative words, I mean *non, ni* and *anc* when they are used with *non, niens,* and *nulhs*. Of the women's *cansos*, half (six) have at least one negative word every 2 or 2.5 lines, four more have one in every 4 or 5 lines, only one has as few as one in 12 lines, while two are heavily negative, nine words in 8 lines (Tibors) and twenty in 28 lines (Clara). Every stanza but one (and two envois) of the Comtessa's four poems contains negatives, all but one and the envoi of Azalais's six stanzas, all but two stanzas of Castelloza's four poems, and all four of Clara's stanzas. The number of negatives per stanza is generally low, with only one in ten stanzas, two in thirteen, three in eight; four, five, six, or seven in only three stanzas; nine negatives in one, and eleven in one. That is, the negatives tend to run through the poems, rather than to dominate one or more stanzas, as they sometimes do in the men's poetry.

The men occasionally have one or more heavily negative stanzas, but they do not use the same proportion of negatives and they all have a higher proportion of stanzas without any negatives.[4] It seems that the women are somewhat more negative in their expression than the men. Of course, like the men, they sometimes use negatives to assert particularly strong feelings: Tibors: "ni anc no fo qu'ieu non agues talan" ("never have I been without desire"); Castelloza: "ni drutz de negun paratge/ per me non fo encobitz" ("no lover of any rank has been desired by me"). But more often they use them to express frustration or deprivation: the Comtessa: "vas lui no'm val merces ni cortesia/ ni ma beltatz ni mos pretz ni mos sens" ("nothing works with him, not mercy or courtesy, not my beauty or my prestige or my sense").[5]

Since the same sense of frustration has been said to lead women to use the subjunctive or optative more than their male counterparts, I also looked at the frequency of use of certain verb forms: the present indicative, the subjunctive and conditional, the various past tenses, and the future. The relative frequency of use of all tenses is the same for men and women, insofar as all of them use the present most, the subjunctive and conditional[6] next, the past next, and the future least. However, the ratio of one tense to another differs between men and women. As against some 273 occurrences of the present tense in the women's poems, there are some 99 subjunctives; in other words, more than one-third as many contrary-to-fact verbs as verbs of current reality (and if one were to take account of the negatives operating with the present tense, the ratio would be closer still).

Among the men, Bernart has some 442 subjunctives against some 1,706 presents, about one-fourth as many. Peire d'Alvernhe, 92 subjunctives against 352 presents, slightly more than one-fourth; Arnaut, 144 subjunctives to 672 presents, more than one-fifth; Peire Cardenal, 34 subjunctives to 138 presents, about one-fourth; and Sordello, 82 to 455, less than one-fifth. So, although one cannot say that women prefer the contrary-to-fact mode, they certainly use it more than the men do. They also seem to use the past tenses more frequently: 58 pasts to 273 presents in their poems (that is, a ratio of 0.21), as against Bernart's 209 to 1,706 (0.12), Peire d'Alvernhe's 50 to 352 (0.14), Arnaut's 97 to 672 (0.14), Peire Cardenal's 25 to 138 (0.18), and Sordello's 34 to 455 (0.07). This reinforces the sense that the women are concerned with real relationships, relationships that have a past.[7]

Though the women may use the subjunctive, wishing for something that is not so, and the past, lamenting something that once was, they are not tentative in their tone or in their voice. They find the devices that best express their needs. They do not adopt complicated rhyme schemes (which may be connected with the fact that they address themselves to their lovers rather than to the audience or their fellow poets). Most of the trobairitz poems are quite simple combinations of two to four rhyme sounds. Only one, Castelloza, uses a dissolute rhyme, in one poem, and only once per stanza. (I do not include Tibors' fragment, which is not a complete stanza.) That means, since most of their poems are *unissonans*, that what variety in sound there is comes in the rhyme sounds, usually four per stanza. Of the twenty poems (*cansos* and *tensos*), fourteen are *unissonans,* eleven have four rhymes per stanza, four have two per stanza, three have five, and two have three. On the other hand, there is some play with consonance or assonance, particularly in the *tensos,* which ties the different rhymes together. (This is a technique Arnaut also uses, but he does it to tie dissolute rhymes together.)[8]

Castelloza and the Comtessa de Dia play with sounds more than the others, Castelloza with inner rhymes and with plays on rhyme words with the same root. The Comtessa plays with related sounds (*anssa, aia, an, men*) in "Fin joi me don alegranssa," the *aia* words "esglaia" and "gaia" picking up the *aia* sound from the first *men* word, "gaiamen." She also uses *rimas derivatius,* paired words that do not rhyme but have the same root: "apais," "apaia," "gais," "guaia," "veraia," "verais," "estrais," "estraia" (in "Ab joi et ab joven m'apais").[9] This technique gives her some interesting possibilities, such as juxtaposing "mais" ("more") with "m'aia" ("that he have me"). Since one expects a derivative rhyme, the unexpected meaning is more emphatic, particularly since it follows a line with much inner rhyme: "mout mi plai, quar sai, que val mais/ cel qu'ieu plus desir que m'aia." The Comtessa varies this close connection between the *a* and *b* rhymes only once in the poem, with a word that is not the same root or sound, using "avinenssa" instead of "valenssa" after "valen." Since this is the only such occurrence in the poem, it calls attention to the difference in meaning between the word she uses and the word she chooses not to use: "ja pois li pro ni li valen/ no'n dirant mas avinenssa," ("the good and worthy will say nothing but agreeable [or suitable] things") of a lady who loves openly, "agreeable" but not ascribing real worth, not "valenssa." Is this a way of implying that others may not share her view of the part she thinks the woman should play in love?

There is another aspect of this particular rhyme scheme worth noting, the play on masculine and feminine forms, particularly in the first stanza with the adjectives "gais/guaia" and "veraia/verais." Since her lover is gay, she is gay; since she is true to him it *would be fitting* for him to be true to her, "be's taing qu'el me *sia* verais," but no assurance that he is. Having established the masculine/feminine pairing, the Comtessa plays off it with her verbs: "qu'anc de lui amar non m'estrais,/ ni ai cor que m'en estraia" ("I have never stopped loving him nor do I have the heart to stop"), both forms "masculine" and "feminine," so to speak, referring to her love for him. Then she continues: "cel qu'ieu plus desir que m'aia,/ e cel que primiers lo m'atrais/ Dieu prec que gran joi l'atraia" ("the one I most desire that he have me, he who first attracted me, I pray God that great joy may attract him"). Here the "masculine" form ("atrais") describes his effect on her, the "feminine" ("m'aia," "atraia"), the possible, the desired but not at all certain effect she may have on him.

The clear assertion of a feminine voice may also be found in the Lombarda poem, in the play with the feminine form of names, emphasized by their importance as rhyme words. The man says he would like to be a Lombard because of Lombarda ("Lombards volgr'eu esser per na Lombarda"), since no German or Guiscard pleases him as much; but the woman changes the identity from a national to a personal one, "no'm volgr'aver per Bernard na Bernarda/ e per n'Arnaut n'Arnauda appellada" ("I would not want to be called Bernarda for Bernard or Arnauda for Arnaut"). That is, presumably, she does not want to give up her own identity to be subsumed under a man's; he would change his location to be near her, but she does not want to lose her identity to become his. He calls her a "mirail de prez" (a "mirror of value"); she wants to know what mirror he looks in and reminds him of the disruptiveness of failing to see in a mirror, that is, of not seeing what is there, or what he should see, in a stanza in which she plays on the words "descorda/acord/desacorda," "record/recorda," and "acord/acorda," the *orda* words being the rhyme words, while *ord* is the inner rhyme. Huchet's comment on this word-play is that it shows how the poem generates the feminine from the masculine (85), but it also shows how fragile the harmony between male and female can be. His defect (not seeing) destroys ("descorda") her harmony ("mon acord"). But in the last line of the stanza, "en bon acord totz mons pensars s'acorda," the "feminine" form is the verb, the active force creating the "masculine" noun, the state of being.

If the female voice can be asserted through such grammatical play, it can also be heard more directly in comments about what is expected of women. Thus Castelloza (I):

> . . . A mi esta gen,
> si ben dison tuig que mout descove
> que dompna prec ja cavalier de se,
> . . . .
> mas cil c'o diz non sap gez ben chausir;

[It pleases me, even though everyone says that it is very improper for a lady to plead her own cause with a knight . . . but whoever says that does not know how to discern well at all;]

and again (III):

> Mout aurei mes mal usatge
> a las autras amairitz,
> c'hom sol trametre mesatge,
> . . . .
> es ieu tenc me per gerida,
> . . . .
> . . . c'aissi'm cove;

[I shall have set a very bad example for other women in love, because it is the man who usually sends the message . . . yet I consider myself cured . . . because this way is right for me.]

Women can also assert the female voice by attacking the male voice, the rhetorical posture adopted by the poet/lover in the courtly love game. This can be a ticklish area, because it is something male writers use from very early on in Provençal poetry.[10] In the *pastorelas* where, unlike the *cansos,* the woman is allowed to speak for herself and answer the man's pleas for her love, she usually does so by cutting through his rhetoric and getting straight to the reality of the situation. This use of the woman to ridicule the extremes of the poet's own postures has a healthy tradition in literature written by men through the Middle Ages and the Renaissance, from the earliest *pastorelas,* the dialogues in Andreas Capellanus, the debate poems of Italian poets, through Boccaccio, Castiglione, and Shakespeare. It probably reflects the reality of life at court much more closely than the distance between the poet and the idealized figure of the *canso* lady does. As Andreas notes, noble women are quick to censure and ridicule the words and deeds of men (ed. Walsh 158–59). The chances are that women did make fun of courtly love rhetoric, even if they encouraged it, precisely because it was so removed from the reality of life. If this debunking characteristic of women in men's poetry is a reflection of life—a big "if" but highly plausible—then it would not be surprising to find women speaking the same way in their own poetry.

To some extent, that is what Castelloza does when she says it may not be proper for women to court, but that is what the situation demands, so she will. It certainly is what the women do in the *tensos.* When Maria de Ventadorn debates with Gui d'Ussel on equality between lovers, he claiming that between lovers there can be no seignory, she that the lady must retain a certain power, being "dompna" and "amiga" while the man can be "amic" but not "seignor" in the love situation, she is throwing the whole rhetoric of the courtly love game in his face. He says they must be equal if they have "made one heart of two" ("faich un cor de dos"), relying on the very unrealistic cliché. He implies that if they are not equal, it is unjust because he is required to love more loyally ("O vos diretz, e no·us estara gen,/que·l drutz la deu amar plus leialmen"), whereas he had earlier said that if *she* feels more love, she should show it ("s'esdeven que l'am plus finamen,/ e·l faich e·l dich en deu far aparen"). In other words, it is all right for her to love more but not for him. He also says that if she is false, she should hide it with a "bel semblan," suggesting that as long as he gets what he wants, it does not matter what she feels or does. But Maria points out that to win the lady the man promises to serve her as her man, her vassal ("mans jointas e de genolhos"), echoing a position Bernart de Ventadorn offers to take; if he has promised himself as a servant but then, when he gets her, acts as her equal, he is a traitor ("ieu lo jutge per dreich a trahitor,/ si·s rend pariers ei·s det per servidor"). Underlying this remark is the truth that promises are all part of the game, of the rhetoric of love, meaningless in the reality of an affair. Perhaps Domna H. is making a similar point in a contrary way when she argues that the man who breaks his word not to do more than hold hands and kiss is a bolder lover than the one who refuses to swear because he is afraid he cannot keep his word. She is simply acknowledging the fact that no matter what the man says about his desires, what he wants is total satisfaction; this recalls the lady in Andreas who says men can talk about *amor purus* and *amor mixtus,* but what they want is *amor mixtus.*

Other *tensos* focus on other aspects of the game or the opposing reality: Isabella shows up the man's pretence, having him admit that he praised her not for love but for his own honor and profit ("s'ieu en dizia lauzor/ . . . no·l dis per drudaria,/ mas per honor e pro qu'ieu n'atendia"). Alamanda tells the man who has lost his lady, who happens to be her lady, how the game is played ("s'ela·us ditz d'aut puoig que sia landa,/ vos la'n crezatz,"—"if she tells you that a high mountain is a plain, you must believe her") and implies that she is more concerned to stay in her lady's good graces than to help him back into them; he betrays his own fickleness by his readiness to look elsewhere for what she will not give him (the help he wants), just as he presumably did with the lady he claims to love ("D'autra amistat ai talan qu'ie·us enquiera,/ si no·us calatz"). And in what is perhaps the most cynical poem of all about male-female relations, though it is concerned with marriage and not with the love-game, Carenza tells the two girls who wonder about marrying and having babies that if they want their qualities to be properly appreciated (and they are the qualities of a courtly lady, "ensenhamen,/ pretz e beltatz, joven, frescas colors/ . . . cortezi' e valors"), they had best marry Christ.

One cannot, of course, know if the poems we still have of the trobairitz are representative of all the women composing in Provençal, or even if they are representative of the works of these women. We cannot know if these poems were preserved because they were the most popular of their kind, or because they were different from the conventional products. But they are all we have, so we are forced to draw whatever conclusions we can from them, however hesitantly. And from this preliminary survey of some aspects of their style and techniques, I would say that there is evidence of a somewhat different rhetoric among the women, a much greater tendency to address the lover directly, to refer to a past state that no longer obtains, a more negative expression of feeling, if not attitude, through both the persistent use of negatives and the greater use of contrary-to-fact verb forms, and at the same time an assertion of the female voice in wordplay and rhymes, and in the attacks on the conventions of the courtly game.

Notes

1. As Huchet points out (78), the spring opening occurs only once among the women poets, and then in an inverted form; he discusses various aspects of their style and characterizes their poverty of expression not as a weakness, but as "une marche vers le silence" (84). Shapiro suggests that the Comtessa internalizes the process of encomiastic description of the lady (566), and also notes the high incidence of direct address to the lover among the women poets (570).

2. Bec notes that the average number of poems for the women is not all that different from that of most of their male counterparts, since there are only some two dozen poets for whom we have twenty poems or more ("'Trobairitz' et chansons de femme" 236). He credits Tavera ("À la recherche des troubadours maudits" 146) with the observation. Dietmar Rieger points out that the manuscripts indicate a greater interest in the vidas of the trobairitz than in their poems; of the twenty-four manuscripts containing women's poems, eight have only one, three only two ("Die trobairitz in Italien").

3. I have consulted the editions by Lazar for Bernart de Ventadorn, by Del Monte for Peire d'Alvernhe, by Wilhelm for Arnaut Daniel, by Lavaud for Peire Cardenal, and by Boni for Sordello. For the trobairitz, I used the Schultz texts as reprinted in Bogin and the edition by Paden et al. for Castelloza. I have not included Azalais's poem to Clara because it is neither a canso nor in stanzaic form.

4. Bernart de Ventadorn in his 41 cansos, which are normally from 6 to 8 stanzas long, has 10 negatives in one stanza, 8 in 3, 7 in 3, 6 in 9, 5 in 16, 4 in 30, 3 in 31, 2 in 59, 1 in 56, and 48 full stanzas and 25 envois with no negatives at all. There are negative words in 1 of every 2 lines in 9 of his 41 cansos; roughly 1 in 3 in 5 of them, 2 in 5 in 3 poems, 1 in 4 in 3, 1 in 4.5 in 2, 1 in 5 in 9 poems, 1 in 6 in 4, 1 in 7, 10 and 12 in one poem each, and 1 in 11 in 2 poems. Peire d'Alvernhe has no heavily negative poems, 1 occurrence in 5 or 6 lines in 6 poems, slightly more in 2 others (2 in 7, 5 in 17), and fewer in the remaining 2 (1 in 7, 1 in 9). He has 16 full stanzas and 4 envois with no negatives, 20 stanzas and 2 envois with only 1, 12 with 2, 12 with 3, 3 stanzas with 4 negatives, and 2 with 6. Arnaut Daniel has 2 stanzas with 8 negatives, 1 with 9, 1 with 10, one heavily negative poem (32 in 45 lines), the rest much less so (1 negative in 2 lines in 3 poems, 3 or 4 in 10 lines in 4 poems, 1 in 4 or 5 lines in 6 poems, 1 in 6, 7, or 8 lines in 3 poems). Arnaut has no negatives at all in 17 full stanzas and in 8 envois, only 1 in 12 stanzas and 6 envois, 2 in 28 stanzas and 3 envois, 3 in 22 stanzas, 4 in 9, 5 in 8, and 6 in only 2 stanzas. Peire Cardenal has one heavily negative poem, with almost 1 per line (51 negatives in 53 lines and stanzas with 15, 16, and 18 negatives); the rest are rather light, 1.5 per 10 lines, 2 in 9, 1 in 8, 1 in 7, as much as 3 in 7 in only one, and none in the 9 lines of two others. Sordello has as many as 8, 7, or 6 per stanza only once each, 5 per stanza 3 times, 4 twice, 3 and 2 fifteen times each, 1 nine times (plus 3 envois or refrains), and none at all in 11 stanzas and 8 envois; he has 1 in 3 lines 4 times, 2 in 5 twice, about 1 in 4 three times, 1 in 6, 10, and 13 lines once each.

5. [On negativity in Castelloza see Siskin and Storme in Part 2 of this volume.—Editor's Note]

6. I deal with these two together since both indicate something that is not so. Henceforth when I say subjunctive, I mean both subjunctive and conditional, and I do not distinguish mood and tense in my text in order to simplify my expression.

7. Paden suggests that the man suffers before love, the woman after, because the cultural model of love calls for the man to be active, the woman passive ("*Utrum copularentur*").

8. In the Alais, Iselda, Carenza *tenso*, the sounds are *en, ors, enza, os,* with vowel and one-consonant sounds connecting non-rhymes. Alamanda's poem, which is in *coblas doblas,* connects three of her *a* rhymes this way (*anda, onda, uda*), while the *b* rhyme stays the same throughout. In the Lombarda exchange, which is in *coblas singulars,* the *a* rhymes are *arda, agna, ada, orda,* the *b* rhymes *er, ez, az, es.*

9. [See also the essay on derived rhyme by Sarah Kay in Part 2 of this volume.—Editor's Note]

10. See my "Male Fantasy and Female Reality in Courtly Literature" for a fuller discussion of the points alluded to in this section.

4 Was Bieiris de Romans Lesbian? Women's Relations with Each Other in the World of the Troubadours

"Na Maria, pretz e fina valors," the only surviving poem of Bieiris de Romans, is among the most frequently discussed love-songs of troubadour lyric poetry, and one may well ask why so much research has been undertaken on a poem that certainly does not belong among the masterpieces of its age.

Composed by a woman and addressed to another, it acquires a special position not only within the works of the trobairitz but within the entire Occitan literature of the thirteenth century. Since the troubadour typically speaks to the *domna,* it is clear that the inversion of this configuration in the poems of the trobairitz may be regarded as a marginal phenomenon; that the masculine element should be eliminated, however, so that the lyrical dialogue takes place exclusively between one woman and another, is an extraordinary rarity. Other than in Bieiris's *canso,* this is the case in only four other Old Occitan pieces. Three of these are *tensos,* genuine dialogues between two or three female interlocutors: the exchanges between Almuc de Castelnou and Iseut de Capio, Carenza and Alaisina Iselda, and an anonymous *domna* and her *donzela.* The fourth concerns a *salut,* a letter whose author, Azalais d'Altier, appears as the ambassadress of a male "client," striving to gain his reconciliation with the addressee of the letter, *domna* Clara.[1] But only Bieiris turns directly to another woman with a *canso,* the typical genre for a love-poem. While the structure of the text and manuscript tradition do not allow for any certainty, the way is open to speculation that the modern reader is witness here to a medieval lesbian relationship.

In order to give the discussion a sound foundation, we should begin with the question of the historical reality of lesbian relationships in the

Occitan Middle Ages. Unfortunately, historians supply little information on the matter.[2] Yet John Boswell's work, *Christianity, Social Tolerance and Homosexuality,* comprehensive in both time and geography, describes the phenomenon of homosexuality as belonging to the Hellenic-Roman culture group, giving examples, however—all in Latin—from the early Christian and early medieval periods, and goes on to describe the later marginalization of homosexuality, even in literary tradition, together with the growing intolerance and sanctioning on the social plane from the thirteenth century onward:[3]

> Given the complexity of the political scene at the time and the infinite variety of response, it is startling how completely and dramatically the gay artistic tradition was broken off. A few poems exemplifying this tradition survive from the first half of the thirteenth century, including what may be the sole extant example of medieval love poetry written in the vernacular language by one woman to another.[4]

This statement concerning none other than Bieiris shows that with regard to lesbian love in the thirteenth century one comes up against considerable difficulties of documentation, indeed that research goes round in circles. The evidence we have turned up by falling back on reality is exactly the poem that we had hoped to illuminate—which is far from a reliable document.

So we direct our search once more to the literary phenomenon in order to assess the position of homosexuality within troubadour poetry. It is well known that the latter is characterized by a latent ambiguity.[5] Among other things, this is made apparent in the terms used for the beloved lady: although the troubadour's predominantly "normal" address for his lady is (*ma*) *domna* or *bona/bella domna,* it is often replaced by the grammatically masculine form *mi dons* as in the famous *canso* of Bernart de Ventadorn, "Can vei la lauzeta mover":

> Pus ab *midons* no·m pot valer
> precs ni merces ni·l dreihz qu'eu ai,
> ni a *leis* no ven a plazer
> qu'eu l'am, ja mais no·l o dirai.[6]

> [Since prayer or mercy or the right that I have cannot help me with my lady, and it doesn't please her that I love her, I shall never tell her.]

Here it is still clear from the context of the language that the beloved person is female ("leis"), but there are cases in which this cannot be determined with certainty, as in Guillem de Cabestany's *tornada* from "Lo dous cossire":

> En Raimon, la belheza
> e·l bes qu'en *midons* es
> m'a gen lassat e pres.[7]
>
> [Sir Raimon, the beauty and the good that are in my lady have gently bound and captured me.]

Here the gender becomes clear only from the situational context (if it were a man one would hardly praise his "belheza"), but nevertheless in this instance one may rule out the possibility of a homosexual relationship with certainty. Such masculine address for a real woman may seem strange to the modern reader; stranger still, however, if the social context required such a playful inversion of the convention, *midons* could have been used to refer to a real man in a homosexual relation. The same holds true for masculine *senhals* of the ladies addressed, for example, "Mos Belhs Deportz,"[8] and here too the ambiguity of the address may on occasion be played upon at great length, as in Peire Vidal's *canso* "Bels Amics cars, ven s'en vas vos estius."[9] Although the *senhal* "bels Amics cars" is identified by Avalle as a "pseudonimo forse di Eudossia di Constantinopoli,"[10] the fact that Peire's complaint about the indifference of his beloved, "Na Vierna," is addressed to a lady, becomes apparent only because he uses the term "sisters" for both of them:

> Per que devetz nom de *serors* aver
> qu'ambas essems vos fai Dieus mais valer. (vv. 40–41)
>
> [So that you must be called sisters because God makes you take precedence together.]

Even if the related wording in praise of the "Amic" befits a woman better than it does a man, as, for example:

> E volh vos tan, bels Amics car, vezer,
> qu'a penas puesc sai mos huelhs retener, (vv. 13–14)
>
> [And I want to see you so much, handsome, dear Friend, that I can hardly keep my eyes here,]

the first of the two quotations is the only sure ground for supposing that the "amic" concerns an "amiga," and that the choice of *senhals* is primarily intended to emphasize the poet's friendly attachment to the woman addressed, for he could actually confess his lovesickness to a male confidant as well.

These examples may suffice to illustrate that although the masculine *senhals* used by the troubadours could be interpreted at first glance as expressing a covert homosexuality, this poetry is not generally homosexual but (and this is of great importance) plays constantly upon linguistic ambiguity in ways that now and then become visible even in manuscript transmission. This is made particularly apparent in the obscene *cobla dobla* (P-C 461,241) where the sole manuscript, G, replaces the refrain:

> E [lo fotaire] ditz que mal mòr e peiz viu
> qui non fot *la* qui ama (vv. 8–9)
>
> [And (the fucker) says he dies badly and lives worse who does not fuck her whom he loves]

or

> E ditz qui non fot que mal viu
> noit e jorn *la* que ama (vv. 17–18),
>
> [And he says that he lives badly who does not fuck her night and day whom he loves,]

with "*le* qui ama," which means literally "*him* whom he loves;" to which Pierre Bec puts the provocative question, "Faute de grammaire ou tendance homosexuelle?" (*Burlesque* 169)

Before we look into the possible homosexual tendencies in Bieiris's *canso* we must also ascertain whether, apart from these ambiguities, there are any other examples in troubadour poetry where homosexuality appears quite explicitly. Another *cobla dobla* (P-C 461,127) has been handed down to us in which the theme is touched upon directly, independent of the question of the sex of its author. We will cite only the first of the two *coblas*, as the second, exclusively devoted to food, has nothing to do with our study.

> Ges no m'eschiu nuls per no mondas mans
> ab mi manjar ni de seder ades,
> q'hanc ab mas mans no fis faitz descortez,
> ni toll ieu l'ars qi sol far las putans.

Ben ai tochada ganba blanc'e lissa,   5
pitz, tintinas e trezas e mentos
de toseta joven mas no de tos—
abanz fos eu crematz sor la cenisa![11]

[No one on account of my unwashed hands
should refuse to eat or sit down readily with me,
for I have never done anything unpleasant with my hands,
neither have I learned the art that whores practice.
I have indeed touched the white smooth leg,
the breasts, nipples, plaited hair and the chin
of a young girl, but not of a boy—
I would rather be burned beneath the ashes!]

In this case it is obviously a male author who wishes to give proof of his moral integrity in that he vehemently denies having had any homosexual experience. Apart from the insight that in the world of the troubadours male, and indeed female, homosexuality was not exactly held in high esteem—after all, the anonymous poet wishes to be burned (like a heretic) rather than touch a boy—this *cobla* places such conduct on the same level as whoring, and designates the entire matter as "faitz *descortez*." The possibility of a lesbian poem thus cannot be denied on the grounds of a complete absence of homosexuality in troubadour poetry.

Because a lesbian interpretation of "Na Maria, pretz e fina valors" does not at all fit the traditional image of the *domna* in Old Occitan poetry, the very possibility has naturally made scholars uncomfortable. Nelli's comment on the reaction of critics is entirely accurate when he says, "Les philologues ont essayé, bien sûr, de réduire ce 'scandale'" (301). We shall only glance at the manner in which they organized this attempt. Bieiris's first commentator, Sainte-Palaye, evaded comment most elegantly by making the amorous trobairitz the ambassadress of a male lover: "Elle loue une autre dame, dans une pièce, où elle semble parler au nom d'un amoureux qui fait sa déclaration d'amour" (3:379). Schultz-Gora, the first editor of a collection of trobairitz texts, originally described the love-song as "von der Bieiris de Romans im zärtlichsten Tone an eine andere Dame gerichtetes" (6). Under pressure from critics, however, he subsequently revised this judgment and attempted, by means of a philological tour de force, to make a troubadour out of the trobairitz, an "Alberics" out of "Bieiris."[12] For Schultz-Gora's successors the problem was reduced to the question of whether the author was really a woman or, as seemed more likely, a man; not until almost a hundred years later was the discussion again taken up by Bogin, Nelli, and Bec (in *Burlesque et obscénité*).

Even Bogin, who vigorously defends the lesbian interpretation, does not avoid the discussion of Bieiris's controversial female authorship (176–77, 99–100 in the French edition). Nelli presents a broad range of possible interpretations of the poem; although he takes no definite position, it becomes clear from his remarks that he would like to attribute the *canso* to a woman.[13] In contrast, Bec reaches the conclusion that a definite classification on the basis of purely philological evidence is impossible, but argues that the poem is interesting only if it is truly by a woman:

> S'il est l'oeuvre d'un homme, il est quelconque, s'il est l'oeuvre d'une femme, il serait le type même d'un contre-texte particulièrement séditieux, ou plus simplement ludique: dans les deux cas un texte de rupture.[14]

In spite of these differing approaches and interpretations, study of the poem has, as yet, failed to bring about any clarification. Consequently, it does not appear to me to be of interest to continue the discussion of the gender of the author of "Na Maria, pretz e fina valors." In my opinion, the record of the manuscript speaks for itself and attests quite adequately that the author was female, so that henceforth I shall take this as given. Yet the question remains whether the author was lesbian. As I pointed out in my introductory remarks, neither the literary tradition nor the social situation speaks for such an interpretation. It is possible that we may get an answer from a contrastive comparison of the text with the four poems cited earlier that involve exclusively women, though any (homo)erotic content is excluded from them by the thematic context. But first let us turn once more to the one sure document, the text itself.[15]

The poem's transmission is not particularly good. Manuscript *T* is not among the most reliable, being full of Italianisms and providing us only with the heading "nabieiris de roman"[16] over a very corrupt text. In this manuscript one could doubt even the attribution, since in another place a song that is definitely by a trobairitz, "A chantar m'er" (P-C 46,1) by the Comtessa de Dia, is ascribed to the troubadour Uc de Saint-Circ. From this circumstance, two possible conclusions may be drawn with regard to Bieiris:

1. The author did not take much note of the poet's gender, and just as the poem attributed to Uc is by a woman, the one attributed to Bieiris could be by a man.

Or, what seems more plausible to me:

2.   If the scribe attempts to assign to a troubadour a poem clearly com-
     posed by a trobairitz, why should he then invent a woman just for
     Bieiris's canso?

The latter consideration implies that for him the existence of the trobairitz lay beyond any doubt.

    In the following edition of the text I have altered the *T* version as
little as possible and have carried out only the most necessary corrections.
I wish to direct the reader's attention from the outset to the critical passages, lines 12 to 16 and the second *tornada*.

I   Na Maria, pretz e fina valors
        e·l gioi e·l sen e la fina beutatz,
        e l'acuglir e·l pretz e las onors
        e·l gent parlar e l'avinen solatz,
        e la do*us* cara, la gaia *c*uendanza,   5
        e·l d*ouz* esgart e l'amoros se*m*blan
        que son e*n* vos, don non avetz egansa,
        me fa*n* traire vas vos s*e*s cor truan.

II   Per *qu*e vos prec, si·*us* platz, que fin'amors
        e gausiment e douz umilitatz   10
        me puosca far ab vos tan de socors
        *qu*e mi donetz, bella domna, si·*us* platz,
        so don plus *a*i d'aver gioi esperansa;
        car en vos ai mon cor e mon talan
        e per vos ai t*o*t so *qu*'ai d'alegransa,   15
        e per vos vauc mantas vez sospiran.

III   E car beutatz e valors vos onransa
        sobra totas, *qu*'una no·*us* *e*s denan,
        vos prec, si·*us* pla*t*z, per so que·us es onransa
        que non ametz entendidor truan.   20

IV   Bella dompna, cui pretz e gioi *e*nanza
        e gent parlar, a vos mas coblas man,
        car en vos es *s*aessa et alegransa
        e tot lo ben *qu*'om e*n* dona deman.

[I   Maria, merit and true worth
        and joy and sense and true beauty,
        hospitality and merit and honor
        and elegant speech and pleasant society,
        and the sweet face, the merriment,   5
        and the sweet look and the loving manner

that are in you, in which you have no equal,
make me draw toward you without deceit.

II   Therefore I beg you, if you please, that true love
and rejoicing and sweet humility   10
may bring me so much help with you
that you grant me, noble lady, if you please,
what is my greatest hope of having joy;
for my heart and my mind are set on you,
and I get all the happiness I have from you,   15
and [yet] you often make me sigh.

III   And since beauty and virtue honor you
above all other women (for not one stands before
    you),
I beg you, if you please, for your honor's sake,
not to love a deceitful lover.   20

IV   Beautiful lady, whom virtue and joy distinguish
and noble speech, to you I send my stanzas,
for in you are wisdom and rejoicing
and all the good qualities one wishes in a lady.]

1 e fina] e la fina *T (hypermetric).*
5 dous] doz *T, a rare form which recurs with orthographic variation in line 10; another*
    possible correction would read: la dousa car'e.
6 douz] ducz *T;* semblan] seblan *T.*
7 en vos] e vos *T;* egansa *T was corrected to* engansa *by Bogin, following the erroneous*
    reading by Schultz-Gora.
8 fan] fay *T;* ses] sis *T.*
9 que] ce *T* (cf. 12, 15, 18); si·us] siuos *T (hypermetric, cf. 12, 19).*
10 douz] doutz *T.*
12 que] ce *T;* si·us] siuos *T.*
13 ai] ni *T. This incorrect and dubious line, for which we are obliged, since* ni *does not make*
    any sense, to adopt Schultz-Gora's by no means compelling emendation, is unfortunately
    one of the decisive passages for the poem's interpretation.
14 car] & car *T (hypermetric).*
15 tot] tut *T;* qu] c *T.*
17 onransa *T] Corrected by Schultz-Gora to* enansa; *although* onransar *is not found as a*
    verb elsewhere, we have kept to the manuscript version as the rhyme of the verb with the
    noun (v. 19) is to be preferred to the rhyme with the same word enansa (v. 21).
18 qu] c *T;* no·us es denan] nouos ouos denan *T. I have adopted Schultz-Gora's correction*
    for the quite incorrect line with two syllables too many.
19 si·us] se uos *T;* platz] plaç *T.*
21 enansa] onansa *T.*
23 es saessa] es aessa *T. I depart from Schultz-Gora's reading* gajess', *too far from the*
    manuscript reading.
24 qu'om en dona] com e dona *T. I accept Schultz-Gora's emendation to* en *and the result-*
    ing translation "that one wishes of a woman," although the ms. version is not entirely
    impossible and in translation would read "what a man and a woman (lady) wish for."

> This reading would support the homoerotic interpretation, but it is improbable since the counterpart to domna would not be (h)om, but senher/don.

From close examination of this poem, three working hypotheses may be deduced, the last of which we will consider more carefully:

1. It is in fact a lesbian love-poem; this hypothesis can be supported by two, or possibly even three, places in the text where the erotic element is unmistakable:

Vv. 12–16: Bieiris asks of Maria that she grant her the longed-for fulfillment of her love (*gioi*) and gives expression to her anxious hope when she pleads,

> que mi donetz, bella domna, si·us platz,
> so don plus ai d'aver gioi esperansa. (vv. 12–13)

and:

> e per vos vauc mantas vez sospiran. (v. 16)

V. 20: The poetess urges Maria not to love a deceitful admirer, which may be interpreted as implying that men are altogether bad, and therefore she should decide in favor of a woman.[17]

V. 24: If one accepts the version presented in the notes,

> car en vos es saessa et alegransa
> et tot lo ben qu'om e dona deman, (vv. 23–24)

in the interpretation: "You unite all the goodness in yourself that a man *and* a woman can wish for," thus: "You are pleasing to the (bad) men but to the (good) women too," it might also explain the contrast—which would therefore be stylistically intended—in the conceptual pairing of *om* (negative connotation) with *domna* (positive connotation).

2. The second working hypothesis holds that the song cannot be regarded as an example of lesbian love poetry, since this view is necessarily based upon the particular stanza that has come down to us in the most uncertain form; and that consequently the homosexuality can be corrected "in" or "out" according to the editor's fancy by means of inevitable emendations:

V. 13: Only through the somewhat risky emendation of *ni* into *ai* does one arrive at the explicitly erotic phrase *ai esperansa d'aver gioi;* as the syntax is anything but regular, it remains questionable whether this really is the right correction and whether the stanza might not read completely differently. As a result, all the places in the text cited under the first hypothesis lose their eroticizing context.

V. 24: Again, the first hypothesis may be rejected not only on the grounds that the opposition *om-domna* is semantically wrong, but also on the grounds that in the manuscript the nasals *m* and *n*, or their contractions, are frequently missing, as in verses 6 (se*m*blan) and 7 (e*n* vos).

3. We now come to our third working hypothesis. The poem is indeed by a woman, addressed to another, but nevertheless does not concern a lesbian relationship. In addition to the already-mentioned rejection of homosexuality within troubadour poetry, which makes a public, positive depiction of such a relationship very improbable, the poem does not contain any indecent passages either. Bieiris addresses Maria only in a manner customary for her time and her world; she expresses her sympathy for her in a conventionally codified form—which the choice of genre would also support—just as one, or better, a woman, speaks with a female acquaintance, friend, confidante, or close relative.

In short, the colloquial tone used between women differed from that used today, and what modern readers deem erotic was simply tender, to keep Schultz-Gora's very apt term ("zärtlichsten" 6). Troubadour research has yet to tackle the problem of the expression of female affectivity in Old Occitan. In contrast to the troubadours,[18] little has been said on this theme regarding the trobairitz, and where it is touched upon it is done with reference to their addressees—who are usually male. On that account, I would like to pursue the question here as to how in the troubadours' world a woman addresses another, or rather, may address another, that is, what conventions exist and what preconditions they imply.

For example, it is evident that a lady's maid would not address her mistress in the same tone as a great lady would her friend. Further, it is clear that dialogue between one woman and another in prose texts such as the *vidas* and *razos* or in a nonlyric text such as *Flamenca* differs from lyrical dialogue. Two factors, then, determine the expression of female affectivity: first, the social positions of the woman who speaks and of the woman addressed, and their level of familiarity; and second, the literary context in which their dialogue occurs.

As we are primarily concerned here with the trobairitz and lyric poetry we can only venture briefly into the nonlyric domain, although more thorough investigation concerning the following points would be most worthwhile:

1. What account do (male) third parties give of the relations between women? Many *vidas* and *razos* take up the theme.[19] Consider Clara d'Anduza, the trobairitz who is probably the addressee of the *salut* from Azalais d'Altier discussed below, and of whom the author of the *razo* to Uc de Saint-Circ's "Anc mais non vi temps ni sason" (P-C 457,4) reports as follows:

> Et [N'Uc de Saint-Circ] si amava una do[m]pna d'Andutz, qe avea nom ma dompna Clara. Mout fo adrecha et ensenhada et avinenz e bella; et ac gran volontat de pretz et [d']esser auzida loing et pres, et d'aver l'amistat et la domestighessa de las bonas do[m]pnas et dels valenz homes. Et N'Uc conoc la volontat d'ella et saup li ben servir d'aiso q'ella plus volia; qe non ac bona dompna en totas aqellas encontradas con qal ell non fezes qe l'agues amor et domestigessa, et no·ill fezes mandar letras et salutz et joias, per acordansa et per honor. Et N'Uc be fasia las lettras de la[s] responsions qe convenian a faire a las dompnas dels plasers q'ellas li mandavan. (Boutière and Schutz 244)

> [And (Sir Uc de Saint Circ) loved a lady of Andutz who was called lady Clara. She was very clever and well-read and attractive and beautiful; and she had a great desire for good reputation and to be heard of far and near, and to have the friendship and the familiarity of the good ladies and the worthy men. And Sir Uc understood her desire and knew how to serve her well in what she wanted most; for there was not a good lady in all those regions with whom he did not bring it about that she had love and familiarity, and whom he did not cause to send her letters and greetings and presents, in harmony and honor. And Sir Uc wrote the letters in response that were suitable to write to the ladies about the presents that they sent her.]

There are two matters of significance in this quotation: first, that the relations of friendship between women from the upper social classes were widely varied, and could include both admiration and expression of open affection (*amors, plasers, joias*), which could also manifest themselves in literary activities (*letras, salutz, responsions*); and second, that these literary activities in the form of attestations of honor, friendship, and love (which, as we see, could also be delegated to professional troubadours) were subject to specific conventions that it was necessary to master: "las lettras de la[s] responsions qe *convenian* a faire a las dompnas."

2. What form does this standardized dialogue between women take? Various *ensenhamens*[20] could supply some information on the matter, but a *sirventes* ascribed (probably mistakenly) to Raimon Jordan provides a fine example of female manners, for it closes with the words:

> E s'eu per so volh far razonamen
> a las domnas, no m'o reptes nien;

car domna deu a–z autra far onransa,
e per aisso ai·n eu dig ma semblansa.[21]

[And if for that reason I wish to make a defense for women, do not criticize
me for it at all; for a lady must show honor for another, which is why I have
given my opinion.]

An anonymous *cobla* also takes up the question and stresses the loyalty
of a woman in her dealings with another as a special virtue:

Dompna qe d'autra s'escuda
    ni cuid' amorsar
son crim per autr' encolpar
faill trop, a ma conoguda;
qar dompna deu esquivar   5
    malditz d'autr' et elognar.
E pos malditz d'autra·il passa las denz,
De si eissa sapcha q'es maldizens.[22]

[A woman who conceals herself behind another one and proposes to wipe
out her offense by accusing another makes a great mistake, in my opinion;
for a woman ought to shun and avoid abusing another. But if she speaks ill
of another woman, may she know that for her part she is a malicious gossip.]

3. Finally, how is feminine dialogue expressed in literature apart
from lyric poetry? An example may be found in *Flamenca,* in the relationship of Flamenca, Alais, and Margarida (the *domna* and her two
maids), who even wrote together,[23] and also in the lightly ironic portrayal of the female rivalry at Flamenca's wedding:

Quan las domnas sa beutat lauzon
Ben podes saber bela es,
Qu'en tot lo mon non n'a ges tres
En que las autras s'acordesson
Que del tot lur beutat lauzesson. (vv. 558–562)

[When ladies praise her beauty you can be sure she is beautiful, for in all the
world there are scarcely three about whom the others could agree to praise
their beauty at all.]

These lines illustrate that outside of lyric poetry, besides all the light in
the relations between women there are also shadows. In the lyric poetry
of the trobairitz, however, there is no place for such rivalries and petty
jealousies.

To what extent does the woman's social position affect the manner in which she addresses another? Let us begin with women of different position, the noble lady and her underling, the *donzela,* who stands below the married woman if only because she is unmarried, but nonetheless may, from being a maid, become a confidante. Our example is the anonymous *tenso* "Bona domna, tant vos ai fin coratge" (ed. Schultz-Gora 29–30). The way in which the *donzela* addresses her lady is immediately apparent in the title, the respectful *Bona domna* (vv. 1, 12, 50) with which we are well acquainted in troubadour songs, and which, precisely like the phrase *tant vos ai fin coratge,* belongs to the conventional lexicon of troubadour terms for praising women. Only on one occasion, when the *donzela* allows herself to become familiar and asks the lady to speak quietly, is the form of address abbreviated to *domna:*

> Süau parlem, domna, qu'om no·us entenda, (v. 33)
>
> [Let us speak softly, lady, so no one will hear us,]

and in spite of the relationship portrayed as intimate between *domna* and *donzela* (the latter permits herself to offer the lady some good advice, and begins her intervention on behalf of the lover who has fallen out of favor with the words "Non puesc mudar no·us cosselh vostre be" (v. 2) [I cannot keep from advising you for your good]), the *dompna* emphasizes the social difference between them with the forms of address "Na donzela" (vv. 9, 25, 41) and "donzela" (v. 52), without adding the first name. She behaves just as majestically toward her as she does toward her rejected admirer, whose advocate she puts back in her place with plain words:

> Na donzela, non m'en podetz rependre. (v. 25)
>
> [Young lady, you cannot criticize me.]

Toward the end, however, even she shows that she regards her *donzela* almost as a friend (as does Flamenca, who calls her maid Margarida *amiga* in verses 4570 and 4572) and takes her advice:

> Bona es la fin, donzela, ab que s'atenda
> e vos siatz garda entre nos dos,
> e que·us tengatz ab aquel que·l tort prenda. (vv. 52–54)
>
> [The end is good, maiden, if only we wait for it, and you be guard between us two, and stay with the one who suffers wrong.]

In the dialogue between lady and servant we find on the one hand the conventional manners that also hold good for lady and troubadour, and on the other, a certain degree of intimacy which eases the class difference. This may also be seen in our next example, the *tenso* of Carenza, "sur un sujet qui est vraisemblablement une parodie ironique des discussions traditionnelles de casuistique amoureuse entre troubadours masculins," a theme Bec subsumes under the title, "Avoir des enfants ou rester vierge?" (Bec, *Mittelalter* 30)

The two sisters seeking advice on this question—of whom, according to Bec (24–25), only the one called Alaisina Iselda speaks—approach Carenza with great respect and courtly formality:

> Na Carenza *al bèl còrs avenenz*
> donatz conselh a nos doas serors. . . . (Bec 22–23, vv. 1–2)

> [Lady Carenza of the beautiful, attractive person, give counsel to us two sisters. . . .]

Na Carenza is obviously an experienced woman who can advise the *pulcela* (v. 6) on marriage or children. Nevertheless the social difference is not as great as in the previous example: here it manifests itself in Na Carenza's greater experience, which is that of a married woman or perhaps even of a nun (even if the religious interpretation of the *tenso* is refused), and probably in the age difference as well (cf. *jovenz* v. 10). It is conceivable that an older relative is involved, the mother[24] or an older sister. This comes out, above all, when Carenza treats her interlocutor as of equal birth, addressing her with the following courtly compliments:

> N'Alaisina Iselda, 'nsenhamenz
> prètz e beltatz, jovenz, frescas colors
> conosc qu'avetz, cortisia e valors,
> sobre totas las autras conoissenz; (vv. 9–12)

> [Lady Alaisina Iselda, I know you have learning, merit and beauty, youth, fresh complexion, courtesy and worth, more than all other knowledgeable women;]

In view of this arsenal of conventional troubadour courtesy we should briefly recall Bieiris's first *cobla:*

> Na Maria, pretz e fina valors
> e·l gioi e·l sen e la fina beutatz, (vv. 1–2)

as well as the line:

E car beutatz e valors vos onransa
sobra totas, qu'una no·us es denan, (vv. 17–18)

and it becomes all too apparent that Bieiris adopts an entirely normal, even conventional, colloquial tone that was required by good manners between women, particularly between women of equal social position.

In contrast to the (thematically related) *tenso* between *domna* and *donzella,* the dialogue between Almuc de Castelnou and Iseut de Capio takes place between women of equal standing. Each one addresses the other using *dompna* with *na* and her first name—"Dompna n'Almucs" (v. 1) and "Dompna n'Iseus" (v. 11)—and the latter shows herself to be conciliatory and quite in favor of her friend's argument:

mas si vos faitz lui pentir
leu podretz mi convertir. (vv. 19–20)

[But if you make him repent, you will be able to convert me easily.]

The familiarity, even intimacy of the colloquial tone increases markedly between women of equal social rank who thereby clearly foster a friendly relationship. This is made still clearer in Azalais d'Altier's *salut* to domna Clara. As this little-known text is of special interest here, I shall quote the entire first part and provide a translation:

Tanz salutz e tantas amors
e tanz bens e tantas honors
e tantas finas amistaz
e tanz gauz com vos volrïaz
e tanz ris e tant d'alegrier   5
vos tramet n'Azalais d'Altier,
a vos, donna, cui ilh volria
mais vezer qe ren q'el mon sia;
qe tant n'ai auzit de ben dire
a ceilh qe·us es hom e servire   10
qe per lo ben qu'el me n'a dich
ai tant inz en mon cor escrich
vostre senblant qe si·us vezia,
entre milh vos conoisseria;
e dic vos ben aitan en ver   15
qez anc donna, senes vezer,
non amei tan d'amor coral;

e dic vos ben, si Deus me sal,
quez el mon non es nulla res
q'eu penses qez a vos plagues   20
qez eu non fezes volentiera,
senes mant e senes preguiera.
Et ai, donna, trop gran desire
quez eu vos vis, e·us pogues dire
tot mon cor e tot mon voler,   25
e pogues lo vostre saber. 25

[So many greetings and so much love
and so much goodness and so much honor
and so much friendship
and as much joy as you could wish for
and so much laughing and so much merriment   5
Azalais d'Altier sends to you;
to you, noble lady, whom she
would rather see than anything else in the world;
for I have heard so many good things of you
from him who is your vassal and servant   10
that because of the good things he has told me about you
I have so impressed your image upon my heart
that if I were to see you,
I would know you in the midst of a thousand;
and I tell you quite truly   15
that never before have I, without seeing a lady,
loved her so from my heart;
and I assure you, so help me God,
there is nothing in the world
which I think might please you   20
that I would not gladly do,
without demand and without pleading.
I wish so much, noble lady,
to see you and to be able to tell you
all that lies in my heart and all my desires,   25
and to learn the same from you.]

This outright declaration of love is addressed to the friend whose
first name, Clara, is only given indirectly in lines 98 and 99,

anz li sias fina e clara
q·el noms ni·l semblans no·us desmenta,

[Rather be true and and bright (Clara) to him, so your name and appearance
will not give you the lie,]

and who is addressed at the beginning only as *donna* (vv. 7, 23, 27, 39) and at the end as *bona donna* (v. 101). The attestation of sympathy in verses 1–25 thus introduces Azalais's actual matter of concern, the portrayal of the rejected lover whom Clara must accept again, which begins in line 27 with the words,

> Aras, donna, es enaissi. . . .

In this *salut* Azalais is not afraid to pull out all the stops in praising the woman in order to reach her goal. First she appeals to the *sen, ensengnamen* and *valor* of her "friend":

> [qe] vos aves ben tan de *sen*
> de *valor* e d'*ensengnamen* (vv. 41–42)
>
> [For you have indeed so much wit, worth, and learning]

—let us recall the comparable passage in Bieiris:

> Bella dompna, cui *pretz* e gioi enanza,
> e *gent parlar,* a vos mas coblas man,
> car en vos es *saessa* e alegransa. (vv. 21–23)

Finally Azalais beseeches Clara to pardon the lover for her sake:

> Per qu'eu vos prec, per gran *merce*
> qe vos, tot *per amor de me*
> li perdones . . . (vv. 89–90)
>
> [And so I pray you, for mercy's sake to pardon him just for love of me . . .]

—and here the usage of semantically complex troubadour concepts such as *merce* and *amor* (cf. also *amor coral,* v. 17) must be pointed out. Bieiris's *fin' amors* and *socors* belong in the same category:

> Per que vos prec, si·us platz, que *fin' amors*
> e gausiment e douz umilitaz
> me puosca far ab vos tan de *socors* . . . (vv. 7–10)

In the case of Azalais's "dear friend" we are concerned with a woman whom she knows only by hearsay, from the descriptions given by the unhappy lover:

> [. . .] vos donna, cui ilh volria
> mais vezer que ren q'el mon sia;
> qe tant n'ai auzit de ben dire
> a ceilh que·us es hom e servire. (vv. 7–10)

Nevertheless, Azalais gives vehement protestations of her affection, even confessing to Clara:

> entre milh vos conoisseria
> e dic vos ben, aitan en ver
> qez anc donna, senes vezer,
> non amei tan d'*amor coral* . . . (vv. 14–17)

and

> quez el mon non es nulla res
> q'eu penses qez a vos plagues
> qez eu non fezes volentiera. (vv. 19–21)

One may well conclude that the colloquial tone adopted by women among themselves in the world of the troubadours allowed for—and also called for—considerably more affectivity than modern reception imagines. Moreover, when Azalais introduces concepts like *desire, cor* and *voler* into her *salut:*

> Et ai, donna, trop gran *desire*
> qez eu vos vis, e·us pogues dire
> tot mon *cor* et tot mon *voler* . . . , (vv. 23–25)

it is no longer at all surprising that Bieiris addresses Maria, who is obviously her intimate friend, as follows:

> Per que vos prec . . .
> que mi donetz, bella domna, si·us platz,
> so don plus ai d'aver gioi esperansa. (vv. 9, 12–13)

Regardless of the uncertainty of line 13, already discussed, it may be established that even if the object of the request expressed by the impersonal *so* remains unidentified, this does not justify the assumption that erotic desires are intimated here. Rather, the impersonal *so* appears to refer to a familiar fact that needs no further clarification for either the author or the woman addressed. Azalais also refers obliquely to the "guilt" of Clara's rejected lover with a similar phrase:

> . . . non podes jes per raizon
> azirar lui *per l'ucaison,*
> q'eu sai, ez elh e vos sabes. (vv. 47–49)

[You cannot rightly hate him for this pretext—that I know and he and you know.]

So what do we actually learn in Bieiris's poem to Maria? The author certainly conveys sympathy and affection, but, as we have seen, she does not exceed the normal degree of affectivity usual between women. In addition, the *canso* is the bearer of a request that is not clearly specified, as its meaning is well understood by both women and therefore is simply reduced to *so*. All the same, in what follows we learn that Bieiris attaches great importance to the fulfillment of her request, that she places great hopes in Maria, and that her uncertainty regarding the latter's reaction fills her with concern:

> car en vos ai mon cor e mon talan
> e per vos ai tot so qu'ai d'alegransa,
> e per vos vauc mantas vez sospiran. (vv. 14–16)

The seeming "érotisme de ces vers" (Bec, *Burlesque* 200) is lost against the backdrop of the strongly affective and, one might say, generally eroticized colloquial tone of the women. If we now consider Bieiris's first *tornada* against the same backdrop, we become aware that all the other trobairitz except Na Carenza address persons of their own sex, either attempting to bring about a reconciliation with a rejected lover (the *donzela,* Almuc de Castelnou, Azalais d'Altier), or else reacting to such an attempt at mediation (the *dompna,* Iseut de Capio). Only Bieiris's *canso* seems to fall outside this thematic framework. By contrast, she speaks out against any love for an *entendidor truan:*

> vos prec, si·us platz, per so que·us es onransa
> que non ametz entendidor truan. (vv. 19–20)

On the assumption that the key to the poem's interpretation lies here, much has been written about the expression *entendidor truan* (Bec, *Bur-*

lesque et obscénité 200, Nelli 305). But however one may choose to read it, as disparaging men in general or as an attempt at categorizing good and evil, the fact is that the male element is introduced by this phrase, albeit in a manner contrary to that of the other texts. The secret (*so*) that both women are hiding is therefore connected with a man or with men in general. We will not be able to resolve it, since all the conjectures in this triangle must remain hypotheses: Does Maria have a choice between several admirers, and is she to decide on the "right one," and are Bieiris's words spoken out of a sort of maternal concern that this young, beautiful, and intelligent woman might choose the wrong one? Or does the man in question stand between the two women, and is Bieiris's poem an appeal to Maria not to take him, thereby making herself and Bieiris unhappy? The list of possible situations could certainly go on, but the two cited may suffice to demonstrate that Bieiris's *canso*—following the feminine lyrical tradition—revolves around the absent third party, the man. The possibility of an element of female jealousy (which might even bear lightly homoerotic characteristics) need not be ruled out entirely. Despite out best efforts, however, the text provides no more circumstantial detail.

It has been worthwhile, nevertheless, to substantiate that Bieiris's poetic motivation does not spring from a lesbian relationship, and that, although the "tender tone" between women may have been lost over the course of centuries, among the trobairitz and persons of their sex it was very common. And this conclusion is perhaps not without interest even for our present.

Notes

1. For editions, see the Checklist under the names of these trobairitz.
2. See Bonnet; Bullough, esp. 117–27: "Lesbianism"; Foster; and Radcliff-Umstead.
3. Boswell 220, where he nonetheless cites a clearly erotic poem from one woman to another from the twelfth century; regarding the sanctions, cf. also 290. Stehling 100–05, "Two Lesbian Love Letters from a German Manuscript (twelfth or thirteenth century)." According to Kuster and Cormier (598–99), ecclesiastical authorities were more lenient toward lesbianism than toward male homosexuality, although lay authorities were not.
4. Boswell 265. Boswell himself points to critics' doubt over the identity of the author (n. 79).

5. Nelli establishes this clearly: "Il y aurait un livre à écrire, non pas sur l'homosexualité (rare dans la littérature d'Oc), mais sur les *tendances* manifestement homosexuelles de toute érotique épurée" (1:303). Nelli also mentions that the troubadours sometimes assumed women's names as *senhals,* or pseudonyms (301). It is regrettable that he does not specify which ones did so. See also Marchello-Nizia.

6. P-C 70,43, vv. 49–52, ed. Riquer 1:386.

7. P-C 213,5, vv. 96–98, ed. Riquer 2:1076.

8. P-C 248,9, v. 27. For further examples see Bergert; also Chambers, *Proper Names*.

9. P-C 364,9, ed. Avalle 1:26–32; likewise Anglade 8–11.

10. Avalle 1:29. Cf. also his summary of the discussion as to whether the *senhal* signifies a man or a woman (1:27–28).

11. The diplomatic edition of the text, which has hitherto never been critically edited, is as follows:

Ges com eschiu nuls per no mondas mans
ab ni maniar ni de seder ades
qhanc ab mas mans no fis faiz descortez
ni toll ieu lars qi sol far las putans
ben ai tochada ganba blanche lissa   5
pitz tintinas e trezas e mentos
de toseta iouen mas no de tos
abanz fos eu crematz sor la cenisa.

Cf. Stengel, *Archiv* 265, corrected here according to ms. (*P*) at v. 5 to read *ganba* in place of *gauba*. Editorial modifications: 1 ges no m'eschiu] ges com eschiu *P*. 2 mi] ni *P*. 4 l'ars] lars *P*.

12. Schultz-Gora, "Nabieiris de roman;" see also P-C 16a on Alberico da Romano. None of the later philologists have accepted this derivation.

13. For example: "Si, comme je le pense, Bieiris est une féministe convaincue, *entendidor truan* désigne tout amant . . . de sexe masculin" (305).

14. *Burlesque* 198. Nevertheless the poem is to be found under the heading "Un poème homosexuel?" in Bec's anthology of counter-texts (197–200).

15. I shall give here my own edition and translation from my forthcoming complete edition of the trobairitz: *Die liebende Frau als lyrisches Ich in der altokzitanischen höfischen Lyrik*. For previous editions, see the Checklist of Poems by the Trobairitz (in this volume).

16. *Sic.* Bec (*Burlesque* 197) is mistaken when he shortens the heading to "de r.," believing that only in analogy to "folquet de r." can Romans be inferred as the place of origin of the trobairitz.

17. Cf. Bec, *Burlesque* 200 and Nelli 305, quoted above in note 13.

18. Studies on the vocabulary of male affectivity include those of Cropp and Lavis.

19. E.g. the *razos* to Raimbaut de Vaqueiras, P-C 392,9, or to Pons de Capdoill or Rigaut de Berbezill; see Boutière and Schutz 465, 315, 154–55.

20. E.g. the "Ensenhamen de la donzela" of Amanieu des Escas, ed. Bartsch, *Chrestomathie* 355–58. See the study of the *ensenhamens* by Monson.

21. Ed. Kjellmann 61–63, vv. 37–40; cf. also A. Rieger, "Un *sirventes* féminin—la *trobairitz* Gormonda de Monpeslier."

22. Ed. Kolsen, *Zwei provenzalische Sirventese* 17–18.

23. Ed. Lavaud and Nelli vv. 4529–79.

24. Vv. 21–24 have a rather maternal ring to them, and imply, in any event, a difference in age:

N'Alaisina Iselda sovinença
ajatz de mi e'us membre de guirença:
quant i seretz prejatz lo Glorïos
qu'al departir mi ritenga près vos.

[Lady Alaisina Iselda, remember me and remember salvation; when you are there, pray to the Glorious one to keep me near you when we part.]

(Bec, *Burlesque et obscénité* 203.)

25. From my own edition; the diplomatic edition by Crescini is unfortunately somewhat unreliable.

AMELIA E. VAN VLECK

5   "Tost me trobaretz fenida":
     Reciprocating Composition
     in the Songs of Castelloza

Castelloza's lyrics depict a woman driven as much by exasperation as by
joi to justify her breach of silence against the charge that she should not,
in conscience, sing. Trespassing the boundaries of self-expression is a
conventional motif in troubadour lyric, yet one here sharpened by an
unconventionality that applies to all trobairitz: Castelloza more than once
addresses the view that the role of active, outspoken suitor does not befit
a woman. What makes the trobairitz unconventional is not "une éternelle
féminité" guaranteeing "spontaneity" or "unliterariness"—presumptions
against which Pierre Bec aptly cautions ("Trobairitz et chansons" 248)—
but the redistribution of power, by force of speech, that is occasioned by
the woman's song. Ironically, however, in this lyric context the usurpa-
tion of poetic speech does not empower the woman. Quite the contrary,
as Marianne Shapiro describes the situation:

> The displacement of the male lyricist by a female lyricist is the basic shift
> that generates a number of other modifications within the available repertory
> of *topoi* in the system of *fin'amor*. That a woman had become the subject of
> the enunciation meant that she posited herself as a suppliant and her lover as
> recipient, thus reversing the two polar humilities and neutralizing her domi-
> nation through her femaleness. (562)

Despite Castelloza's repeated defense of the woman's right to sing love-
pleas, she also recognizes and enacts the powerlessness of the suppliant;
the persuasive line in her work, I maintain, moves to restore power to
her poetry's speaker by reinstating the conventional roles. She uses a variety of persuasive techniques, from promises to memories, from hints
to commands, to prompt the addressee (*amic*) to act as *amador* / *preja-*

dor—and thus, by voicing love-pleas, as *trobador*—so that she can vacate the demoralizing post of *amairitz / trobairitz* and claim the powerful position of *domna* now occupied by another. Thus, the exchange of words between *amairitz* and *amics* takes center stage, particularly the poetic speech of the *prec* or love-plea.

Concern with verbal power is prominent enough among Castelloza's broad themes to suggest its operation also in details of her language. Attention to the way Castelloza's lyrics sound notes from the register of speech and poetry will add a dimension to our reading of them: songs where we have primarily observed how she realizes the topoi of *amor*— the "medicine" of love, the request for a reward (*merce*) from the beloved, and so on—offer also Castelloza's own versions of the topoi of *trobar*.[1]

Castelloza's preoccupation with speech and poetic composition is well represented in each of the four songs attributable to her.[2] By focusing on speech as the medium of whatever love or antagonism passes among the characters of her cansos, she leads us quickly to a second level in which the terms for speech and silence act as equivalents of the terms for life and death, or for love and indifference. In Poem I, "Amics, s'ie·us trobes avinen," Castelloza examines her own formal, poetic speech in contrast to other real or imagined counter-speeches. Not only can she control what *she* says; she manifests a compulsion to create and manage also what is to be said by others.

Acknowledging disaccord between her glowing verse portraits of her loved one and the mean model he provides, the speaker presents her lyric composition as a proportional response ("On plus . . . "), though an inappropriate one, to her *amic*'s behavior:

> . . . —cant era m'en sove
> Qu'ie·us trop ves mi mal e sebenc e ric,
> E·n fatz chansons per tal que fass'ausir
> Vostre bon pretz; don eu nom puesc sofrir
> Q'eu no·us fasa lausar a tota gen
> On plus me faitz mal ez asiramen. (I, 3–8)

[—since now I am mindful that I find you mean and spiteful and proud, and yet I make songs such that I make your good name heard; so, I cannot forbear to make you praised by all people, the more you deal out pain and anger to me.]

Her response reverberates to the greater public: not only does she praise this angry man, but under her influence so does everyone else ("tota gen").

She thus finds her composing poetry to him to be incongruous with his merit though not with her own compulsion ("nom puesc sofrir"); further, she shows herself facing a widely held view ("dison tuig") that it is inappropriate in another way—simply because she is a lady, and ladies should not compose poems presenting love-arguments (*prejar*) to men:

> Eu sai ben qu'a mi esta gen,
> Si ben dison tuig que mout descove
> Que dompna prec ja cavalier de se,
> Ni que·l tenga totz tems tam lonc pressic. (I, 17–20)

> ["I know well that it pleases me, even though everyone says that it's very improper for a lady to plead her own cause with a knight, and make him so long a sermon all the time."]

How easily she could shape "what everyone says" in the exordium, persuading all to praise a manifestly unredeemed sinner against lyric virtues—yet too soon public opinion passes out of her command. The speaker anticipates antagonistic discourses, not only the one just cited (by which *tuig* would disapprove all trobairitz[3]) but also the objections of a generalized individual antagonist to her particular passion:

> Asatz es fols qui m'en repren
> De vos amar, pos tan gen me conve;
> E cel c'o diz no sap co s'es de me,
> Ni no·us ve ges a·ls uels ab qu'ieu vos vic . . . (I, 25–28)

> ["He is quite a fool who reproaches me for loving you, since it is so very pleasing to me; and he who says it doesn't know how it is with me, nor has he seen you with the eyes I saw you with . . ."]

This imagined reproach, which spells out (and puts into the mouth of an anonymous third party) all that is wrong in the speaker's choice of an addressee, implicitly limits the man's beauty to the eyes of a single beholder—thus limiting the validity of her praise-song's argument. Loving him is fitting specifically to her ("pos tan gen me conve"), and counters general "folly" based on the majority view from unenamored eyes. Thus, although she has claimed the power to "make him praised by all" (v. 7), she points out that a good case can be made against him—and presented in public. His worthiness to be praised or blamed depends upon what *he* says:

. . . Ni no·us ve ges a·ls uels ab qu'ieu vos vic
Quan me dissez que non agues consir,
Que calc'ora pori'endevenir
Que n'auria enquera jausimen.
De sol lo dig n'ai eu lo cor jausen. (I, 28–32)

[. . . Nor has he seen you with the eyes with which I saw you when you told me that I should not worry, for at some time it might come to pass that I might yet have enjoyment. From the saying alone I have a rejoicing heart.]

This speech he once made could disprove the unfavorable line of speech of "whatever fool" reproaches her love. The nameless slanderer, "cel c'o diz," "did not see him with the eyes with which she saw him" when her *amic* spoke those words of solace. Having portrayed him as an ogre in the eyes of many, herself included, the lady offers him a way to transform his own image, guiding him in what kinds of words it would be advisable for him to say. If he would console her in public, all would see him through those adoring eyes.

The speaker's imagining of antagonistic discourses extends to the beloved himself:

—Non farai ja, qu'eu non vueill puscaz dir
Qu'eu anc ves vos agues cor de faillir;
C'auriaz i qualque razonamen,
S'ieu avia ves vos fait faillimen. (I, 13–16)

[I will never do it, for I do not want you to be able to say that I ever had the intention of doing you wrong; for you would have some justification if I had made an error toward you.]

What her *amic* "will be able to say" is something the speaker moves vigorously to control. She has threatened him with a soiled reputation; she defies him to soil hers. Her proof that she has *not* made an error (*faillimen*) is the unlikelihood that his hypothetical discourse against her could bear any *razonamen* whatever. While she refuses to enable a fault-finding response to herself or to her song (derivatives of *faillir* can also refer to metrical or logical flaws in troubadour verse[4]), she praises him for a kind of speech he has made toward her in the past and encourages him to repeat it. His comforting words, remembered, counterweigh his potential, hostile *razonamen*.

Thus the song is a complex of speeches: potential, remembered, and actual lines of argument. For their resolution, Castelloza urges the man to take back the properly male role of *prejador,* since doing so will mend his reputation and her health. So her demand for consolation, with *jausir* in the final stanza, is a demand for *dig*—for a reply, for an act of speech corresponding to her own act in singing:

> E no·us o man, qu'eu meseisa·us o dic:
> E morai me si no·m volez jausir
> De qualque joi. . . . (I, 44–46)

> [And I do not send it to you, for I myself recite it to you: and I will die if you are not willing to give me the pleasure of some *joi*. . . .]

If her recitation were the question, the man's reply would be a donation of *joy,* that nebulous elation which troubadour poetry typically gives to and takes from its audience, and which is often associated with literary enjoyment (the *joy de trobar*). In the context of this poem, actions will not speak loudly enough, for speech alone—the man's or her own?—consoles her: "De sol lo dig n'ai eu lo cor jausen" (v. 32). We find, in Huchet's words, "la langue devenue l'objet de désir" (84).

Poem II, "Ja de chantar non degr'aver talan," poses several alternate discourses running parallel to that of the poem itself. The speaker's own inarticulate utterances, opposed to the formally controlled song realized in words, appear as a specter threatening the success of the song-as-love-argument (*prec*):

> Que *plaing e plor*
> Fan en mi lor estage . . . (II, 4–5)

> [For complaint and weeping take their state in me . . .]

> . . . E s'en breu no·m rete
> Trop ai fag long *badatge*. (II, 8–9)

> [. . . And if he does not soon retain me, I have waited too long in vain.]

Badar, "gape," means to stand idly with one's mouth open, waiting in vain. It has been used by other poets to refer to ineffectual singing, the production of bad or useless songs.[5] *Badatge,* then, adds to Castelloza's list of gestures that fail of speech. These subverbal "gestures of the lips"—*plaing e plor* and *badatge*—are, within the context of the stanza, the speaker's disparaging terms for her poetry: when it does not promote her success in love, her song fails to claim, and press into service, the powers of the words it is made of.[6]

The speaker sketches out two songs, in the genre of the *prec* or love-argument, that might have been. Regrettably (from the speaker's point of view), circumstances have not left room for these songs to exist. The first is the poem her lover might have sent to her:

> Que prejador
> No·m fan ren, ni mesatge
> Que ja·m virets lo fre. (II, 31–33)

> ["For suitors have brought me nothing, nor messengers saying that you will ever turn your bridle toward me."]

The second song ostensibly not sung by the speaker herself would have argued the love-plea by recalling a contractual agreement, an exchange of tokens, that would obligate the lover to be loyal to her:

> Se pro·i agues, be·us membrera chantan—
>   Aic vostre gan
> Qu'enblei ab gran tremor. (II, 37–39)

> ["If there was any use in it I would indeed remind you as I sing—I got your glove, which I stole with great trembling."]

Yet having avowed the uselessness of full recall, she sketches out the story of why she returned his glove to the other woman. The stolen token of a contract had bound no oaths in the first place: a one-sided pledge gave her no dominion ("cre / Que no·i ai podiratge," vv. 44–45). Instead of composing an entire Glove-song, like those of Giraut de Bornelh, she has compressed the whole argument into a stanza prefaced by its own disparagement. Both of these unsung songs, by their mere mention, accentuate the addressee's silence. He refuses to reciprocate her song, either by participating in a mutual pledge or by sending *prejador ni mesatge* with promises, or at least rebuttals, in his own words.

A final stanza compares the *precs* composed by knights and by ladies. Men should not outdo their ladies in presenting love-arguments; ladies should *prejar* in proportion as they love. If we take *prejar* as a specific kind of *trobar*, namely, as the composition of lyrics that plead the case for love, then Castelloza is again making the argument that women should compose their share of the world's love-poetry:

> Dels cavaliers conosc que·i fan lor dan,
>   Car ja prejan

> Domnas plus qu'elas lor,
>   C'autra ricor
> No·i an ni seignoratge.
> Que plus dompna s'ave
> D'amar, prejar deu be
> Cavalier, si·n lui ve
> Proess'e vasalatge. (II, 46–54)

[I know some knights who act to their own harm, for they continually court ladies more than ladies court them, because they have no other wealth nor lordship. For the more it happens that a lady loves, the more she ought to make pleas to knights, if there comes into her any sense of courage and service.]

The value attached to *prejar* in both cases—*ricor, seignoratge,* and *proess'e vasalatge*—connects verbal superiority with feudal virtues. *Ricor* suggests *trobar ric*, and *seignoratge* is associated with poetic mastery.[7] The pair *seignoratge/vasalatge* defines the love-plea as both a service and a means of mastery: the "polar humilities," reversed by her stance as *prejairitz,* hang in an uneasy balance.

The stanza explains and answers the charge of conscience, raised in the exordium, that the (female) speaker should not be singing: resuming the verb *dever,* she has changed her own mind. At the same time, it participates in the debate between Bernart de Ventadorn and Peire, restating Bernart's comic vision of a world made-over, for a year or two, to his pleasure.

> Peire, si fos dos ans o tres
> Lo segles faihz al meu plazer,
> De domnas vos dic eu lo ver:
> Non foran mais preyadas ges,
>   Ans sostengran tan greu pena
> Qu'elas nos feiran tan d'onor
> C'ans nos prejaran que nos lor.[8]

[Peire, if for two or three years the world were made to my pleasure, I'll tell you the truth about (how it would be for) ladies: they would no longer be beseeched at all, but rather they would sustain such serious trouble that they would do us the great honor of beseeching us before we beseech them.][9]

Calling to mind both the lightness of Bernart's proposal, and Peire's affirmation that making *precs* is man's work, Castelloza's speaker is far from making a feminist claim to equal rights. Rather, she underlines the reversal that has made her the petitioner, the powerless one. By describing a class of men to which her lover pointedly does not belong, those who send love-poems to their ladies, she congratulates him for avoiding the *dan* they incur, but at the same time points out the *ricor* and *seignoratge* of poetry that he is missing. If it is not only the poor and worthless who *prejan,* let him speak up; if he wishes to refute her upside-down view of the world, where ladies woo and men are weak, he will have to join that class of men who woo. The stanza thus continues Castelloza's persistent effort to evoke, or if necessary to provoke, an "enriching" response from the addressee: that "parallel text" to be composed by him, but which he has thus far neglected to compose.

In Poem III, "Mout aurez fag lonc estage," the song by example (*usatge*) potentially converts a whole class of human beings from *amairitz* to *trobairitz* who "send messengers and carefully chosen rhyme words":

> Mout aurei mes mal usatge
> A las autras amairitz,
> C'om sol trametre mesatge,
> E motz triaz e chauzitz. (III, 21–24)

> [I will have set a very bad example to other women-lovers, for a man usually sends a messenger, and carefully selected rhymes.]

As in Poem II, she directs the man addressed toward his unfulfilled role: a proper *amador* should act the part of *trobador,* composing careful rhymes and employing a messenger (rather than going himself) to sing them.[10] If she sets a poor example for the other *amairitz* by singing, her lover sets an equally bad example for the other *amadors* by not singing. Rather than reinforce the implicit reproach, the speaker settles for less than what *om sol far,* praising her *amic* as best she can for charms that do not include sending love-messages. Again, the stanza both defends the lady's right to make a *prec,* and reproaches the man's silence:

> Es ieu tenc me per gerida,
> Amics, a la mia fe,
> Can vos prec—c'aissi·m conve;
> Que plus pros n'es enriquida
> S'a de vos calqu'aondansa
> De baisar o de coindansa. (III, 25–30)

> [And I consider myself acquitted, my friend, by my faith, when I make love-pleas to you—for this is suitable to me; for the most valiant woman is en-

riched by it, if she has from you some generosity of kissing or of pleasant behavior.]

Her *proeza* will be enriched—and her song successful—if the man can be made to respond to it. This is what justifies her knowingly "setting a bad example" by making a song: its potential to restore the woman to the position of *domna, pro e rica*. In this case, the "abundance" or "generosity" (*aondansa*) she seeks from him is at the level of verbal or sub-verbal gestures: the kiss, as movement of the lips, belongs to the realm of un-articulated, soundless pronunciation; *coindansa,* a general category of nice behavior, could include the speech appropriate to courtship.

Despair over his unresponsiveness leads her to the topos of love's med-icine, including an apparent threat of suicide and request for "surgery":[11]

> Anz son pensiv'e marida
> Car de m'amor no·us sove;
> E si de vos jois no·m ve
> Tost me trobaretz fenida,
> C'ab petit de malanansa
> Mor dompna s'om no cal lansa. (III, 35–40)

> [Instead I am thoughtful and grieved, because you do not remember my love; and if joy does not come to me from you, soon you will find me dead, for with a little sickness, a lady dies if someone does not apply the lancet.]

Line 38, "soon you will find me dead," plays upon an ambiguity that becomes unavoidable in the context of Castelloza's persistent effort to elicit a counter-text from her lover. *Trobar,* of course, means to compose poetry, and *fenida* is the accepted term for a specific unit of poetry: the *tornada*.[12] We can take the line to mean, "Soon you will compose a *tornada* for this poem" or "Soon you will compose a farewell couplet for me," an *envoi* commending her to another addressee (perhaps to God, to whom ladies untended by love's physicians go: *fenida* also means death-knell, "glas funèbre" [FEW, s.v. fīnīre 2 "sterben"]). To "compose a *fenida*" may also stand in metonymy for "to compose a whole song," since one doesn't reach the end without first passing through the begin-ning and the middle. In either case, the line paradoxically sees the speak-er's final failure to get *joi* from this recalcitrant lover as, at the same time, success in her project of obliging him to compose verses for her.

Alone, the ambiguous line "Tost me trobaretz fenida" might not seem a clear request that the addressee compose a *tornada* for the poem.

But the speaker reinforces this request. The final stanza carries out the functions of a *tornada* (by anticipating the song's reception) and thus does duty for the missing *fenida* she apparently is asking him to compose; it reasserts her demand for a "reciprocating text" to be composed by the *amic:*

> E prec que veingnaz a me
> Depueis que aurez ausida
> Ma chanson, que·us faz fiansa—
> Trobarez bella semblansa. (III, 47–50)

> [And I beg that you come to me as soon as you will have heard my song, for I make you a pledge: you will find a fair appearance.]

We recall that in Poem I the speaker did not employ a *joglar* but delivered the song in person ("Qu'eu meseisa·us o dic").[13] Now she asks that the addressee "come to her" as soon as he has heard her song. Not only will he "find a good reception" with her ("trobarez bella semblansa") but, if we again read *trobar* as "to make a song," she expects he will "compose a beautiful *semblansa*" to her song—that is, a mirror-image, a likeness, that parallel text she has been urging him to compose, the response she has waited for. Her vow, *fiansa,* thus is both an offer and a threat: "I guarantee that, when you visit me, you will compose a likeness of this song." Pierre Bec observes of trobairitz poetry that "on n'y relève jamais le terme de *trobar* . . . " ("Trobairitz et chansons" 241). This song of Castelloza uses it twice, if we accept *trobar fenida* and *trobar semblansa* as alluding to poetic composition.

Poem IV, "Per joi que d'amor m'avegna," which strongly resembles the other three songs in its style and themes, ends in a similar request for a *bel semblan*—either a "friendly greeting" or, as before, a beautiful likeness of her own song, a set of words that parallel her text and thereby reward it. That this *bel semblan* will make the difference between life and death,[14] reviving *me* and "killing" *consir,* proposes (within the schema I have suggested) that the counter-text swing the balance between trobairitz and *domna,* animating the latter while letting the former take her turn at silence, given the whole song has been one long *consir:*

> Amics, no·m laissatz morir,
> Pueis de vos no·m puesc gandir
> Un bel semblan que·m revegna
> E que·m ausiza·l consir. (IV, 47–50)

[Friend, do not let me die, since from you I cannot obtain a *bel semblan* that would revive me and that would kill my worry.]

Like the other songs, this one demands that the man act upon her poetry, even "obey" it:

> Qu'eu non cre qu'en grat me tegna
> Cel c'anc non volc hobesir
> Mos bos motz ni mas chansos. (IV, 3–5)

["For I don't believe that he finds me pleasing, he who never wanted to heed my good words or my songs."]

Returning to this "obedience," she makes clear that what she wants from him is a reply:

> E pos no·ill platz que·m retegna,
> Vueilla·m d'aitant hobesir
> C'ab sos avinenz respos
> Me tegna mon cor joios. (IV, 13–16)

["And since it doesn't please him to keep me, he might at least want to heed me enough to keep my heart joyful with his inviting responses."]

By specifying that his *respos* should be *avinenz,* the speaker again directs the man in the kind of speech she wishes him to produce.

In soliciting a verbal response, she seeks to transfer the powerless position of the suppliant, the spokesman for *amar* and *trobar,* to the poem's recipient. She thus in a sense rejects the unconventional roles (those other than the *domna*'s) that the female speaker creates: of the *amairitz / trobairitz,* and even of the "passionate woman" whose complaints have their roots in the *albas, chansons de toile,* and *chansons de malmariée.*[15] Although Castelloza's poetry usurps the power of words and glories in it, it does so ambivalently; it strives to use that strength toward a return to the silent, but more powerful position of *domna.* With his *bella semblansa* and his *avinenz respos,* her *amics* can take back the suppliant role of *amador / trobador,* with its attendant pains. When he does so, he either kills her *consir* or advises her not to *cossirar,* thus dispensing with the type of poetry her supplication produces: complaint. At the same time, he will inspire her to *jauzir,* which is what *amadors* do for their ladies, and what *trobadors* do for the audiences to which they sing. Castelloza tries out the fantasy-world envisioned by Bernart de Ventadorn, exemplifies Bernart's forecast of the great suffering entailed for ladies in this reversal of the roles, and uses the unconventionality of her female voice to urge the proper thing: "ans conve / c'om las prec e lor clam merce." She cannot ask for a *merce* in the sense of a tangible reward; the answering *precs* will be her *merce*.

Having surveyed the evidence, in these four lyrics, of Castelloza's apparent efforts to elicit responding texts from her hearers, one must ask whether it is plausible that a trobairitz might urge an addressee to compose her a poem—or to compose just a *tornada*. She could of course, in all instances, be speaking figuratively. But particularly in Poem III, "Mout aurez fag lonc estage," the request is so striking—with "Tost me trobaretz fenida" and the final lines, challenging the hearer to appear before her as soon as he has heard her song and to *trobar bella semblansa* (*sai* "here" in the manuscripts)—that it is worthwhile to consider the grounds for (and against) believing that she could actually have expected an addressee to add a rhyming half-stanza to her poem.

Numerous troubadour lyric songs ask their addressees to learn and sing them.[16] The addressee is thus treated not simply as a song's receiver, but also as a potential performer. Sometimes there are also indications that the poet expects the addressee to respond to the poem by improving it,[17] adding to it, sending it on to another addressee (which could involve attaching another *tornada* as one might "forward" a letter by writing another address and adding another stamp), or by replying to it. In the starling poems of Marcabru and Peire d'Alvernhe, the birds return with answering poems; Guilhem IX asks that the final *destinataire* of his riddle-poem send back to him its counterpart, *la contraclau*.[18]

The case for accepting *trobar fenida* as a poetic term in Poem III would gain strength, in considering whether Castelloza predicts her *amic* will "compose an ending" or "find her dead" or both, if the *tornada* was felt to be a detachable part of the poem. If poets treat it as an "option," if transmitters treat it as a snippet of verse requiring less stringent fidelity than usual to the "original" version, then we have some reason to think Castelloza may have viewed the *fenida* as an occasion for impromptu additions.

Azalais de Porcairagues does speak of the *fenida* as if it were detachable, requesting that her song be conveyed *with* it, as if it could be conveyed *without* it:

> Joglar, que avetz cor gai,
> Ves Narbona portatz lai

Ma chanson ab la fenida
Lei cui Jois e Jovens guida. [19]

[Joglar, you who have a lively spirit, take there to Narbonne my song, with the ending, to her whom *Jois* and Youth guide.]

Indeed, the *chansonniers* provide hundreds of instances in which the same song was carried both with and without *tornadas*. The *tornada*, of all the stanzas in troubadour songs, is most likely to vary from one manuscript to another—not to vary in its position within the poem, but to be omitted or to exist in several different versions. [20] Even the most stable poems, spared from stanzaic transposition in the manuscripts, frequently come down in at least one manuscript with the *tornada* missing (such is the case with Arnaut Daniel's sestina where *V* lacks the *tornada*, and Peire d'Alvernhe's "Cantarai d'aqestz trobadors" where *CRa* lack the *tornada*) [21] or with alternate *tornadas*. A song of Guilhem de Saint-Didier, one that by its lyric persona gives the performer a field day, comes equipped with four different "tornades apocryphes" in *COQ, V, AB,* and *Sg,* respectively, in addition to the one Sakari deems "authentique" in *ABGIKOQ.* [22] The six versions of the famous *tornada* of Jaufre Rudel's "Quan lo rius de la fontana":

Senes breu de pergamina
tramet lo vers . . . ,

name two to three different addressees, two different *joglars*, and seven different regional destinations among them (P.-C. 262,5 ed. Pickens 88–89). It is as if the *tornada* changed with the song's circulation, depending upon the audience for whom it was to be sung.

Clearly, it is conceivable that some addressees would accept an invitation to compose a *tornada* for another person's composition. But this brings us to the question of Castelloza's audience: what kind of public would appreciate this endeavor to return the role of *prejador* to the male *amic*? The rarity of songs by trobairitz, and their lack of "courtly ambiance," has led scholars to discuss the notion (which seems to have originated with Bogin, on the grounds of the women troubadours' supposed "candor") that they had no "audiences" as such: that their songs were performed "privately" or were given very limited circulation, primarily in written form (Shapiro 569–70; Bec, "Trobairitz et chansons" 240). Castelloza, though, lays claim to a substantial audience, since she causes her praise of her *amic* to be heard and repeated by *tota gen,* "everyone":

E·n fatz chansons per tal que fass'ausir
Vostre bon pretz; don eu nom puesc sofrir
Qu'eu no·us fasa lausar a tota gen (I, 5–7)

["Yet I make songs to make your good name heard; which is why I cannot keep from making everyone praise you."]

That she sees herself as "setting an example for other women in love" (III, 21–22) means that she considers *las autras amairitz* an important sector of her audience; her position before them gives her the responsibility of leadership. For a general audience unaccustomed to songs sung in the voice of a woman, Castelloza's strategy of offering the role of *prejador* to the man, since she accepts the belief that it is rightfully his, might alleviate the sense that the *convenances* have been unpardonably violated. It could thus facilitate her poetry's acceptance by an audience composed of men and women.

If we assume a more exclusive circulation, an audience that was probably of great importance to the women troubadours was that "club d'affiliés," as Bec calls them, of other poets (240). Given Castelloza's "accès à cet univers socio-poétique somme toute assez clos qu'était le monde troubadouresque" (Bec 240), we can be sure that she had some literary contacts. Supposing that "Mout aurez fag lonc estage" were composed for other poets to hear, what better mark of respect for her peers could she make than to ask her hearer to "compose her a *fenida*"? We can infer from other sources that the trobairitz probably had considerable literary contact with the troubadours: from the high proportion of trobairitz compositions that are *tensos* with men, and from the *vidas* which frequently depict the trobairitz as consorting with male poets and composing poems for them. Other circumstantial evidence points to literary exchange between at least one trobairitz and a troubadour: if Azalais de Porcairagues was the "Joglar" of Raimbaut d'Aurenga as Sakari argued ("Azalais de Porcairagues, le Joglar de Raimbaut d'Orange"), then the large number of songs he sent her (more than a dozen according to Pattison [451]), along with the high level of poetic skill evident in her one surviving song, suggests that the two exchanged songs regularly over a period of several years. Only one of Castelloza's songs comes down to us with *tornadas* (Poem II), but there she confirms that other poets composed part of her audience by naming the trobairitz Almois de Castelnou as one of two addressees (Paden et al. 162–63). That the troubadour as *destinataire* took some part in the audience of the trobairitz, then, is not an unreasonable supposition.

When miniatures in the chansonniers depict trobairitz they usually show them alone, either declaiming with raised hands or holding some symbol of distinction such as a rod, a scepter, or a falcon (A. Rieger, "Ins e·l cor" 391–92). But women recognizable as trobairitz appear with men in at least three miniatures—two where the men are unquestionably troubadours. The picture in manuscript *A,* fol. 168v, of Castelloza "en train de 'domnejar' avec un chevalier" (A. Rieger 393 and Fig. 1) appears, because of the positioning of the figure's hands, to make her the listener while the man declaims; the illustrator, placing her within this "couple complémentaire," thus grants her the reciprocation her poetry envisions. Among eight illustrations in the manuscripts *A, I,* and *K* showing troubadours accompanied by ladies, two show ladies attired as trobairitz: portraits of Pons de Capdoill *(A,* f. 45v) and of Rigaut de Berbezilh *(A,* f. 164v), who "sont représentés debout, en train de converser avec une noble dame blonde qui porte le manteau que nous connaissons pour être celui des *trobairitz* et une couronne" (A. Rieger 394).

In sum, Castelloza's request for a "responding text" from her addressee would have been appropriate either for the usual audience of the *canso,* accustomed to the self-reflection of troubadour lyric but perhaps less comfortable with the character of the female *prejador,* or for a specialized audience composed mainly of other poets. Her strategy of seizing the right to *prejar* in *motz triatz e chauzitz* and then graciously offering to give it back creates a unique place for a trobairitz—a temporary place, she might protest, but a few of her lyrics *have* lasted—among the variety of stances available for the speaker in the Old Provençal *canso.*

Notes

1. For the intersection of terms in the fields of *amor* and of *trobar,* see Zumthor, "Circularité" as well as Van Vleck 14–26.

2. Paden et al. present the evidence for and against the attibution of P-C 461,191 to her (163–65). All citations of Castelloza's poetry refer to the texts in this critical edition. Translations within quotation marks, following the Old Occitan texts, are Paden's.

3. Bruckner points out that Castelloza uses the very terms of Peire d'Alvernhe—*"avinen, cove, pregar"*—"to refashion her own sense of the respectable," and that "it is precisely the tradition that acts as *lausengier* (gossip monger, deceiver, and potential rival)" (241).

4. E. g., Azalais de Porcairagues:
E s'ieu faill ab motz verais,

D'Aurenga me moc l'esglais. (P-C 43,1 vv. 13–14)
[And if I err with true words, my sadness came from Orange.]
I am ignoring Sakari's punctuation (colon after *verais*), since his translation calls for a comma in the text ("Le Joglar" 184).

5. Cf. Marcabru:
Si l'us musa, l'autre bada
E ieu sui del dich pechaire
[Si l'un muse, l'autre bâille, et moi, je pèche en le disant] (tr. Dejeanne)
(P-C 293,51, ed. Dejeanne vv. 29–30);
Mas menut trobador bergau
    Entrebesquill,
Mi tornon mon chant en badau
    En fant gratill
[Mais de menus troubadours frelons et brouillons ridiculisent mon chant et en font des gorges chaudes] (tr. Dejeanne)
(P-C 293,32 ed. Dejeanne, vv. 9–12).

6. That sighs and tears interfere with eloquence can be seen in Raimbaut d'Aurenga's *carta* where they force him to end the letter:
Sospir mi fan fenir mon comde . . . ;
Plor mi tol q'eu non puos plus dire
Mas cho q'eu volgra dir, conssire
[Sighs make me finish my account . . . ; tears keep me from saying more to you but I think that which I should like to say] (tr. Pattison)
(ed. Pattison 149, vv. 181, 183–84).

7. Cf. Grimoart:
Sobre·ls melhors senhoreja
mos chans, en qual guiza·m vuelha,
e·ls motz laissans senhorei
e·ls sai dir aissi cum vuelh
[My song dominates the best in whatever fashion I choose, and I dominate the words by tying them up, and I know how to say them just as I want]
(P-C 190,1 ed. Riquer 1:273–75, vv. 57–60), and Bernart Marti:
E qui belhs motz lass'e lia
de belh'art s'es entremes;
Mas non cove q'us disses
que de totz n'a senhoria
[And he who ties and binds beautiful words has taken up a beautiful art; but it is not fitting for anyone to say that he surpasses everyone]
(P-C 63,6 ed. Riquer 1:254–57, vv. 75–78).

8. P-C 323,4 ed. Appel 10–13, vv. 22–28.

9. Peire appears to be speaking from the more common view when he counters that ladies should not make pleas, since that is a job for men (vv. 29–31):
Bernatz, so non es d'avinen
que domnas preyon; ans cove
c'om las prec e lor clam merce.
[Bernart, it is not fitting that ladies should beseech; instead it is seemly that men beseech them and beg mercy from them.]

10. The lines could indicate that, for this song, she does employ a messenger, since she now does what "om sol far."

11. See discussion in Paden et al. 167. An alternative explanation for Castelloza's request, if one doubts "lancet" for *lansa,* is a possible allusion to a lance that wounds with the first blow, then heals with the second, named by Bernart de Ventadorn as "the lance of Peläus":

Anc sa bela bocha rizens
non cuidei, baizan me träis,
    car ab un doutz baizar m'aucis,
    si ab autre no m'es guirens;
        c'atretal m'es per semblansa
        com de Peläus la lansa
que del seu colp no podi'om garir,
si autra vetz no s'en fezes ferir.

[I never thought her beautiful, laughing mouth would betray me with a kiss, yet with a sweet kiss she slays me, unless she revives me with another. Her kiss, I think, is like the lance of Peleus, from whose thrust a man could not be cured unless he were wounded by it once again.] (tr. Nichols et al.) (P-C 70,1 ed. Appel 1–10, vv. 41–48.)

12. Raynouard, *Lexique Roman* (3:329), cites two passages where *fenida* means "ending" and, in context, specifically the concluding part of a poem: "Lo vers vay a la fenida" in Peire Raimon de Tolosa (P-C 355,12) and "Ves Narbona portatz lai / Ma chanson ab la fenida" in Azalais de Porcairagues (P-C 43,1).

13. This line does indicate that, at least within the poem's own fiction, she did not employ a joglar to deliver the song; however, there is nothing in "eu meseisa·us o dic" to suggest that she transmitted the poem in writing. On the contrary, Castelloza refers specifically to a "first," oral performance in which speaker, poet, and performer claimed identity. The inclusion of such a claim would lend immediacy and authenticity to any performance or reading—even a silent reading from a written text.

14. Cf. Poem II, vv. 10–11:

Ai bels amics, sivals un bels semblan
    Me faitz enan
    Qu'eu mueira de dolor.

15. Bruckner believes Castelloza "reject[s] the image of the haughty lady" but integrates the other roles into one coherent lyric persona (251). She might dispute my distinction between the motives of the speaker (to avoid composing *precs*) and those of the poet (to compose *precs* well).

16. E.g., the following explicit requests: Peire Vidal (P-C 364,48 vv. 3–4), Berenger de Palazol (P-C 47,10 vv. 34–36), Peire Rogier (356,8 vv. 67–68 and 356,4 vv. 57–58), Peire d'Alvernhe or Bernart de Venzac (323,6).

17. Pickens, "Jaufre Rudel et la poétique de la mouvance." For Old French, Dragonetti 347.

18. P-C 293,25 and 26; P-C 323,23; P-C 183,7.

19. P-C 43,1 ed. Sakari, "Le Joglar" 184–97, vv. 49–52.

20. Dragonetti discusses the similar situation in Old French, where *envois* were sometimes omitted or the *destinataire* changed (306–07).

21. P-C 29,14 ed. Toja 378 variants; P-C 323,11.

22. P-C 234,7 ed. Sakari 103, 109–111.

H. JAY SISKIN

JULIE A. STORME

6   Suffering Love: The Reversed Order in the Poetry of Na Castelloza

Rarely has a lover suffered as relentlessly as the thirteenth-century tro-bairitz known as Na Castelloza.[1] Indeed, the few critics who have studied her poetry have consistently noted her unhappiness in love: they see her as subservient or even tormented and masochistic.[2] The most casual reading confirms the critics' observations and furthermore reveals another characteristic that is seldom mentioned: the complexity of her expression. Castelloza frequently baffles her reader by her contradictions, paradoxes, and enigmatic statements.[3] Perhaps this complexity explains why critics have not ventured beyond the observation that Castelloza is unhappy in love and yet strangely content to remain so.

Past descriptions of Castelloza's suffering disappoint us in their failure to explain its predominance. That Castelloza suffers and exhibits masochistic behavior is perfectly evident to the reader. Not so evident is the reason for this persistent behavior, an issue not addressed as yet. A closer examination of her expression reveals the compulsive nature of her masochism. The poet describes her behavior as uncontrollable, as actions she cannot help performing because they are beyond her intellectual and emotional power. Her lack of control is manifested linguistically by the preponderance of the negative:

Oimais *non sai* que·us me presen . . . (I, 41; emphasis added)

[From now on, *I don't know why* I present myself to you . . .]

Ja de chantar *non degr'aver talan* . . . (II, 1; emphasis added)

[*I should never have any desire* to sing . . .]

The poet tells us that she cannot control her self-destructive behavior:

> E·m cug ades per plain e lais jausir
> De vos, amics, qu'eu *nom puesc* convertir . . . (I, 37–38; emphasis added)

> [By my lamentation and lays I always hope to enjoy you, friend, because *I cannot* convert . . .]

Although she has been mistreated, although her singing will not advance her cause, and in spite of her suffering, her masochism drives her to compulsive actions that will only increase her despair.

Castelloza's compulsion is also exhibited on the level of syntax. In the following example, the poet contrasts the hypothetical and desired behavior on the part of her lover with the behavior he exhibits in reality, along with the consequences of such behavior:

> Amics, s'ie·us trobes avinen,
> Humil e franc e de bona merce,
> Be·us amera—cant era m'en sove
> Qu'ie·us trop ves mi mal e sebenc e ric . . . (I,1–4)

> [Friend, if I found you charming, humble, open, and compassionate, I would love you indeed—since now I realize that I find you wicked, despicable and haughty toward me . . .]

A closer analysis of this contrast reveals a discordance between form and content. Castelloza uses nearly identical propositional structures and syntactic patterns to describe two sets of contradictory conditions and behaviors, one hypothetical and one real. The parallelism on the syntagmatic axis contrasts with the opposition on the paradigmatic axis. Castelloza prepares the following linguistic equation and teases the reader to solve for X:

Conditions		*Lover's Behavior*		*Consequences*
(hypothetical)		(courtly)		(reward)
s'ie·us trobes	+	humil e franc e de bona merce	=	be·us amera
(reality)		(noncourtly)		(X)
cant era ie·us trop	+	mal e sebenc e ric	=	X

In Castelloza's hypothetical world, courtly behavior is rewarded with love. Since in reality her lover exhibits the opposite behavior, should we not expect the contrary punishment, that is, a withholding of love? But

Castelloza destroys her equation, and jars our expectations by complet-ing it in the following way:

> E·n fatz chansons per tal que fass'ausir
> Vostre bon prez . . . (I, 5–6)
>
> [yet I make songs to make your good name heard . . .]

Castelloza is out of control:

> . . . don *eu no·m puesc* sofrir
> Qu'eu no·us fasa lausar a tota gen
> On plus me faitz mal ez asiramen. (I, 6–8; emphasis added)
>
> [which is why I cannot keep from making everyone praise you when most you cause me harm and anger.]

She compulsively collapses her argumentation, seeking the exaltation of her lover at the expense of her emotional needs.

Often, Castelloza manifests her suffering in a feudal context (cf. Paden et al. 167). As a submissive vassal, she catalogues the wrongs her lord has committed against her: while he has sworn and pledged ("*jurar e plevir,*" III, 4) to love no other woman, he consistently violates this pledge. The poet claims that this behavior will result in her death and betrayal ("mi avez mort'e *traida,*" III, 8). She has loved in good faith ("per *bona fe,*" II, 17) but is not retained ("*retener,*" IV, 13) in his service. She can expect no help ("*socors,*" I, 39), and despairs because she knows that displaying a cruel heart ("cor *felon,*" I, 12) would not help her cause.[4]

Castelloza's lover has broken the reciprocal ties which bind vassal to lord: he has violated his pledge, betrayed her, not returned her good faith, refused help. Under these circumstances, a suffering vassal could legitimately renounce his allegiance (*recreire*).[5] But Castelloza persists:

> Que saiat ai ez a mal ez a be
> Vostre dur cor—don lo mieus *no·s recre.*
> (I, 42–43; emphasis added here and in the following citations)
>
> [For I've tested with evil and with good your hard heart—which my own *doesn't renounce.*]

> Car joia no·m ave
> De vos—don *no·m recre*
> D'amar per bona fe . . . (II, 15–17)

[Since no joy comes to me from you, yet *I don't renounce* loving you in good faith.]

E si·m fasetz mal per be
Be·us am mas. *No m'en recre.* (III, 16–17)

[And even though you do me ill for good, I only love you the more. *I don't renounce it.*]

Castelloza chooses not to avail herself of her rights to renounce her lover even as she acknowledges the lack of reciprocity in their relationship, thus proving once again that despite repeated incidents of cruelty and neglect, she stubbornly persists in the behavior that causes her suffering.

In other instances, Castelloza consciously encourages a nonreciprocal relationship: after describing the ill treatment she receives at the hands of her lover, she advises him: "Amics, non fasatz re!" ("Friend, don't do anything!" II, 34). In this example, she goes a step beyond the involuntary, unreflected statements in our earlier citations ("I don't know why, I cannot help myself"). By instructing her lover not to change his behavior, Castelloza both acknowledges the source of her suffering and makes a deliberate choice to insure its continuance.

Suffering is the unifying thread running through Castelloza's poetry, but as we delve deeper into its nature we find that it is only a single element of a larger design, merely a symptom of a graver disorder. Castelloza creates a poetic universe that is fundamentally negative, a universe in which there is no alternative to the suffering she so frequently expresses.

The governing principle of this negative world is deconstruction: whatever is done will be undone. Her deconstructive order is too self-conscious to be truly Derridean.[6] In its simplest and most conscious form, deconstruction is embodied in the mechanism of reversal. Castelloza consciously reverses her actions: if she is bold enough to take her lover's glove, she is also timid enough to return it (II, 38–44); immediately after telling her lover that she intends to show him a hard heart, she proclaims: "Non farei ja" ("I will never do it," I, 13).

In addition to undoing her actions or proposed actions, Castelloza frequently reverses descriptions of her emotional state. In stanza IV of Poem I, for instance, she implies that she has hope and that she derives joy from that hope:

Que calc'ora pori'endevenir
Que n'auria enquera jausimen.
De sol lo dig n'ai eu lo cor jausen. (I, 30–32)

[For at any time it could happen that I would again have joy. From your mere word I have a rejoicing heart.]

Yet a few lines later, she proclaims that she has neither joy nor hope since she does not expect her lover to respond to her pleas:

Ni joi non ai, ni socors non aten. (I, 39)

[I have no joy, nor do I expect help.]

Within the poetic universe of Castelloza, the poles of positive and negative are reversed. The negativity of her poetic universe is all-encompassing, allowing no escape from its influence. Positive emotions become negative within her world. As Paden et al. have pointed out (165), there is little happiness in Castelloza's poetry, and she restricts the use of the word *joi* to negative contexts. As a symbol of escape from sorrow, pain, and despair, hope has no place within Castelloza's negative universe; like *joi,* hope is conspicuously rare in her vocabulary (166). When she speaks of hope, she most frequently refers to her lack of it.[7] Furthermore, what hope she has is strangely negative, sometimes taking the ironic form of lament:

E·m cug ades per plain e lais jausir
De vos, amics . . . (I, 37–38)

[By my lamentation and lays I always hope to enjoy you, friend . . .][8]

Hope's positive essence lies in its association with the future. Castelloza imbues her hope with negativity by expressing it in the past tense:

C'avi'en vos m'esperansa
Que m'amasetz ses doptansa. (III, 9–10)

[For I had in you my hope that you would love me without a doubt.]

A hope that is past no longer offers the possibility of an end to present pain and sorrow; rather, it confirms and underscores the existence of disappointed wishes and unfulfilled expectations.

Deconstruction occurs on the level of syntax through expressions that eliminate the possibility of an orderly and balanced universe. Castelloza undermines the distinction between the hypothetical and the real.[9] We refer once again to the episode of the glove. The poet tells her lover:

> Si pro·i agues, be·us membrera chantan—
> 　　Aic vostre gan . . . (II, 37–38)

> [If there were any use in it, I would indeed remind you as I sing—I got your glove . . .]

Of course, Castelloza is in fact performing the action that she describes as hypothetical, making this typical lament rhetorical; she uses the hypothetical structure to stress the absence of the conditions that would justify her action. For Castelloza, the consequence of a hypothetical structure does not depend upon its preliminary conditions; her hypotheses are empty structures having only the appearance and not the substance of a hypothesis. In the above instance, the action is clearly real despite its description as hypothetical.

In other instances, Castelloza describes actions as hypothetical after having implied that they have actually taken place. The first stanza of Poem III illustrates such a double description. Castelloza first implies that her lover has been unfaithful:

> Ez es me grieu e salvatge
> Car me juretz e·m pleviz
> Que als jorns de vostra vida
> Non acses dompna mas me. (III, 3–6)

> [And it is grievous and cruel for me, because you swore and pledged to me that in the days of your life you would love no woman but me.]

No sooner do we believe her lover unfaithful than she casts doubt on his infidelity by putting it in a hypothetical form:

> E si d'autra vos perte . . . (III, 7)

> [And if you care about any other woman . . .]

Our doubt increases in the fifth stanza when Castelloza writes,

> E s'anc fes ves me faillida . . . (III, 45)

> [Yet if ever you sinned against me . . .]

By describing an action as both virtual and real, Castelloza has created a confusion between the hypothetical and the real, making such a distinction meaningless.[10]

Reality eludes the reader. In Poem I, it is impossible for the reader to know whether or not Castelloza has tested her lover's heart, since she tells us that she has done so after having proclaimed that she would never do it (I, 11–13 and 42–43). In Poem II, Castelloza argues that a lady should woo a knight if she sees in him prowess and heroism (II, 51–54). She clearly woos her knight, but it is not clear whether or not he possesses prowess and merit. She speaks of his *ric preç* (II, 25), but others feel that his cruelty and indifference towards her make him *salvatge* (II, 14). Thus, the reader cannot easily determine whether Castelloza loves her knight because of his merit or despite his lack of it.[11] Her illogical laments to her lover in Poem IV represent a complete breakdown of order. She threatens to leave him, but this would seem impossible since he has already left her and lives with another woman (IV, 9–10 and 11). She begs him to allow her to keep on loving him and no other (IV, 25–27), and then complains that he will not show her how to free herself from her passion for him (IV, 28–30).

Castelloza's portrayal of love serves as the center toward which the elements of her poetry examined thus far converge. Hers is a suffering, negative love that reflects the disorder of her poetic universe, a universe in which reversal and irreality reign and from which hope and joy have been exiled. It perplexes by virtue of its paradoxes and illogical principles. Her love increases rather than decreases with ill-treatment (III, 16–17); she threatens to leave a lover who has already left her (IV, 11–13); and she expects her lover to want to make her happy even though he has betrayed and abandoned her:

> E pos no·ill platz que·m retegna,
> Vueilla·m d'aitant hobesir
> C'ab sos avinenz respos
> Me tegna mon cor joios . . . (IV, 13–16)

[and since it doesn't please him to keep me, he might at least want to heed me enough to keep my heart joyful with his inviting responses . . .]

By looking at Castelloza's portrait of love, we can detect a strong omnipresent ego behind the timid and suffering lover. Her portrait of love is egocentrical; it holds no place for a lover or any actor other than the self. Throughout Castelloza's poetry the lover is missing,[12] his actions are non-actions. His absence and lack of active role permit Castelloza to dwell on *her* emotions, *her* reactions, *her* chosen course of action.[13] Her love does not require a lover since she continues to love regardless of her lover's behavior, be it indifferent or cruel. She writes songs about her lover even though he is "mal e sebenc e ric" (I, 4–6).[14] This nonreciprocal love places the self at its center; suffering is its main expression because suffering does not depend upon the lover's presence, but rather his absence. Even the lover's ill-treatment is described in a way that eliminates his active role. Castelloza writes:

> Car en mala merce
> Ai mes mon cor e me. (II, 6–7)
>
> [since I have put my heart and myself in ill favor.]

She consistently effaces the lover's role. Rather than praying for her lover's response, Castelloza prays for prayer itself. Her prayer is an auto-affective gesture that brings its own relief regardless of the lover's reply or lack of reply:

> Qu'ieu vueil preiar ennanz que·m lais morir,
> Qu'el preiar ai maing douz revenimen,
> Can prec sellui don ai gran pessamen. (I, 22–24)
>
> [I want to pray before I let myself die, since in prayer I find such sweet healing, when I pray to the one from whom I get great care.]

The "sweet healing" comes from the prayer itself and not the answer to it:

> Es ieu tenc me per gerida,
> Amics, a la mia fe,
> Can vos prec—c'aissi·m conve. . . . (III, 25–27)
>
> [Yet I consider myself cured, friend, by my faith, when I pray to you—because this way is right for me. . . .]

If Castelloza attaches no conditions to her offer of love, as Paden et. al. have observed (169), this omission springs from her egocentrism. Conditions call for response. Unlike the Comtessa de Dia and Bernart de Ventadorn, Castelloza provides her lover no such opportunity to respond.

It is strange to find such an egocentrical love in the subservient, self-effacing, and unhappy persona of Castelloza. This enigmatic combination of strong and weak expressions of self leads us to a new interpretation of her suffering. We propose that within the reversed order of Castelloza, suffering and self-effacement become positive expressions of the self. Her poetry hints at the psychological rewards she gains from her suffering. In the midst of her anguish, she thanks her tormentor:

> Grasisc vos, con que m'en pregna,
> Tot lo maltrag e·l consir. (IV, 31–32)
>
> [I thank you, no matter what befalls me, for all my suffering and worry.]

In another statement, the poet seems conscious of a positive side to her suffering:

> De vos amar, pos tan gen me conve . . . (I, 26)
>
> [Since loving you is so very pleasing to me . . .]

Indeed, later statements are more revealing. For Castelloza, suffering permits the exaltation of her virtue, righteousness, and magnanimity. If she took control of her emotions and showed her lover a hard heart, she would give him reason to complain of ill-treatment (I, 13–16). She rejects this choice. Paradoxically, by choosing suffering, Castelloza increases her self-esteem. She can self-righteously proclaim her untarnished record of unabated anguish:

> Bels Noms, ges no·m recre
> De vos amar jasse,
> Car i truep bona fe
> Totz temps, e ferm coratge. (II, 59–62; see also 16–18)
>
> [Fair Name, I do not at all renounce loving you always, for in doing so I always find good faith and a steadfast heart.]

The good faith and steadfast heart are her own. She forfeits control over her emotions, but by doing so gains psychological gratification. Although her willingness to suffer would seem to stem from low self-esteem, it actually permits her to establish her moral superiority.[15] Thus she transforms her negative world into a positive self-image.

This reversal typically occurs when Castelloza contrasts her own ap–

proach to love with conventional behavior (see I, 25–27). She would seem to be denigrating her own behavior through these comparisons:

> Mout aurei mes mal usatge
> A las autras amairitz,
> C'hom sol trametre mesatge,
> E motz triaz et chauzitz. (III, 21–24)

> [I shall have set a very bad example for other women in love, because it's the man who usually sends a message, and words picked and selected.]

These apparent denigrations, however, are always accompanied by the claim that her unusual approach to love, however different from accepted behavior, is appropriate for her; thus the above citation is soon followed by the declaration "c'aissi·m conve" (because this way is right for me, III, 27). Furthermore, she rejects anyone else's authority with regard to her own behavior:

> Eu sai ben qu'a mi esta gen,
> Si ben dison tuig que mout descove
> Que dompna prec ja cavalier de se,
> Ni que·l tenga totz tems tam lonc pressic.
> Mas cil c'o diz non sap gez ben chausir. (I, 17–21)

> [I know well that it pleases me, even though everyone says that it's very improper for a lady to plead her own cause with a knight, and make him so long a sermon all the time. But whoever says that doesn't know how to discern well at all.]

Castelloza describes her own behavior as inferior to the convention and yet persists in its practice. By so doing she shows both respect and disdain for convention. This simultaneous expression of contrary opinions equates denigration and respect, thus effacing the distinction between them. Within the disordered poetic universe of Castelloza the difference between respect and denigration is undone. Consequently the negative descriptions of her behavior become declarations of the "rightness" of her behavior since self-denigration must also be an expression of self-esteem. Castelloza's self-effacing comparisons are not simply the torment of a subservient woman—they are, to her, proof of her superiority.

Castelloza not only gains self-esteem through her suffering, she inflicts guilt on others while remaining blameless. Indeed, her torment will cause torment for others, and she will be rewarded:

E morai me si no·m volez jausir
De qualque joi; e si·m laissatz morir
Farez pecat, e serez n'en turmen,
E serai mos quesid'a·l jutjamen. (I, 45–48)

[I shall die if you don't want to make me rejoice with whatever joy; and if
you let me die you will commit a sin, and you'll be in torment for it, and I'll
be more sought after at Judgment.]

Her choice to allow ill-treatment to continue permits the denigration of
others to her apparent blamelessness. By forfeiting control over her suffering, she gains control, that is, the power to inflict guilt. Her negative
universe is once again transformed into a positive one. This mechanism
of reversal changes degradation into honor:

E ja ves vos non aurai cor truan
        Ni plen d'enjan,
    Si tot vos n'ai pior,
        Qu'a grant honor
M'o teing e mon coratge. (II, 19–23)

[Toward you I will never have a treacherous heart or a heart full of deception,
even though you treat me badly, because I consider it a great honor in my
heart.]

Degradation provides the opportunity for transforming the negative into
the positive with regard to self-esteem.

It is easy, then, to explain Castelloza's response to ill-treatment. Her
masochistic behavior gains her the luxury of self-justification. When
Castelloza states

    Asatz es fols qui m'en repren
De vos amar, pos tan gen me conve;
E cel c'o diz no sap co s'es de me . . . (I, 25–27)

[He is quite a fool who reproaches me for loving you, since it is so very
pleasing to me; and he who says it doesn't know how it is with me. . . .]

she is alluding to her reversed order. Her love is nourished by suffering
and abuse, which are perversely generative of self-esteem. This is "how
it is" with Castelloza.

It is clear, then, that Castelloza is not merely the suffering lover portrayed by past critics, nor do we see her expression as the "willed sim-

plicity" described by Dronke ("The Provençal *Trobairitz:* Castelloza,"
134). Indeed, her formal complexity rivals the complexity of her portrayal of suffering love.[16] A brief analysis of Poem III, which shows a
number of important formal characteristics, confirms this observation.
Most noteworthy is the alternation of the first person singular proclitics,
disjunctive pronouns, and possessive adjectives (mi, me, m') with the
second person plural corresponding forms (·us, vos). Stanza I patterns
this way:

    2 mi—·us
    3 me
    4 me—'m
    5 vostra
    6 me
    7 vos
    8 mi
    9 vos
    10 m'

This alternation gives forward movement to the stanza. In stanza IV, a
similar alternation culminates in chiasmus:

    32 vos
    34 mi
    36 Car de m'amor no·us sove.
    37 E si de vos jois no·m ve . . .

The chiasmus, along with the common rhyme, links lines 36 and 37
together. Such alternation can further link verses through the identity of
the common vowel sound or the initial consonant, which can also enter
into series of alliterations or assonances:

    Que per *vos* m'es escaritz—
    Vos fai grasir *mos* lignage
    E sobre totz *mos* maritz!
    E s'anc *fes* ves mi *faillida* . . . (III, 42–45)

As illustrated above, alliteration and assonance are prominent fea-
tures of Castelloza's verse. These are often combined with a reduplication
of syllables (m'*es es*carnitz) or internal rhyme (mos-vos; fes-ves).[17] These
factors result in rich sonorities. Castelloza particularly favors the vowel *a*
(alone or in dipthongs) and the nasal consonants *m* and *n:*

E si·*m* fasetz *m*al per be,
Be·us *am mas* . . .
*M*as tan *m'a* amor sasida . . . (III, 16–18)

*M*out aurei *m*es *m*al usatge
A las autras amairitz
C'ho*m* sol trametre mesatge . . . (III, 21–23)

The rhyme in -*ansa* in the last two lines of each stanza insures a periodic repetition of these sounds. This interplay of movement and sound suggests an underlying coherence as yet unexplored.

Such formal subtleties should not surprise us. Castelloza's poetic craft is as dense and systematic as the world she so deliberately constructs and deconstructs. Victim that she is, she is not victimized. She transforms her passive self into the active agent who creates a fundamentally negative universe. In this negative world, pain becomes pleasure, degradation leads to honor and abuse establishes self-esteem. It is through this reversed order that the positive self emerges in Castelloza's poetry.

Notes

1. For remarks on the name *Na Castelloza,* see Paden et al., "The Poems of the *Trobairitz* Na Castelloza," 158–59. The activity of the trobairitz has been dated at the beginning of the thirteenth century by Schultz-Gora, *Die provenzalischen Dichterinnen* 12; Bertoni, "Il vestito della trovatrice Castelloza," 228; and Bogin 118.

2. Among these critics are Bertoni, who calls her "sospirosa" (228), and Schultz-Gora, who sees her as subservient (quoted in Lavaud 85–86). Bogin says very little about Castelloza except that she is unhappy (66). Bruckner concludes that Castelloza's poetic voice is a reversal of the male/female roles in the troubadour lyric. This reversal nonetheless modifies the servile male role by incorporating feminine stereotypes that exist outside of the lyric, including the passionate woman of the *alba* and the social model of female subordination. According to Dronke ("The Provençal *Trobairitz*: Castelloza," 132), she "shows intense single-mindedness," never straying from the subject of her suffering. He contends that her four songs represent a brief lyrical cycle which develops the theme of her unhappiness. Paden et al., "The Poems of the *Trobairitz* Na Castelloza," argue that Castelloza not only suffers in love, but does so masochistically. We refer to the edition and translation by Paden et al. Like them, we choose to include the fourth poem ("Per joi que d'amor m'avegna") in our study, even though it lacks an attribution in the manuscript, because it echoes many of the elements we find in the three poems of certain attribution.

3. For example:

E sapchaz ben que mais jois no·m soste,
Mas lo vostre que m'alegr'e·m reve
On mais m'en ven d'afan e de destric. (I, 34–36)

[So know well that joy no longer sustains me, but for yours which delights me and heals me when most pain and distress come to me.]

Vos fai grasir mos lignage
E sobre totz mos maritz! (III, 43–44)

[My family makes you welcome, and especially my husband!]

Per joi que d'amor m'avegna
No·m calgr'ogan esbaudir . . . (IV, 1–2)

[Whatever joy may come to me from love, from now on I don't care to rejoice . . .]

4. Cropp discusses the following terms: *jurar* (148 and 476); *plevir* (476); *traida* (130 and 445); *bona fe* (404 and 478); *retener* (372 and 475); *felon* (135, 240, and 479).

5. Cropp also discusses *recreire* (228).

6. Derrida, of course, searches for the point at which an author inadvertently deconstructs his philosophical system by saying what "he does not wish to say," being led to this point by his incomplete mastery of his language (152 and 227). One need not seek out the "weak" spot in Castelloza's mastery of her language in order to observe the deconstruction of her poetic world, since she reverses her language at every moment in a very apparent, and thus we assume self-conscious, manner.

7. See I, 9–10; I, 39; I, 41–43; II, 35–39; III, 35–38; IV, 1–8; IV, 23–24.

8. Of course, "cug" need not be translated as "hope," but the translation does not alter the argument since, however translated, these lines express a hopeful expectation.

9. Dronke observes a similar collapse between the notion of public and private that renders any distinction between them meaningless ("The Provençal *Trobairitz:* Castelloza," 136, 139).

10. The difficulty in determining exactly what has transpired in Poem III is reflected in critics' summaries; Paden et al. write of this episode, "He left her on one occasion with a promise that he would never have any other woman (III 2–4), but this is a promise which he has *evidently* broken (III 7, cf. II 42, IV 9). It is characteristic of Na Castelloza that she says nothing about the time when they *must have been* together" ("The Poems of the *Trobairitz* Na Castelloza," 166; emphasis added).

11. Castelloza makes the task even more difficult by defending "a lady's" right to woo a knight rather than defending her personal right to do what she is doing, i.e., wooing a knight.

12. Bogin argues that the lover is frequently absent in all trobairitz poetry (69). Our point, however, is not the same as Bogin's, who describes the fact that the lovers are apart. Although Castelloza refers to such separations, the question is not so much one of distance as one of existence. Castelloza's lover is a hollow figure whose only role is to provide a springboard for her suffering.

13. Dronke tells us that "her fulfillment lies far more in herself, and in her poetry than in her man" ("The Provençal *Trobairitz:* Castelloza," 137). He argues that this is one of her "pervasive themes." Paden et al. confirm this egocentrical aspect of Castelloza's sorrow, pointing out that she does not use the term *lauzengier* "since her suffering originates in her *amic* and in herself, not in a hostile social environment" ("The Poems of the *Trobairitz* Na Castelloza," 168). Their observation that she frequently threatens suicide and applies the verb *morir* only to herself and not to her lover (166) can also be explained by her egocentrical form of love.

14. For additional references to her lover's failings, see II, 28–33; III, 1–10; III, 16–17; IV, 31–40.

15. Paden et al. point out that in contrast, the Comtessa de Dia, "In her distress, . . . is able to fall back upon a firm sense of her own worth" ("The Poems of the *Trobairitz* Na Castelloza," 168). Castelloza does not "fall back" on anything in the face of distress because she derives her firm sense of worth from her suffering.

16. On the originality of her rhyme schemes and syllabic formulae, see Paden et al., "The Poems of the *Trobairitz* Na Castelloza," 163.

17. Further examples of these elements include the following:
E *sai* que *fait ai f*olatge;
Que plus m'*en es en*carzits . . . (III, 13–14)

Mal ag'ieu s'*anc co*r *vo*latge
Vos aic ni·*os* fui *can*jairiz! (III, 31–32)

Per mi *non fon en*cobitz. (III, 34)

7   The *Sirventes* by Gormonda de Monpeslier

For Karl Kohut in Eichstätt

The only Provençal *sirventes* attributed in the manuscripts to a woman, and apparently the "first French political poem by a woman,"[1] is, according to manuscript *R,* by Gormonda de Monpeslier, about whom nothing else is known.[2] In view of her ties to Rome and its politics as well as to the French king, she may well have belonged to the circles of the Roman orthodox clergy of southern France.[3]

It is in the political-satirical nature of the genre that Gormonda's *sirventes* contains numerous allusions to historical events which make it possible to determine the approximate period of the poem's origin. In the year 1209, Pope Innocent III took the occasion of the murder at Saint-Gilles of his legate, Pierre de Castelnau, to proclaim a crusade against the heretics, among whom were both Cathars and Waldensians, who had long existed in Languedoc and Gascony. A large contingent of the northern French nobility took part in these Albigensian crusades, but so did many of the lesser counts and barons of the south. The wars ultimately led to the disintegration of the great county of Toulouse, and to the affiliation of the Midi with the French kingdom following the terms of the treaty of Meaux in 1229. The count of Toulouse, Raimon VII, supported by the populace of the city, which was favorably disposed toward the Cathars, withstood the crusading army's attacks on the city until he was obliged to surrender the city on April 11, 1229. Gormonda's *sirventes* must have appeared in the last months of the Albigensian war, since she "wished the very worst misfortune upon the inhabitants of Toulouse, while she certainly would have adopted a triumphant tone had she composed the poem after that event."[4]

Another allusion concerns the death of the French king, Louis VIII, in Montpensier in the year 1226:

VI   Mas so que Merlis
            prophetizan dis
            del bon rei Lois,
        que morira en pansa,
        aras s'esclarzis.

[But what Merlin prophesied of the good King Louis, that he would die in Pansa, now becomes clear.]

According to *La Chronique de Reims,* the soothsayer and magician Merlin had prophesied "que li dous lions de France morroit a Montpancier" (that the gentle lion of France would die at Montpancier) (ed. Paris 178). Louis's death was thought to have been the fulfillment of the oracle, whose double meaning Gormonda plays upon here (*en pansa* "in the stomach" or "in [Mont-] Pensier"). It is remarkable that the poet who is otherwise so entirely partial to the affairs of Rome should attach such great significance to the words of a magician belonging to Celtic folklore. We will, however, find an explanation for this upon turning to examine the whole poem.

Guilhem Figueira[5]

Gormonda de Monpeslier[6]

I   D'un sirventes far   Greu m'es a durar,
      en est son que m'agenssa   quar aug tal dezcrezensa
        no·m vuolh plus tarzar   dir ni semenar,
      ni far longa bistenssa,   e no·m platz ni m'agensa;
        e sai ses doptar   qu'om non deu amar
      qu'ieu n'aurai malvolenssa,   qui fai desmantenensa
        si fas sirventes   a so don totz bes
        dels fals, d'enjans ples,   ven e nais, et es
        de Roma, que es   salvamens e fes.
      caps de la dechansenssa,   Per qu'ieu farai parvensa
        on dechai totz bes.   e semblan que·m pes.

[It is difficult for me to bear it when I hear such disbelief spoken and spread about, and it neither pleases me nor suits me; for one should not love anyone who renounces that from which all goodness comes and is born, and (which) is salvation and faith. Therefore I shall show and make known what oppresses me.]

II   No·m meravilh ges,   No·us meravilhes
      Roma, si la gens erra,   negus, si eu muou guerra
        que·l segle avetz mes   ab fals mal apres
      en trebalh et en guerra,   qu'a son poder soterra

e pretz e merces
mor per vos e sosterra,
Roma enganairitz,
qu'etz de totz mals guitz
e cima e razitz,
que·l bons reis d'Englaterra
fon per vos trahitz.

totz bos faitz cortes
e·ls encauss' e·ls enserra.
Trop se fenh arditz,
quar de Roma ditz
mal, qu'es caps e guitz
de totz selhs que en terra
an bos esperitz.

[None of you should wonder if I go to war against a false, ignorant one who does his best to bury all good courtly deeds, and to persecute and imprison them. He pretends to be very brave, for he speaks ill of Rome, which is the head and leader of all those on earth who have good souls.]

III   Roma enganairitz,
cobeitatz vos engana,
c'a vostras berbitz
tondetz trop de la lana.
Lo Sains Esperitz,
que receup carn humana,
entenda mos precs
e franha tos becs.
Roma, no m'entrecs,
car es falsa e trafana
vas nos e vas grecs.

En Roma es complitz
totz bes, e qui·ls li pana,
sos sens l'es falhitz,
quar si meteis enguana;
qu'elh n'er sebelitz,
don perdra sa ufana.
Dieus auja mos precx:
que selhs qu'an mals becx,
joves e senecs,
contra la lei romana,
cajon dels bavecx.

[In Rome all goodness is perfected, and whoever denies it has impaired understanding, for he deceives himself; and he will be buried for it, and will lose his arrogance. May God hear my request: that those with nasty tongues, both young and old, who speak wickedly against the Roman faith may fall from the balance (of Judgment).]

IV   Roma, als homes pecs
rozetz la carn e l'ossa,
e guidatz los secs
ab vos inz en la fossa:
trop passatz los decs
de Dieu, car trop es grossa
vostra cobeitatz,
car vos perdonatz
per deniers pechatz.
Roma, de gran trasdossa
de mal vos cargatz.

Roma, selhs per pecx
tenc totz e per gent grossa,
per orbs e per secx,
que lur carn e lur ossa
carguon d'avols decx
don cazon en la fossa
on lur es sermatz
pudens focx malvatz;
don mais desliatz
no seran del trasdossa,
qu'an de lurs peccatz.

[Rome, I consider them to be stupid and rude people, blind and gaunt, who burden their flesh and bones with low vices that make them fall into the pit where a stinking, evil fire is prepared for them, so that they will never be freed of the burden of their sins.]

V   Roma, ben sapchatz   Roma, ges no·m platz
    que vostra avols barata   qu'avols hom vos combata;
    e vostra foudatz   dels bos avetz patz,
    fetz perdre Damiata.   qu'usquecx ab vos s'aflata.
    Malamen renhatz,   Dels fols lurs foldatz
    Roma. Dieus vos abata   fes perdre Damiata,
    en dechazemen,   mas li vostre sen
    car trop falsamen   fan sel ses conten
    renhatz per argen,   caitiu e dolen
    Roma de mal'esclata   que contra vos deslata
    e de mal coven.   ni renha greumen.

[Rome, it does not please me at all that a vulgar man attacks you; you are at
peace with the good, for each of them makes himself pleasing to you. The
folly of the fools caused the loss of Damiette, but your wisdom makes him
irresistibly wretched and sorrowful who is arrogant toward you and lives
wickedly.]

VI   Roma, veramen   Roma, veramen
     sai eu senes doptanssa   sai e cre ses duptansa
     c'ab galiamen   qu'a ver salvamen
     de falsa perdonanssa   aduretz tota Fransa;
     liuretz a turmen   oc, e l'autra gen
     lo barnatge de Franssa   que·us vol far ajudansa.
     lonh de paradis,   Mas so que Merlis
     e·l bon rei Lois,   prophetizan dis
     Roma, avetz aucis,   del bon rei Lois,
     c'ab falsa predicanssa   que morira en pansa,
     ·l traissetz de Paris.   aras s'esclarzis.

[Rome, I truly know and believe without doubt that you shall lead all France
to true salvation; yes, and (so too) the others who seek to help you. But
what Merlin prophesied of the good King Louis, that he would die in Pansa,
now becomes clear.]

VII   Roma, als sarrazis   Piegz de Sarrazis
      faitz vos pauc de dampnatge,   e de pus fals coratge
      mas grecs e latis   heretjes mesquis
      liuratz a carnalatge.   son. Qui vol lur estatge,
      Inz el foc d'abis,   ins el foc d'abis
      Roma, faitz vostre estatge   vais, en loc salvatge,
      en perdicion.   en dampnatio.
      Ja Dieus part no·m don,   A selhs d'Avinho
      Roma, del perdon   baisses, don m'es bo,
      ni del pelegrinatge   Roma, lo mal pezatge,
      que fetz d'Avinhon.   don grans merces fo.

[Worse than the Saracens and of more deceitful mind are the pitiful heretics. Whoever wants (to know) their dwelling should go into the fire of the abyss, to the hostile place, to damnation. I am pleased to know, Rome, that for those from Avignon you lowered the evil toll, which was a great mercy.]

VIII
Roma, ses razon
avetz mainta gen morta,
e jes no·m sab bon,
car tenetz via torta,
qu'a salvacion,
Roma, serratz la porta.
Per qu'a mal govern
d'estiu e d'invern
qui sec vostr'estern,
car diables l'en porta
inz el fuoc d'enfern.

Roma, per razo
avetz manta destorta
dressad'a bando
et oberta la porta
de salvatio,
don era la claus torta;
que ab bon govern
baissatz folh esquern.
Qui sec vostr' estern,
l'angel Michel lo·n porta
e·l garda d'ifern.

[Rome, you have rightly made straight many crooked paths and opened salvation's gate, whose key was twisted; for with good governing you humble foolish mockery. The angel Michael carries off and protects from Hell anyone who follows your course.]

IX
Roma, be·is decern
lo mals c'om vos deu dire,
quar faitz per esquern
dels crestians martire.
Mas en cal quadern
trobatz c'om deia aucire,
Roma, ·ls crestians?
Dieus, qu'es verais pans
e cotidians,
me don so qu'eu desire
vezer dels romans.

L'estiu e l'yvern
deu hom, ses contradire,
Roma, lo cazern
legir, si que no·s vire;
e quan ve l'esquern,
cum Jhesus pres martire,
albir se lo cas
si·s bos crestias,
. . . .
s'adoncx non a cossire,
totz es fols e vas.

[Rome, in summer and in winter man must without contradiction read the Book, so that he will not change; and when he sees the scorn, how Jesus was martyred, he should ponder the matter, if he is a good Christian; . . . but if he feels no sorrow then, he is utterly foolish and vain.]

X
Roma, vers es plans
que trop etz angoissosa
dels perdons trafans
que fetz sobre Tolosa.
Trop rosetz las mans
a lei de rabiosa,
Roma descordans.

Roma, lo trefas
e sa leis sospechoza
als fols digz vilas
par que fos de Toloza,
on d'enjans certas
non es doncx vergonhoza.
Ni ans de dos ans

Mas si·l coms prezans   mas si·l coms prezans
viu ancar dos ans,   cove que·ls engans
Fransa n'er dolorosa   lais e la fe duptoza
dels vostres engans.   e restaure·ls dans.

[Rome, the deceiver and his suspicious faith, with its foolish, vulgar language, seems to be from Toulouse, which feels no shame of notorious deceit. Within two years the worthy count must give up the deceptions and the dubious faith and set right the wrongs.]

XI   Roma, tant es grans   Roma, lo reis grans
        la vostra forfaitura   qu'es senhers de dreitura
            que Dieu e sos sans   als falses Tolzans
        en gitatz a non cura,   don gran malaventura,
            tant etz mal renhans,   quar contra sos mans
        Roma falsa e tafura,   fan tan gran desmezura,
            per qu'en vos s'escon   qu'usquecx lo rescon,
        e·is magra e·is cofon   e torbon est mon;
        lo jois d'aquest mon.   e·l comte Raimon,
        E faitz gran desmesura   s'ab elhs plus s'asegura,
        del comte Raimon.   no·l tenrai per bon.

[Rome, may the great king who is lord of justice bring great misfortune upon the false people of Toulouse, for against his commands they commit deeds of such great arrogance that everyone conceals (?) it, and they confuse this world; if Count Raimon further allies himself with them, I will not think it good.]

XII   Roma, Dieus l'aon   Roma, be·s cofon
        e·lh don poder e forsa   e val li pauc sa forsa,
            al comte que ton   qui contra vos gron
        los frances e·ls escorsa,   ni bast castelh ni forsa,
            e fa·n planca e pon,   quar en tan aut mon
        quand ab els se comorsa;   no·s met ni no s'amorsa
        et a mi platz fort.   que Dieus non recort
        Roma, a Dieu recort   son erguelh e·l tort
        del vostre gran tort, ...
        si·l platz; e·l comte estorsa   don pert tota s'escorsa
        de vos e de mort.   e pren dobla mort.

[Rome, he greatly errs and his strength is of little worth, who grumbles against you and builds and conquers fortresses, for he does not establish himself upon such a high mountain that God will not remember his pride and injustice; . . . through which he loses his mortal frame and receives the double death.]

XIII   Roma, be·m conort   Roma, be·m conort
        quez en abans de gaire   que·l coms ni l'emperaire,
        venrez a mal port,   pueis que son destort
        si l'adreitz emperaire   de vos, non valon gaire,
        mena adreich sa sort   quar lur folh deport
        ni fai so que deu faire.   e lur malvat vejaire
        Roma, eu dic ver,   los fa totz cazer
        que·l vostre poder   a vostre plazer,
        veirem dechazer,   qu'us no·s pot tener;
        Roma, lo vers Salvaire   sitot s'es guerrejaire,
        m'o lais tost vezer.   non li val poder.

[Rome, I am well pleased that the count and the emperor, having turned away from you, have lost their strength, for their foolish behavior and their wicked opinions make them (both) fall according to your will, so that not a one may stand; however warlike he may be, his power is worthless.]

XIV   Roma, per aver   Roma, ieu esper
        faitz mainta vilania   que vostra senhoria
        e maint desplazer   e Fransa, per ver
        e mainta fellonia: cui non platz mala via,
        tant voletz aver   fassa dechazer
        del mon la senhoria   l'erguelh e l'eretgia:
        que ren non temetz   fals heretges quetz,
        Dieu ni sos devetz,   que non temon vetz
        anz vei que fazetz   ni crezo·ls secretz,
        mais qu'ieu dir non poiria tan son ple de feunia
        de mal, per un detz.   e de mals pessetz.

[Rome, I hope that your dominion and France, to whom a wicked way is truly not pleasing, will bring to destruction the pride and the heresy: the false, secret heretics, who neither fear prohibitions nor believe in mysteries, they are so full of treachery and wicked thoughts.]

XV   Roma, tan tenetz   Roma, be sabetz
        estreg la vostra grapa   que fort greu lor escapa
        que so que podetz   qui au lor decretz;
        tener, greu vos escapa.   aissi tendon lur trapa
        Si·n breu non perdetz   ab falses trudetz
        poder, a mala trapa   ab que quascus s'arrapa.
        es lo mons cazutz   Totz son sortz e mutz,
        e mortz e vencutz,   qu'el lur tolh salutz,
        e·l pretz confondutz.   don quecx es perdutz,
        Roma, la vostra papa   qu'ilh n'an capelh o capa
        fai aitals vertutz.   e remanon nutz.

[Rome, you know well that hardly anyone escapes from them who hears their teaching; thus they set their traps with false enticements, in which everyone becomes ensnared. All (the victims) are deaf and dumb (when they are told that this teaching) takes away their salvation, and so everyone is lost, for they have neither hat nor cape and remain naked.]

XVI   Roma, Cel qu'es lutz   Clauzis e sauputz
        del mon e vera vida   naisson, senes falhida,
          e vera salutz,   crematz o perdutz
        vos don mal'escarida,   per lur malvada vida.
          car tans mals saubutz   Ans negon vertutz,
        faitz, per que lo mons crida. car fe no·i es—auzida
        Roma desleials,   no n'avem sivals.
          razitz de totz mals,   E si fos lejals
          els focs enfernals   lor vida mortals
        ardretz senes falhida,   Dieus crei l'agra eissauzida,
          si non penssatz d'als.   mas non es cabals.

[They are born hidden yet known, without fault, burnt or destroyed through their wicked lives. Earlier they deny miracles, for they have no faith—at least we have not heard of any. And if their mortal life were upright I believe God would have accepted it, but it is not just.]

XVII   Roma, als cardenals   Qui vol esser sals
        vos pot hom sobreprendre   ades deu la crotz penre
          per los criminals   per heretjes fals
        pecatz que fan entendre,   dechazer e mespenre,
          que non pensan d'als,   que·l Celestials
        mas cum puoscan revendre   hi venc sos bras estendre
        Dieu e sos amics,   tot per sos amicx;
          e no·i val castics.   e pus tals destricx
        Roma, grans fastics   pres, ben es enicx
        es d'auzir e d'entendre   selh que no·l vol entendre
          los vostres prezicx.   ni creire·ls chasticx.

[Whoever wishes to be saved must now take up the cross to overthrow and hurt the false heretics, for the heavenly one came this way to stretch forth his arms, just for his friends; and since He took such torment upon himself, whoever will not hear and believe his teachings is truly wicked.]

XVIII   Roma, eu sui enics,   Roma, si pus gicx
        car vostre poders monta,   renhar selhs que·us fan onta
          e car grans destrics   al Sant Esperitz
        totz ab vos nos afronta,   (quant hom lor o aconta,
          car vos etz abrics   tan son fol mendicx
        e caps d'engan e d'onta   qu'us ab ver no s'afronta),
          e de deshonor;   no·i auras honor.

e·il vostre pastor
son fals trichador,
Roma, e qui·ls aconta
fai trop gran follor.

Roma, li trachor
son tan ples d'error
qu'on plus pot, quascus monta
quec jorn sa folor.

[Rome, if you continue to allow those men to rule who cause you shame before the Holy Ghost (when one tells it to them, they are such foolish scoundrels that none will turn to the truth), you will thereby win no honor. Rome, the traitors are so full of errors that each one pursues his folly every day as far as he can.]

XIX   Roma, mal labor
fa·l papa, quan tensona
ab l'emperador
pel dreich de la corona
ni·l met en error
ni·ls sieus guerriers perdona;
car aitals perdos,
que non sec razos,
Roma, non es bos;
enans que l'en razona
reman vergonhos.

Roma, fol labor
fa [qui ab] vos tensona,
de l'empe[rador
dic, s']ab vos no s'adona,
q[u'en gran] deshonor
ne venra s[a corona—
e] sera razos.
Mas per[o ab vos
leu] troba perdos
qui g[en sos tor]tz razona
ni n'es a[ngoissos].

[Rome, whoever quarrels with you undertakes a foolish task; of the emperor, I say that if he does not unite with you, his crown will fall into great dishonor—and that will be just. But he will easily find forgiveness who nobly perceives his misdeeds, and is anguished by them.]

XX   Roma, ·l glorios,
que sofri mortal pena
en la crotz per nos,
vos done mal'estrena,
car voletz totz jors
portar la borsa plena,
Roma, de mal for,
que tot vostre cor
avetz en tresor;
don cobeitatz vos mena
el fuoc que no mor.

Roma, ·l glorios
que a la Magdalena
perdonet, don nos
esperam bona estrena,
lo folh rabios
que tans ditz fals semena,
fassa d'aital for,
elh e son thezor
e son malvat cor,
morir, e d'aital pena
cum heretjes mor.

[Rome, may the glorious one who forgave Magdalene, from whom we hope for a good gift, cause the foolish, truculent fellow who spreads so much false talk, to die, him and his possessions and his wicked heart, in the same way and with the same pain as when a heretic dies.]

Since Gormonda's apologia is a response to the famous *sirventes* against Rome by Guilhem Figueira,[7] its argumentative and poetic structure becomes fully apparent only when interpreted in contrast to Figueira's song. The imitation may be readily observed in the outer form: the stanza structure and rhyme scheme correspond exactly (*coblas singulars capcaudadas*).[8] That a poet should have imitated another's meter and rhyme scheme was not unusual in Provençal poetry. Indeed, Guilhem Figueira structured his *sirventes* upon the strophic pattern of Gaucelm Faidit's *canso* (P-C 167,2),[9] and he alludes to this in his second line with "en est son que m'agenssa." Diez characterizes the troubadour as follows:

> In the strongest sense of the word, Guilhem was an enemy of the priests and a friend of the emperor; he calls Frederick II his lord and exalts him with passion, though it is not believable that he served him as court poet. His hatred for the clergy and its leader was obviously engendered by the crusade against the Albigensians and the count of Toulouse, his ruler; in a *sirventes*, the longest and most powerful that we know of concerning these matters, he speaks his mind without reserve; yet he did not belong to any of the various heretical sects of southern France.[10]

Guilhem's anti-clericalism provoked Gormonda's *sirventes*. She imitated the form of her model so that her song might be understood immediately as a reply to Guilhem's attack. Schultz-Gora and Riquer mistake this intention when they dismiss the *sirventes* as "ziemlich mißglückt" (rather unsuccessful) and "de muy escaso valor literario" (of very slight literary value) because of its formal correspondence to its predecessor.[11] Gormonda's art consists in creating a new *sirventes* of identical form as Guilhem Figueira's, and even with some literal repetition of his text, but with completely contrary polemical content. Her response is not inferior to Guilhem Figueira's invective in any way.[12]

In the very first stanza, the poet makes her point of view unequivocally clear. She intends to oppose the heresies that have reached her ears, since she is unhappy with the attacks on what she refers to as the source of all goodness, salvation, and faith. Gormonda intentionally does not mention Rome by name here, preferring to paraphrase it with its positive significance to salvation: "so don totz bes / ven e nais, et es / salvamens e fes" (that from which all goodness comes and is born, and [which] is salvation and faith). The implicit reference to Guilhem Figueira's *sirventes* is made here, as the troubadour in his first stanza had drawn up a negative picture of Rome, describing it as "caps de la dechansenssa / on dechai totz bes" (head of decadence, where all goodness decays). Gormonda succeeds in expressing her radical opposition to the poet's position by reevaluating the content of the central subject "Rome."[13] At the same time she condemns the opinion of her opponent as "dezcrezensa" (disbelief) and his behavior as "desmantenensa" (renunciation of faith) and thereby brands him a heretic.

Throughout the *sirventes,* Gormonda makes use of the reevaluating method in various ways. Mostly she takes up Guilhem's rhyme-words to use them in an antithetical context, as for example in the second stanza with *guerra, sosterra,* and *guitz*.[14] Countering the poet's "Roma enganairitz / qu'etz de totz mals guitz / e cima e razitz" (Rome the deceiver, you are the leader, head and root of all evil, II) she introduces "Roma . . . qu'es caps e guitz / de totz selhs que en terra / an bos esperitz" (Rome, the head and leader of all those on earth who have good souls, II) and thus gives a further antithetical definition of Rome. The literal reversal of Guilhem's "totz mals" in stanza II then comes at the beginning of the third stanza: "En Roma es complitz / totz bes" (In Rome all goodness is perfected).

It is interesting that Gormonda, like Guilhem, argues in terms of courtly concepts even when she speaks about religious or moral ideas. While the troubadour pillories Rome as the cause for the decline of "pretz e merces" (worth and grace, II), Gormonda accuses him of destroying "totz bos faitz cortes" (all good courtly deeds, II) and describes the "fals mal apres" (false, ignorant one) in uncourtly terms. She reproaches him and his partisans with irrationality, arrogance, and evil speech (II–III), declares them stupid and coarse (IV), and contrasts them, the "fols" (fools, V) and above all, the "avols hom" (vulgar man, V) with Rome's reason (V) and the good example of those who are "good souls" (II) and therefore live at peace with Rome (V). Since she is an advocate of the "lei romana" (Roman faith, III), for her Rome is naturally the highest feudal lord ("senhoria," XIV), and thus all criticism of its resolutions or actions and all resistance amount to reprehensible arrogance ("erguelh," XII).[15] In contrast, being on good terms with Rome brings honor, as is explained in stanzas V and XVIII.[16] While Gormonda on the one hand urges obedience to the church, on the other she represents Rome itself as a political power in the fight for honor ("honor," XVIII). Here she cleverly makes a standard of behavior bearing high social prestige in chivalrous courtly society binding for the church, but in addition to that, she lends this "honor" a religious character, since only those who advocate Rome's interests and doctrines may achieve it. Contrariwise, if the church fails to defend itself sufficiently against the unbelievers, it cannot lay claim to "honor." Of course, the poet believes that God stands on the side of Rome: "hi venc sos bras estendre / tot per sos amicx" (He came this way to stretch forth his arms, just for his friends, XVII).[17] Since He approves of the Roman cause, the fighter against the heretics wins double glory, human and divine recognition, honor and salvation: "qui vol esser sals / ades deu la crotz penre" (whoever wishes to be saved must now take up the cross, XVII). The call to the crusade contains both the worldly and the spiritual moment, but places the emphasis on the latter.

Gormonda's chief reproach against Rome's enemies invokes pride and heresy, "erguelh" and "eretgia" (XIV), a highly charged accusation in its contemporary context, which will be analyzed in due course.[18] The problematic political and religious areas bound together here can in general be distinguished in the four parts of the *sirventes*: at the beginning comes praise for Rome and invective against her enemies; in stanzas V–XIV the poet answers Guilhem Figueira's incriminations concerning political events point for point, only then to attack, in stanzas XIV–XVIII, the heresy from a religious point of view; in the two final stanzas, she casts a prognostic glance to the future.

Gormonda does not enter into discussion regarding the first three strong reproaches that Guilhem makes in stanzas II–IV of his poem. First of all, Guilhem maintains that the English king had been betrayed by Rome: "·l bons reis d'Englaterra / fon per vos trahitz" (II). Here he is almost certainly referring to the proceedings concerning the contested election of the English cardinal, Stephan Langton, to the archbishopric of Canterbury in the year 1207, which had led to Pope Innocent III's imposing an interdict on England in 1209 and to King John's excommunication one year later. After another four years, under threat of war with France that the Pope had declared to be a crusade, John finally had to make peace with Rome and thereafter retained England and Ireland as a papal fief upon payment of an annual tribute.[19]

In the third stanza, Guilhem raises the reproach that Rome had betrayed the Latins and the Greeks.[20] In conjunction with his equally pronounced accusation of avarice, this allusion can only refer to the plundering of Constantinople in the year 1204, when the Flemish and Frankish crusader armies robbed and completely destroyed the city. Pope Innocent III had called up the European knights to the fourth crusade, but was either unwilling or unable to influence the troops that had set out from Venice in 1202 and sought to regain rule over Constantinople for the Byzantine Alexios IV. The Pope was interested chiefly in subjugating the Eastern church to Rome, and secondly in safeguarding the route to the Holy Land along which the crusade army was accustomed to march. With the establishment of the Latin Empire of Romania in 1204, these goals seemed to be realized for the time being, and the continuation of the crusade was dropped.[21] One last censure that Gormonda never responds to concerns Rome's dealings in indulgences: "car vos perdonatz / per deniers pechatz" (for you forgive sins for money, IV).

Up to this point, the poet has contented herself with execrations and curses that she directs toward Rome's enemies. Her defense at last begins with the fourth critical point raised by Guilhem. The troubadour charges Rome with responsibility for the loss of the city of Damiette: "e vostra foudatz / fetz perdre Damiata" (your foolishness let Damiette be lost, V). Damiette, a strategically advantageous city in Egypt, had been conquered by the armies of the fifth crusade but had to be returned to the Sultan Malik al-Kamil in 1221 after the defeat at Mansurah. The blame for this loss was laid on the Spanish cardinal legate Pelagius, who had not condescended to negotiate peace terms with the sultan.[22] Nevertheless it also involved the complicity of the emperor, Frederick II, whose followers included Guilhem. For her part, Gormonda now leads off with this: "dels fols lurs foldatz / fes perdre Damiata" (the folly of the fools caused the loss of Damiette, V). Frederick had not dispatched adequate support to the battle at Mansurah, and Gormonda now uses this *foldatz* as a reproach against him. While she repudiates Guilhem's assertion that Rome alone bears the guilt, in this stanza she refrains from answering a further criticism by the troubadour when he condemns Rome as an economic power: "trop falsamen / renhatz per argen" (you rule all too falsely by money, V). The next exchange of blows brings onto the scene the central issue of both poems: the Albigensian wars. "Ab galiamen / de falsa perdonanssa / liuretz a turmen / lo barnatge de Franssa / lonh de paradis" (with the deception of false forgiveness you deliver up the French nobility to sorrows far from paradise, VI), curses Guilhem. By "falsa perdonanssa" he means the indulgences that the church granted to those who took part in the crusades against heresy, indulgences that put the war in southern France on a par with the crusades to the Holy Land. "Far from paradise" stands as a paraphrase for the moral injustice of this war, in which the northern French nobility made themselves culpable. How different, by contrast, is Gormonda's summons to the crusade! In her answer to Guilhem's sixth stanza, she emphasizes again that Rome may bring France to salvation, and "tota Fransa" no less, north and

south, as she would have it, bound together in a unity of faith. "L'autra gen / que·us vol far ajudansa" (the others who seek to help you,
VI) might refer to France's neighbors who had promised help, or who
had received petitions from the Pope for help: Otto IV of Brunswick,
Peter II of Aragon, and Alphonse VIII of Castile.[23]

In the second half of the sixth stanza, Gormonda defends Rome—as
just addressed—against Guilhem's accusation that it was responsible for
the death of Louis VIII, having lured the king out of Paris with false
sermons: Guilhem charged, "e·l bon rei Lois, / Roma, avetz aucis, / c'ab
falsa predicanssa / ·l traissetz de Paris" (VI). Louis VIII was the first
French king to become actively involved in the affairs of the Albigensian
wars. Despite sustaining heavy casualties in his own army, he conquered
Avignon and the Languedoc in 1226, issuing an ordinance against the
heretics that led to the establishment of the Inquisition (see Jedin 268).
Gormonda might also have vindicated the death of a warrior so valuable
to the church by pointing out that by his works against the heretics he
had saved his soul and gained eternal salvation. However, she obviously
prefers to refer to the *auctoritas* of a famed magician and to depict Rome
as the fulfiller of the prophecy. Significantly, even for the Christian poet,
the figure of Merlin symbolizes wisdom and soothsaying,[24] in other
words, scholarliness. To this she pays the highest respect, while she herself showed it to no mean degree.

In their respective seventh stanzas, both Guilhem and Gormonda
deal with the themes of the Saracens and Avignon. Guilhem begins:
"Roma, als sarrazis / faitz vos pauc de dampnatge, / mas grecs e latis /
liuratz a carnalatge" (Rome, you inflict few injuries on the Saracens but
yet you deliver up the Greeks and Latins to be massacred, VII). Following the internal logic of the sentence, this accusation must be interpreted in two ways. First, the church left its warriors in the East to be
slaughtered—meaning the Latin crusaders and the Byzantines who constantly had to endure attacks from the Seljuks. With this, Guilhem makes
an indirect complaint against the Popes' warmongering and their reiterated calls to save the Holy Land, which, as exemplified by the fourth
crusade, resulted in injustice and bloodshed. It is also possible that Guilhem was thinking of the atrocities committed in the various Christian
camps during the taking of Constantinople. By the "Saracens," who ostensibly received hardly any trouble from Rome, he does not mean the
crusaders' enemies in the Near East,[25] but rather the Moors on the Iberian
peninsula against whom the Reconquista had already been waged for

almost two hundred years. Throughout this entire period, the Popes had supported the Spanish knightly orders with forces and had continually attempted to unite the kings of the northern Spanish Christian kingdoms; nonetheless, they left the initiative for a war against the Moors to the Spanish themselves. In preparation for the battle of Las Navas de Tolosa, where King Alfonso of Castile conquered the Saracens in 1212, Innocent III contributed nothing beyond conducting a procession in Rome a few days before the battle. His lack of interest in subduing the moorish Saracens was evident (Roscher 172–91). Guilhem's criticism is therefore leveled at the one-sided policy of the papal auxiliary measures in the East.

Gormonda responds directly to the reproach that Rome spares the Saracens by claiming that the problem of the heresy must take precedence: "piegz de Sarrazis / e de pus fals coratge / heretjes mesquis / son" (worse than the Saracens and of more deceitful mind are the pitiful heretics, VII). This curse is more than a mere religious condemnation; it is noteworthy because under both Innocent III and Honorius III, Rome regarded the crusades to the Holy Land as its most important task (cf. Roscher 234–48). If Gormonda means by "Saracens" the Spanish Moors, a precise situation may be found in which the Moorish and Albigensian crusades coincided briefly and the fight against the heretics was given precedence over that against the heathen—namely, the year 1209. At that point, Innocent III hoped that his letters to the kings of Aragon and of Castile would prompt these rulers to take an interest in settling the circumstances in the south of France in order to obtain backing for their own undertakings (Roscher 235). But even if one does not agree with this interpretation, a measure of regional dogmatism may be heard in Gormonda's words, a dogmatism that classifies—perhaps through her own experience—the heretics of her home country as more dangerous to Christianity than the more distant muslims.

To return to Guilhem Figueira. He asks in his seventh stanza: "Ja Dieus part no·m don, / Roma, del perdon / ni del pelegrinatge / que fetz d'Avinhon" (Rome, may God grant me no portion of the indulgence or of the pilgrimage that you have arranged from Avignon, VII). He may well be alluding to the siege of Avignon by Louis VIII in 1226.[26] The citizens of Avignon, favorably disposed towards the heretics and long allied with the count of Toulouse, had made an agreement with the French king in early summer of that year to consult over how the crusading army was to cross the Rhône. Avignon owned the right-of-way over the only stone bridge on the lower Rhône, at Saint-Bénézet, and was not prepared to let the whole army move through the town and across the bridge. The king himself was offered free escort but the army was directed toward another bridge. Why this should have led to a siege of the city has not been determined. Avignon surrendered on September 9, 1226, and thereupon received the *perdon,* the annulment of the papal interdict that had been placed upon it. It also had to promise the *pelegrinatge:* to send thirty crusaders to the Holy Land and to provide for their financial support. Nevertheless, the question arises as to whether Guilhem could know these details of the surrender treaty, or whether instead he is alluding to the better known and politically more important events during and after the taking of Avignon. At that time began the southern French nobility's great "pilgrimage" into Louis VIII's encampment near Avignon, in order to avert, by their submission, the disastrous fate with which other provinces had met at the hands of the crusaders. The French king was the highest feudal lord of the southern counties, yet the visits of the nobility had the indisputable character of pilgrim processions and not that of a warm welcome. Only the bishops of the great cities received Louis well, as the crusade army finally moved through the Languedoc in the direction of Toulouse. At its head rode Arnald-Amauri, abbot of Cîteaux and archbishop of Narbonne, giving indulgence to all deserters from the southern ranks. These spectacular measures of the church, which provoked Guilhem's fury, ended of necessity on November 8, 1226, when Louis VIII died at Montpensier in the Auvergne.

Gormonda's clerical sympathies lead her to praise Rome for abolishing the road tolls in Avignon: "A selhs d'Avinho / baisses, don m'es bo, / Roma, lo mal pezatge, / don gran merces fo" (I am pleased to know, Rome, that for those from Avignon you lowered the evil toll, which was a great mercy, VII). Here it is possible that she is citing two decisions of the third Lateran council of 1179 and the council of Montpellier of 1195, both of which forbade the introduction of road tolls and increases in tariffs; as usual, however, the councils dispensed with names and concrete case-descriptions.[27] It is more probable and more in accordance with Gormonda's emphatically regional loyalty that she is alluding to an event closer to her own time that brought Rome and Avignon into direct confrontation. Two conflicts are pertinent. In 1215, the Archbishop of Aix, acting on behalf of the papal legate, Pierre de Bénévent, established new taxation tariffs and duties for the inhabitants of the city of Avignon, who had petitioned the cardinal for legal assistance.[28] The great noble families thereby lost several of their privileges to the benefit of a business interest group with whom Gormonda's sympathy might consequently appear to lie. Avignon and the church were truly opposing parties only in the treaty of 1226, following the siege of the city. On January 4, 1227, Cardinal Romano Frangipani published the terms:

> The people of Avignon were ordered to cease their support of Raimon VII and his allies . . . , to restore to the bishop and the church of Avignon the goods and rights which had been usurped, not to proceed to the election of municipal magistrates without the consent of the bishop, no longer to subject the canons and religious houses to annoyance, no longer to oblige them to contribute to taxes and no longer to submit them to the jurisdiction of the town, not to interfere in the election of bishops, to suppress tolls not established by the emperor or the king, and not to violate the peace.[29]

These requirements laid down by Rome tie in closely with the earlier council decisions of 1179 and 1195, so that ultimately it cannot be determined with any certainty which of the toll laws Gormonda had in mind when composing her *sirventes*. In any event, here again her familiarity with the political decisions of the Catholic church is apparent.

Stanzas VIII and IX contain nothing new. Once more Guilhem deplores the senseless killing for which Rome has to answer, in particular the martyred deaths of many Christians (fighting against the heathen), and denies that they have any religious justification. Gormonda dismisses this attack as mockery ("esquern," VIII) and points to the duty of obedience to the church: its instructions must be followed "ses contradire," otherwise it resorts to sanctions ("ab bon govern / baissatz folh esquern" [with good governing you humble foolish mockery], VIII). The example for the death of any individual is found in the suffering of Jesus, which every Christian must consider.

Guilhem now turns to the fate of the count of Toulouse, Raimon VII.[30] Raimon's relations with Rome had been so strained even prior to his official accession to power in 1222 that the church relieved him of his lands in October 1221, a measure of no practical consequence. Despite repeated efforts on the part of the count, no reconciliation came about; in 1225, the council of Bourges sanctioned his excommunication and offered indulgence to the French king, Louis VIII, in the event that he should wish to lead the crusade against Raimon. The council most probably acted at the instigation of the papal legate, Romano Frangipani, following the wishes of Amauri de Montfort to have his son Simon de

Montfort, the leader of the crusade army who had been killed in the battle outside Toulouse, recognized as the city's legitimate count. The troubadour rightly condemns this action as a deceit, an offense, and exaggerated severity ("engans," X, "forfaitura," XI, "desmesura," XI). By contrast, as a partisan of the house of Toulouse, he praises the warlike conduct of Count Raimon: " . . . ton / los frances e·ls escorsa, / e fa·n planca e pon, / quand ab els se comorsa; / et a mi platz fort" (he mows down the French and slashes them up and walks upon their corpses, when he goes out to fight them; and that pleases me greatly, XII).

Gormonda also describes Raimon as "guerrejaire" (warlike, XIII), but naturally she stresses that his power is useless against Rome: "non li val poder" (XIII). In the tenth stanza, entirely in keeping with the church's wishes, she demands that the count drop his deceit and false belief, and make good the wrongs that he had inflicted upon the church. This corresponds fairly precisely to the offer that Raimon had put forward to the council of Bourges in 1225:

> He promised to satisfy all the grievances of the clergy and to restore everything that he was accused of taking from the church; heresy would be uprooted from his dominions, and the authority of the church re-established everywhere. (Sumption 215)

Evidently, Gormonda advocated the position of the council's members who were determined to punish the people of Toulouse, and who refused to accept the count's offer of a too easy reconciliation.

In stanza XI she expresses this clearly: "lo reis grans / qu'es senhers de dreitura / als falses Tolzans / don gran malaventura" (may the great king who is lord of justice bring great misfortune upon the false people of Toulouse, XI). Directly after the council of Bourges, the French king began the crusade against Toulouse. The primary aim of his endeavor was to appoint Amauri de Montfort, who had given over all his rights to the king, as the legitimate count of Toulouse, but even more, to conquer the city itself. Throughout the years of the war Toulouse had proved itself to be Raimon's most faithful ally: "e·l comte Raimon, / s'ab elhs plus s'asegura, / no·l tenrai per bon" (if Count Raimon further allies himself with them [the people of Toulouse], I will not think it good, XI). In Gormonda's eyes, such conduct on the part of the city represents great arrogance ("gran desmezura," XI), which is explicable only in view of her fidelity to the king. The second reproach that she levels at the people of Toulouse concerns heresy. She considers Guilhem Figuiera representative of all the city's inhabitants: "lo trefas / e sa leis sospechoza / als fols digz vilas / par que fos de Toloza, / on d'enjans certas / non es doncx vergonhoza" (the deceiver and his suspicious faith, with its foolish, vulgar language, seems to be from Toulouse, which feels no shame of notorious deceit, X). The descriptions in stanza XIV might also apply to the populace of Toulouse, who rebuilt the walls and fortifications after every siege or sacking. "Qui contra vos gron / ni bast castelh ni forsa" (who grumbles against you and builds and conquers fortresses, XII) might also be those barons of the Midi who had castles built to defend themselves against the invasions of the crusade army. The allusion to the high mountain ("aut mon," XII) suggests a fortification like Montségur, which had been erected by 1204 for Ramon de Perella, who was sympathetic toward the Cathars. Just as later on in stanza XVII, in this instance Gormonda knows that God, who is on the side of the church, perceives the pride and injustice ("erguelh e·l tort," XII) of the heretic and will punish him with twofold death, both spiritual and corporal, against which Guilhem thought the count of Toulouse to be immune—with God's help: " . . . e·l comte estorsa / de vos e de mort" (the count will escape both you and death, XII).

The troubadour then broaches the conflict between Rome and the Holy Roman Emperor, Frederick II: "si l'adreitz emperaire / mena adreich sa sort (. . .) que·l vostre poder / veirem dechazer" (when the clever emperor acts cleverly, we shall see your power broken, XIII). We may presume that at the time these lines were written Frederick stood under excommunication, which brought to a preliminary conclusion the dramatic development in relations between emperor and Pope in the years prior to 1227 (see Jedin 241–43). Already, at his coronation as emperor on November 23, 1220, Frederick had promised Pope Honorius III a crusade to the Holy Land, but for various reasons he repeatedly put it off. After his latest attempt to set out in August 1227 he soon returned unwell; meanwhile, the new Pope, Gregory IX, did not let his excuses pass and pronounced the emperor excommunicated on September 29, 1227. But this did not prevent Frederick from making the journey to Palestine in June 1228, there to draw up a treaty with Sultan al-Kamil of Egypt concerning the holy cities of Jerusalem, Bethlehem, and Nazareth, which was signed on February 18, 1229. Guilhem's optimism probably stems from the period between September 29, 1227, and June 28, 1228, when the emperor continued to lead the crusade despite his excommunication. This supposition is further substantiated by stanza XIX:

"mal labor / fa·l papa, quan tensona / ab l'emperador . . . ni·l met en error" (the Pope undertakes a bad venture when he quarrels with the emperor . . . and puts him in the wrong, XIX). Frederick's excommunication had already been pronounced and, naturally, Guilhem was sharply critical.

In her thirteenth stanza, Gormonda counters by saying that both the count of Toulouse and the emperor were to blame for their miseries. She comments on their lack of strength: "be·m conort / que·l coms ni l'emperaire, / pueis que son destort / de vos, non valon gaire" (I am well pleased that the count and the emperor, having turned away from you, have lost their strength, XIII). She calmly states that the "folh deport" (foolish behavior, XIII) and "malvat vejaire" (wicked opinions, XIII) of the enemies of the church put them into their difficult position, and that warlike bearing could be of no help to such fundamentally false attitudes. Again, at the beginning of stanza XIV, she summarizes her wishes: "ieu esper / que vostra senhoria / e Fransa . . . fassa dechazer / l'erguelh e l'eretgia" (I hope that your dominion and France . . . will bring to destruction the pride and the heresy, XIV). It is surely not presumptuous to read into "erguelh" and "eretgia" the two political opponents of the church, Frederick II of Hohenstaufen and Raimon VII of Toulouse.

Guilhem, on his part, had discovered the Catholic church's aspirations to world power: "tant voletz aver / del mon la senhoria" (you strive so much after world dominion, XIV), an imputation that came fairly close to the truth in his time (cf. Jedin 178–91). The inevitable invective against Rome ensues: Rome neither fears God nor keeps His commandments, and with each finger commits more evils than he, Guilhem, can count (XIV).

Of course, Gormonda does not let these insults pass uncontradicted. It is the heretics who do not follow the prohibitions of the church, and who do not believe in mysteries (XIV). It is difficult to make out which heretical doctrine the poet is referring to here, as the heretics of southern France included such diverse groups as the Cathars, the Waldensians, wandering reform preachers, and religious fanatics (Jedin 123–32). They shared a common questioning of ecclesiastical doctrine, rejecting the hierarchy of the bishops, the sacraments, and the worship of relics, and in contrast to the Catholic clergy, they both preached and practiced a life of simplicity and chastity. Their political abstinence lent their religious claims greater credibility. Exactly this made it all but impossible for Gormonda to make accusations against them on any grounds other than dogmatic, which should not be interpreted as a shortcoming or clumsiness on her part.

On the opposing side, it was an easy matter for Guilhem to pillory the obvious mistakes of the Pope, the Curia, and the bishops.[31] In stanza XV, he fancies the whole world will be lost if Rome does not soon lose its power, in particular charging the Pope with the desire to monopolize everything. After another polemic stanza, he attacks the cardinals: "que non pensan d'als, / mas cum puoscan revendre / Dieu e sos amics" (who think of nothing but how they may sell God and his friends, XVII). This refers not so much to the cardinals' practice of employing indulgence as a means of political pressure wherever needed, as to the fact that they would neglect and betray Christian ethics whenever a material advantage was to be gained—as they did in the case cited above of Romano Frangipani at the council of Bourges in 1225. Lest this not be enough, Guilhem adds: "e·il vostre pastor / son fals trichador" (and your shepherds are false deceivers, XVIII). Even the lowest rank of the clerical hierarchy falls to his condemnation, which is quite understandable in view of the behavior of the southern French clergy during the Albigensian wars. At the council of Lavaur in 1213, against their better judgment, the bishops and prelates present accused Raimon VI of Toulouse before the Pope and called for the continuation of the war against him, a demand that Innocent III refused for the time being. Even the fourth Lateran council in Rome in 1215, not to mention other contemporary sources, sharply criticized the lack of discipline among the clergy.

Gormonda answers each of these charges. In stanza XV, she borrows the image of the snare from Guilhem's parallel stanza; for her, the snarers are of course the "fals heretges quetz" (false, secret heretics, XIV) of the previous stanza: "aissi tendon lur trapa . . . ab que quascus s'arrapa" (thus they set their traps . . . in which everyone becomes ensnared, XV).[32] The next stanza likewise condemns the heretics with severe words: "car fe no·i es—auzida / no n'avem sivals" (for they have no faith—at least we have not heard of any, XVI). Gormonda's condemnation culminates in the earlier mentioned summons to the crusade, to which, as she explains, Christians are obliged through the sacrifice of Jesus Christ. Only the fight against the traitors brings honor, "que·us fan onta / al Sant Esperitz" (for they cause you shame before the Holy Ghost, XVIII). The argument has moved from religious polemic back to the plane of chivalrous courtly values.

The nineteenth stanzas of both poems cite one last common issue, the emperor's quarrel with the Pope. "Mal labor / fa·l papa, quan tensona / ab l'emperador / per dreich de la corona" (The Pope undertakes a bad venture when he quarrels with the emperor over the right to the crown, XIX) very likely concerns the crown of Sicily, which was a frequent subject of dissension between the emperor and the papacy. In 1216, Frederick II, who was also king of Sicily, had to assure Pope Innocent III that after being crowned emperor he would hand over the kingdom to his son Henry. Sicily was a fief dependent on Rome, so the Pope always acted as feudal lord to the Sicilian king. After Frederick II had become emperor, he and the Pope almost out of necessity fell into opposite fields of interests and into conflict.

In her answering stanza, Gormonda alludes presumably to their most recent incident, the excommunicated emperor's crusade to the Holy Land, mentioned above. She calls for his submission to the Pope: "de l'emperador / dic, s'ab vos no s'adona, / qu'en gran deshonor / ne venra sa corona" (of the emperor, I say that if he does not unite with you, his crown will fall into great dishonor, XIX). Here, again, it is interesting that she should bring a negative value of chivalric society—the concept of *deshonor*—into the discussion, although she might just as well have held out a prospect of moral or religious punishment to the emperor. Apparently, the topic of discourse, the emperor, and the categories of value in his world influenced the language even of the pious poet.

The final stanza throws significant light onto this piety. While Guilhem wishes Rome with its avarice upon the straight path to purgatory (XX), Gormonda brings up once more the cruel fate of the heretics. In the context of her *sirventes*, the lines "·l glorios / que a la Magdalena / perdonet" (the glorious one who forgave Magdalene, XX) immediately call to mind a key event of the Albigensian wars, the taking and destruction of the city of Béziers by the crusade army on July 22, 1209. The chronicler of the *Chanson de la croisade albigeoise* reports:

> So fo a una festa c'om ditz la Magdalena
> Que l'abas de Cistel sa granda ost amena;
> Trastota entorn Bezers alberga sur l'arena. (ed. Martin-Chabot 52)

> [It was on a holiday which is called (the feast) of Magdalene, when the abbot of Cîteaux led up his great army; it encamped all around Béziers on the sandy soil.]

The papal legate Arnald-Amauri, abbot of Cîteaux, called upon the inhabitants to hand over all heretics within the walls. Without waiting for a reaction, the crusaders then stormed the city, laid it waste and set it on fire. The people, including priests, women, and children who sought refuge in the churches, were slaughtered without mercy. Gormonda wishes the troubadour a death such as that which thousands suffered as the city burned: "·l glorios . . . lo folh rabios . . . fassa d'aital for . . . morir, e d'aital pena / cum heretjes mor" (may the glorious one cause the foolish, truculent fellow to die . . . in the same way and with the same pain as when a heretic dies, XX). A more aggressive cynicism is hardly imaginable.

The sharpness and severity of Gormonda's argument were probably oriented to the expectations of her audience. The poet addresses her listeners directly on one occasion ("no·us meravilhes negus" [none of you should wonder, II]), from which one may infer that she recited her *sirventes* in front of a sizable group. There is also much to suggest that in composing her answer she had Guilhem's poem written down in front of her: the imitation of the rhyme scheme; the borrowing of many rhyme words and, in many instances, of word sequences from the troubadour's text together with close thematic connections; the transformed but similar sounding contradiction of each stanza in the original poet's attack. Precisely this stanza-by-stanza advancing of the argument, Gormonda's perpetual reacting, implies something about the way in which this *sirventes* was produced. It can be imagined as a kind of staged debate, as was customary among scholastics from the twelfth century onwards.[33] It is quite conceivable that Gormonda replied to each stanza from Guilhem's *sirventes*, as it was recited by a teacher or some other partner, with the countering stanza she composed. Thus she breaks into the beginning of her poem having just heard sung or read, it would seem, a stanza of Guilhem's: "Greu m'es a durar, / quar aug tal descrezensa / dir ni semenar" (It is difficult for me to bear it when I hear such disbelief spoken and spread about, I). The audience that may have been present, consisting of monastery pupils or members of an order, is suggested by "per qu'ieu farai parvensa / e semblan que·m pes" (therefore I shall show and make known what oppresses me, I), for both *faire parvensa* and *faire semblan* contain the dramatic moment.

The most important elements in Gormonda's arguments include faithfulness to Rome and to the Pope, obedience to the church, and unity of faith; the fight against the southern French heretics, against Raimon of Toulouse and Frederick II; the view of the French king as an instrument of Providence; knowledge of courtly standards; and a certain penchant toward learning and erudition. If we assume that Gormonda's opinions corresponded with those of her listeners, we can perhaps detect the mentality of a religious community in which the delineated debate may have occurred: the Dominicans. Beginning in the year 1233, the first papal inquisitors were appointed from the ranks of this order. A note of religious and political fanaticism reminiscent of the Dominicans is sometimes to be heard in Gormonda's words. But no more than a cautious suggestion of a Dominican audience may be derived from the text of her *sirventes*, and so the quest must begin again to determine with precision both the person of the poet and the political-theological dimensions of her poem. Numerous problems still confront the literary historian, both concerning the situation of women at this time and concerning the art and the personal inspiration of Gormonda.[34]

Notes

1. "Die erste französische politische Dichtung einer Frau" (D. Rieger, "Die französische Dichterin" 39). [In his contribution to this volume, Zufferey attributes another *sirventes* (P-C 404,5) to an anonymous trobairitz despite the attribution in the manuscripts to Raimon Jordan, and considers the *planh* by another anonymous lady (P-C 461,2) as a variety of *sirventes*.—Editor's note]

2. Cathala-Coture wrote in 1785: "Une dame quercinoise, nommée Dormunda, composa alors sur cette secte [les Albigeois] un poeme dans l'idiôme provençal, qu'elle adressa à la ville de Rome" (1:220). There is considerable likelihood that this refers to Gormonda. Cathala-Coture does not, however, cite a source. See also Malinowski, who would see Gormonda as the author of the *Chanson de la croisade albigeoise.*

3. The *Histoire littéraire de la France* expresses doubt that the author is a woman: "Nous nous persuadons difficilement que l'auteur de cette pièce soit une femme. Ce sera peut-être quelque moine . . . ou quelque autre partisan de la ligue, qui aura voulu se dérober sous un nom supposé aux vengeances des Toulousains et des Avignonnais" (18:665). Even if that were the case, it would still have to be explained just why a woman's name should cause less suspicion than a man's, or rather, why such a pseudonym would be assumed at all.

4. "Sie . . . [wünscht] nur das schlimmste Unglück auf die Toulouser herab, während sie sicher triumphiert hätte, wenn sie das Gedicht nach jenem Ereignis verfaßt hätte" (Levy, *Guilhem Figueira* 8).

5. P-C 217,2. Text according to Riquer, *Trovadores* 3:1272–78.

6. P-C 177,1. Text according to Levy, *Guilhem Figueira* 74–78, with modifications in punctuation, in capitalization, and in the following passages: stanza IV.10, *del trasdossa* follows ms. *R, de la trossa* Levy; stanza VII.6 reads with De Bartholomaeis, cf. *van s'en en loc salvatge* Levy, *vai (vas R) en loc de salvatge*

mss. *CR;* stanza XVI.3 reads *o* as in ms. *R, e* Levy; and XVI.4 reads *per* as in ms. *R, que* Levy. In stanza XIX, square brackets enclose material conjectured by Levy where the manuscript has been damaged. See also the text and translation in De Bartholomaeis, *Poesie provenzali storiche* 2:106–12. Present translation by the author. The edition by A. Rieger, "Un *sirventes* féminin: la *trobairitz* Gormonda de Monpeslier," was not available when this study was completed.

7. Composed between 9 September 1227 and the beginning of 1229; cf. Levy, *Guilhem Figueira* 9. For the interpretation of this *sirventes* see Levy, *Guilhem Figueira* and Klein, *The Partisan Voice* 96–97, and also Jauss and Köhler, eds. *Grundriß* VI.2 item 5204.

8. The two poems are listed by Frank, *Répertoire,* as numbers 272:2 and 3. In explanation of the detail that Gormonda composed only twenty stanzas in contrast to Guilhem Figueira's twenty-three, Levy suggests (*Guilhem Figueira* 8) "that not the entire poem, but only twenty stanzas were well-known, which is supported by the fact that the Ambrosiana manuscript ends just where the Gormonda poem stops" (daß derselben nicht das ganze Gedicht, sondern nur 20 Strophen bekannt waren, wofür die Tatsache spreche, daß die Handschrift der Ambrosiana D 465 inf. ebenda ende, wo auch das Gedicht der Gormonda schließt).

Taking into consideration the criticism of Levy, *Guilhem Figueira,* who set Gormonda's and Guilhem's stanzas into long lines with internal rhyme (11a'-11a'-11a'-5b-5b-11a'-5b), in this study only short lines are used; compare Bartsch's review of Levy as well as Chabaneau's improvement mentioned by Levy in his review of Schultz-Gora 178; likewise *Histoire littéraire de la France* 18:663–65, and further Frank, *Répertoire métrique* 1:49, and Riquer 3:1272–78. De Bartholomaeis (2:106–12) proposes a mixed form (11a'-11a'-11a'-5b-5b-5b-6a'-5b). To avoid confusion in verse numbers, for all quotations in the remainder of this essay references will be given to the respective stanza only.

9. See Frank, *Répertoire* 1:xx; prior to him, Bartsch in his review of Levy. Rajna ("Un serventese contro Roma") and Riquer (3:1272) propose the religious *canso* "Flors de paradis / Regina de bon aire" (P-C 461,123) as Guilhem's model.

10. "Guillem war im strengsten Sinne des Wortes der Pfaffen Feind und des Kaisers Freund; er nennt Friedrich II (!) seinen Herrn und erhebt ihn mit Leidenschaft, wiewohl es nicht glaublich ist, dass er ihm als Hofdichter diente. Sein Hass gegen den Clerus und dessen Oberhaupt ist sichtbarlich durch den Kreuzzug gegen die Albigenser und den Grafen von Toulouse, seinen Landesherrn erzeugt worden; in einem Sirventes, dem längsten und stärksten, welches wir über diese Gegenstände kennen, hat er ihn ohne Rückhalt ausgesprochen; gleichwohl gehörte er zu keiner der verschiedenen südfranzösischen Ketzersecten" (*Leben und Werke* 455).

11. Schultz-Gora, *Die provenzalischen Dichterinnen* 5, and Riquer 3:1272. Diez, *Leben und Werke* 457 and *Histoire littéraire* 18:663 also condemn the quality of Gormonda's poem without citing particulars.

12. Only Thiolier-Méjean 359 defends Gormonda's "violence verbale," "non moins cinglante," but "sans doute moins imagée que celle de Guilhem" against, above all, the judgment of Anglade, *Les troubadours* 195: "La riposte est d'ailleurs loin d'avoir l'allure violente et par moments si éloquente de l'attaque."

13. See Hagan 54–59, who characterizes Gormonda's technique as "repetition with reversal."

14. Altogether, Gormonda borrows 92 of Guilhem's 220 rhymes, including five entire verses (in stanzas VI, VII, VIII, XIII and XX). She transfers 11 rhyme-words to other stanzas.

15. Further examples of uncourtly qualities of anyone who opposes Rome: "fols digz vilas, non es . . . vergonhoza" (X); "falses Tolzans, . . . desmezura" (XI); "non valon gaire, . . . folh deport, . . . guerrejaire" (XIII); "si fos lejals, . . . non . . . cabals" (XVI); "fol mendicx, . . . li trachor, . . . sa folor" (XVIII); "deshonor" (XIX); "folh rabios" (XX).

16. See also stanza VI, where it is said of those who help Rome that they might lead France to true salvation.

17. This is a paraphrase of the Crucifixion.

18. The Old French and Old Provençal literary polemic concerning the Pope and the crusades has been analyzed by Throop, "Criticism of Papal Crusade Policy" and *Criticism of the Crusade,* and by Siberry.

19. See Levy, *Guilhem Figueira* 82; Klein 96–97; Jedin 187–88.

20. By analogy to "grecs e latis" (VII), "vas nos e vas grecs" (III) may be interpreted as "Latins and Greeks." Most probably this means those believers originally of the Latin (Roman) and Greek churches, but in a broader sense also the knights and crusaders of those respective confessions; see Levy, *Guilhem Figueira* 83.

21. See Klein 97; Jedin 191–96; Roscher 99–122.

22. See Jedin 242 and 358; likewise Levy, *Guilhem Figueira* 83–84. Discussions of the loss of Damiette can also be found in the Old French poems about the crusades, on which see Serper.

23. "In March [1209] Otto IV had just agreed at Speyer to give the Pope effective help against the heretics. Moreover, since the kingdom of the Arelate, which bordered on the region of the heretics, was under the Emperor's rule, he was, as worldly sovereign, almost directly affected too." (Otto IV. hatte gerade im März des Jahres [1209] im Speyerer Versprechen dem Papst wirksame Hilfe gegen die Ketzer zugesagt und war außerdem, da das dem Ketzergebiet benachbarte Königreich Arelate dem Kaiser unterstand, auch als weltlicher Oberherr fast schon direkt betroffen) (Roscher 235). Peter II of Aragon, otherwise faithfully obedient to the Pope, came to the aid of his brother-in-law Raimon VII of Toulouse in the fight against Rome and was killed at the battle of Muret in 1213.

24. See Zumthor, *Merlin;* Lejeune, "Les allusions à Merlin."

25. During the first crusade, Nicea, Antioch, and Jerusalem were captured, and in the third crusade, Acre and Cyprus. In addition, the Christian armies triumphed over the Seljuks in numerous battles. Thus Guilhem's accusation might be best understood in the sense that the conquest of the entire Holy Land had not yet succeeded and that Rome had lost interest in fighting the Saracens, above all since the breaking off of the fourth crusade.

26. See Diez, *Leben und Werke* 456. The events mentioned here are described in detail by Sumption (217–20).

27. See Mansi vol. 22, col. 230 (ch. 22) and 669; see also the decision of a *concilium provinciale Narbonense* of 1227: "De novis pedagiis (et) quidagiis statuit

concilium, ut per ecclesiasticum judicem, si necesse fuerit, prohibeantur om-
nino" (vol. 23, col. 24 [ch. 13]). The notes in Levy, *Guilhem Figueira* 84 are not
very helpful.

28. See Labande 20–21, and the accompanying *pièce justificative* (296–304).

29. "Il fut ordonné aux Avignonais d'abandonner Raimond VII et ses al-
liés . . . , de restituer à l'évêque et à l'église d'Avignon les biens et droits usurpés,
de ne pas procéder à l'élection des magistrats municipaux sans l'assentiment de
l'évêque, de ne plus molester les chanoines et maisons religieuses, de ne plus les
obliger à contribuer aux impôts et de ne plus les soumettre à la juridiction de la
commune, de ne pas s'ingérer dans l'élection des évêques, de supprimer les
péages non-établis par l'Empereur ou le roi, de ne pas violer la paix" (Labande
31–32).

30. See Sumption 199–206 for what follows.

31. See Jedin 42: "Die Kurie, Kardinäle oder 'capellani', auch der Papst fan-
den sich jetzt [= Ende 12. Jh.] im Kreuzfeuer der Kritik, ohne wirklich Abwehr
leisten zu können, weil dieser Kritik eben einfache, unbestrittene Tatsachen zu-
grunde lagen." (The Curia, Cardinals or 'capellani', and even the Pope now [at
the end of the twelfth century] found themselves in the cross-fire of criticism
without any real means of defending themselves, because simple undisputed facts
underlaid the attacks.) No details are supplied.

32. The second halves of stanzas XV and XVI, where several details concerning the heretics are enumerated, present a particular problem in interpretation as the text is corrupt; see Chabaneau, "Sur un vers"; Bertoni, "Noterelle."

33. See Grabmann's description (2:20–21): "Es gewährten diese Disputa-
tionen große Vorteile; sie verursachten Schärfung des Verstandes, Schlagfertig-
keit und Wortgewandheit, sie leiteten dazu an, fremde Gedanken rasch und scharf
aufzufassen und zu prüfen. . . . In der Disputation trat das persönliche Können
des Schülers am deutlichsten in die Erscheinung und Öffentlichkeit. . . . Das
Hin- und Herwogen dieses Kampfes, die allmähliche Entwicklung und Verwick-
lung des Problems, die Schlag auf Schlag aufeinander folgenden Einwände und
Lösungen . . . , alle diese und noch andere Momente waren geeignet, die Erwar-
tung und das Interesse der Teilnehmer und Zuschauer bei solchen Disputations-
übungen in Spannung zu halten." (These debates afforded great advantages; they
brought about a sharpening of understanding, quickness of repartee and clever-
ness with words, they instructed one to comprehend and to examine strange
ideas swiftly and keenly. . . In debate the personal ability of the student makes
its appearance most clearly. . . . The fluctuations of this struggle, the gradual
development and complication of the problem, the objections and solutions following upon each other, blow upon blow . . . , all these and even other moments
were suited to holding the attention and the interest of the participant and the
observer in debating exercises.)

34. ". . . et au sujet de la situation de la femme en ce temps-là et au sujet
de l'art et de l'inspiration personnelle de Gormonda" (Camproux, review of
Bogin 417).

8 Derivation, Derived Rhyme, and the Trobairitz

This essay starts from the idea that rhyme, the principal rhetorical orna-ment of the medieval Occitan lyric, functions both as a metaphor for the experience of poetic creation (or reception) and as a metonym for the meaning of the poetic text: the first, because the very act of rhyming—that is, creating sequences of related words—offers an analogue to the combining of motifs, themes, or ideas by the poet as he/she writes, and the audience as they respond; the second, because the rhyme gives prominence and memorability to the rhyme words, so that they come to provide a ready means of access to, or even to stand for, the other words and meanings of the text (see Switten, Smith 94–95).

The kinds of rhyme that can be classed together as "derived rhyme" (*rims derivatius*)[1] fulfil the second of these two functions in a particularly emphatic way, since by definition they accumulate at the rhyme forms derived from the same lexeme or root. In the earliest songs using derived rhymes, the related forms occur in pairs, and this remains characteristic. Access to the semantic substance of the rest of the text is therefore me-diated by these pairs. From Raimbaut d'Aurenga onward, however, rhyme-schemes are devised in which the same rhyme words are repeated throughout the text, as in his famous "Ar s'esplan la flors enversa" (see Appendix 1 to this essay, no. 4); the effect is to prolong the material of the seasonal opening, as resumed by the rhyme words (*enversa, tertres, conglapis, trenca, siscles, giscles*), to create from the landscape a sustained metaphor of the emotional and moral condition of its inhabitants. Alter-natively, the same root can be repeated throughout each stanza, as in Guilhem de Saint-Didier's "Pois tant mi forss'amors" (Appendix 1, no. 10) or Aimeric de Peguilhan's "En amor trob alques en qe·m refraing"

(no. 13), so that each stanza becomes saturated by a particular concept; Aimeric, for example, foregrounds in succession the meanings
<*fraing*>, <*pren*>, <*man*>, <*trai*>, and <*ferm*>, being imitated in this
by Guilhem Anelier de Toulouse (no. 47) who uses three of the same
rhyme roots in his *contrafactum* of Aimeric. In some of the later songs,
the repetition of a root at the rhyme is further reinforced by recurrences
of the same root within the line. An example of this technique is provided by Peire de Blai (no. 34):

> En est son fas cansoneta *novella;*
> *novella* es quar eu cant de *novel;*
> et de *novel* ai cauzida·l plus *bella,*
> *bell'* en tot sens, e tot quan fai es *bel*
> per que m'es *bel* qu'ieu m'alegr' e·m *deport*
> quar en *deport* val pauc qui nos *deporta.* (vv. 1–6)

> [To this tune I compose a new little song; it is new because I sing anew; and
> I have newly set my eyes on the most lovely, lovely in every way, and all
> that she does is lovely; and so I find it lovely to rejoice and be diverted, for
> in (ordinary) diversion there is little to divert one.]

This density of repetition makes the meaning of these roots indissociable
from the song's content, which they come to represent or resume almost
to the point of attaining identity with it. Thus, in the stanza just quoted,
one need only add the notion of "song" repeated in verses 1 and 2 to the
series *novel—bel—deport* to have a fair résumé of its content.

The patterns of derived rhyme can offer an equally prominent metaphor of the kinds of mental act underlying the poem's composition (or
decoding). The most obvious is the operation of pairing like with like,
which is often used as a form of emphasis, notably in the moralistic tradition which stems from the earliest known poem in derived rhyme,
Marcabru's "Contra l'ivern que s'enansa." In the opening stanza of this
song, derived rhyme is used as a form of amplification (*interpretatio*) to
reiterate material in a slightly different guise. This is particularly clear in
verses 2 and 4 where the subject of repeated *asalh-* is itself repeated in
variant forms (*cossir-*):

> (Co)ntra (l'i)vern que s'e(n)ansa
> ab cossi(ri)er que m'as(sa)lh,
> m'es belh (q)ue del chant (m)'enans
> ans (qu)'autres cossirs m'assalha.

[In the face of advancing winter, with the anxious concern which assails me, I like to advance myself in song, before any further concern assails me.]

Similar accumulation is found in verses 25–27 and 43–45:

Per cujatz n'ay esperansa
qu'enquer ab mi s'enguasalh,
mas tan n'ay bons esperans . . .

[Through foolish fancy I hope that she may yet join company with me, but I have such fine hopes of this . . .]

D'aquesta qu'ieu chant sobransa
sos pretz, senes devinalh,
et en valor es sobrans . . .

[The merit of the one of whom I sing is supreme, I speak without fond imagining, and her worth is supreme . . .]

Converse to this equating or reduplication is the use of derived rhyme to accentuate a contrast. Bernart de Ventadorn's "Ara no vei luzir solelh" (Appendix 1, no. 2) opens with the opposition between the radiance of love and the consequent eclipse of the rays of the sun:

Ara no vei luzir solelh,
tan me son escurzit li rai;
e ges per aisso no·m esmai,
c'una clardatz me solelha
d'amor, qu'in el cor me raya . . . (vv. 1–5)

[Now I cannot see the sun shining, so obscured are its beams for me; and yet I do not feel at all dismayed, because a brightness of love which beams in my heart acts as a sun for me . . .]

Grimoart Gausmar's moralizing love song "Lanquan lo temps renovelha" (no. 12) contains an example in which the contrary nature of *amor* and *malvestatz* is reinforced by the rhyme:

amors si senh ab joi fi
e jois fa d'amor capdelh,
e malvestatz, que no fina,
baissa pretz e·l descapdelha. (vv. 29–32)

[Love girds itself with true joy, and joy makes love its captain, whereas evil, which knows no end, debases merit and leaves it captainless.]

It is worth noting that in this example the contrast is expressed by the use of a prefix (*des-capdelha*) as well as by the suffix required by the rhyme. In Guiraut Riquier's "Lo mons par" (no. 41), where all the derivation is by prefixation, the prefix *des-* is used to convey the disorder and disruption of the world.

The grammatical categories of the forms repeated in derived rhyme can serve to nuance the relations of equivalence or difference just described. Roncaglia (personal communication cited by Lawner 521) has suggested that Marcabru's rhymes in "Contra l'ivern" are a reflection of a philosophical analysis of grammatical categories, attested in Bernard of Chartres and John of Salisbury, according to which "the noun contains the real substance, the adjective and the verb being subsequent attenuations of that substance through conmixture with accidental elements such as the 'person.'" Since Marcabru's text does not as a rule pair noun with verb or noun with adjective, this observation seems less applicable to it than to those of later poets such as Elias Fonsalada (Appendix 1, no. 22) or Raimon Bistortz d'Arles (no. 35), both of whom combine at the rhyme adjectives with their corresponding abstract nouns. Verses 7–12 of stanza I of Elias Fonsalada's song, for instance, run as follows:

> Sivals entre·ls valens
> aura mos chans valensa;
> Qu'ieu vuelh als sapiens
> mostrar ma sapiensa;
> quar ab los conoyssens
> deu aver conoyssensa.
>
> [At least among the worthy my song will have worth; for I wish to show my wisdom to the wise; for it must find discernment among the discerning.]

The rhyme words, which recur in all stanzas, here suggest a relationship of mutual reinforcement between the values upheld by the poet's community and their realization in his text. In Roncaglia's formulation, the "substance" represented by the series of abstract nouns (*valensa, sapiensa, conoyssensa*) is exemplified, in a form diluted by personal reference, in the corresponding series of adjectives.

Another kind of semantic relation for which certain morphological exponents of derived rhyme can serve as a metaphor is reciprocity—or, more commonly in the lyric, the lack of it. The morphological opposition between masculine and feminine provides an obvious expression of this relation, as in Guiraut d'Espanha's *dansa* "Dona, si tot no·us es preza" (Appendix 1, no. 38):

> Dona, si tot no·us es preza
> de l'Amor don ieu soi pres,
> autra no·m pot far conqueza
> tal per qu'eu sia conques. (vv. 1–4)

> [Lady, although you are not taken by the love that has taken me, I cannot make a conquest of another lady, such that she could make a conquest of me.]

Alternation between first and third person singular verb forms is another, very common, means of giving poetic relief to this most standard of *topoi*. An early example occurs in Bernart de Ventadorn's "Bel m'es can eu vei la brolha" (no. 3):

> . . . tuih mei dezir
> son de lei per cui sospir.
> E car ela no sospira . . . (vv. 36–38)

> [. . . All my desires are for her for whom I sigh. And since she does not sigh . . .]

The technique is particularly clear and well-sustained in Daude Pradas, "De lai on son" (no. 28):

> De lai on son tug miei desir,
>   car sai que cill no·m desira
> per qu'ieu soven plaing e sospir;
>   mas ill non plaign ni sospira.
> . . . .
> Qu'ieu non pens d'autra ren ni cur
>   et ill de mi non a cura. (vv. 1–4, 7–8)

> [There where all my desires are placed, since I know that she has no desire for me, that is why I keep lamenting and sighing, and yet she does not lament or sigh. . . . For I think of and care for nothing else whereas she has no care for me.]

A theme commonly associated with that of reciprocity, the discrepancy between desire and experience, or fantasy and reality, can also be articulated by a morphological opposition: that between indicative and subjunctive. Here is Bernart de Ventadorn's accomplished manipulation of this discrepancy in "Bel m'es":

. . . . Per so m'acolha
ma domna, pois tan l'acolh
c'a totas autras me tolh
per lei, cui Deus no me tolha.
Ans li do cor qu'en grat colha
so que totz jorns s'amor colh. (vv. 11–16)

[And so may my lady make me welcome, since she is so welcome to me that
I deprive myself of all others on account of her whom God grant I may never
be deprived of; may He instead give her a mind to graciously accept the fact
that I accept to love her eternally.]

It is worth noting that the phonetic material which characteristically
marks the oppositions here associated with the theme of reciprocation,
real or desired, is the same: final -*a*, alternating with either zero or (in the
case of nominal flexions) final -*s*. (This is of course not the way first/third
verb endings are marked for all conjugations, but it is for the majority
class in -*ar*.) A glance at the final column of the table in Appendix 1 will
confirm that these are by far the commonest exponents of derived
rhyme.

Is there any indication that the troubadours were conscious of the
effects that could be derived from this opposition? The treatises, it must
be admitted, offer no account of derived rhyme as a semantic system.
The concern of the author of the *Leys d'Amors* is to classify its formal
operations, which he does under three heads: (*rima*) *derivada* (addition or
removal of one letter or syllable, e.g., *mort* > *mort-a*), *maridada* (addition
or removal of more than one syllable, e.g., *humil* > *humil-itat*), and
entretracha (substitution of one segment for another, e.g., *capdel-s* >
capdel-a).[2] Among the troubadours themselves there is, not surprisingly,
almost no discussion. The one exception is Gavaudan who, in "Lo vers
dech far en tal rima" (Appendix 1, no. 19), writes as follows:

Lo vers dech far en tal rima,
mascl'e femel que ben rim,
qu'ieu trac lo gran de la palha,
de sen qu'om no ss'i empalh. (vv. 1–4)

[I should compose a *vers* with such a rhyme scheme, masculine and feminine
that it will rhyme well, for I separate the grain from the chaff so that no one
of sense can be incommoded by it (the chaff).]

The rhyme scheme is presented as one suited to drawing distinctions, in particular to separating grain from chaff; it also combines *mascl'* and *femel*. The analytical aspect of the song consists in contrasting sweet and bitter love (v. 7), and then proceeding to denounce the latter as *fals'amistat amara* (v.8), *putia* (v. 14), *fals'amors* (v. 31, 68). Bitter love is well-armed with deceits to which men repeatedly fall victim:

> Et yeu fug a la trebalha
> qu'als sieus fa tostemps trebalh,
> a jove, vielh e senec.
> Anc Nero, c'aussi Seneca,
> non ac un jorn son cor clar. (vv. 63–67)

> [And I flee the torment (of love), which always causes torment to its adherents, young, old, and aged. Never did Nero, who killed Seneca, have his heart unsullied by love for so much as a day.]

It acts, of course, through immoral women:

> Sella qu'ab dos s'entressima
> greu er del ters no·s tressim . . . (vv. 21–22)

> [She who couples with two will hardly keep from cleaving to a third. . . .]

Could this theme have any bearing on the terms *mascl'* and *femel*?

The terms are also used by Aimeric de Peguilhan in the second stanza of "Mangtas vetz sui enqueritz":

> Qu'ieu ai motz mascles auzitz
> en chansonetas assatz
> e motz feminis pausatz
> en verses bos e grazitz. (vv. 9–12)

> [For I have heard many masculine words in *chansonetas,* and feminine ones set in good and agreeable *vers.*]

Aimeric's editors note that *mascles* and *feminis* "refer of course to masculine and feminine *rimes.*" Their observation, though accepted by other scholars,[3] is not self-evidently true, since the Occitan treatises on versification describe rhyme in terms of the position of tonic stress (*accen*), what we call "masculine" rhymes being specified as oxytonic, or having an *accen agut,* and "feminine" ones as paroxytonic, or with an *accen greu.*[4]

They reserve the terms *mascles* and *feminin* for gender *stricto sensu*, in the noun and adjective.[5] It seems more likely, then, that Aimeric and Gavaudan are invoking a notion associated more with gender than with the position of stress in relation to rhyme.

If we suppose that Aimeric's editors are correct in glossing *motz* as "rhyme words," then the sections on gender in the treatises may throw some light on what "masculine" and "feminine" rhyme words might mean. The *Leys* distinguish arbitrary (*vocal*) from motivated (*real*) gender.[6] The latter are illustrated by lists of nouns and proper names, mostly ending in -*a* as well as referring to women or female creatures, for instance, Gatien-Arnoult 2:68 "*Saurimonda. Helena. Alamanda. fina. Aycelina.*"[7] The former are identifiable because as the *Leys* (Gatien-Arnoult 2:66) have it, "Si tant es que la votz sia mays convenable al femini quez al masculi. cum son li nom termenat en .a. coma *taula. porta. banca. cadiera. terra. ayga. poma. arca.*" Anglade's text of the *Leys* treats feminine words which do not end in -*a* and masculine words that do as exceptional (3:76f.). The strength of association between *real* and *vocal* gender ascription is demonstrated by the attraction of certain masculine nouns in -*a* (*gaita, garda,* etc.) into the feminine.[8] It seems clear that to the grammarians the principal marker of feminine was final -*a,* and that its strength of formal (*vocal*) association with this category was sufficiently strong to override etymological or *real* gender. One possibility, then, is that by "masculine" and "feminine" rhymes Aimeric and Gavaudan are referring to rhymes with and without -*a*. Gavaudan's "mascl' e femel que ben rim" (see above) is calling attention not to the phonological structure of his rhymes, but to their morphological structure (and perhaps by extension also its semantic implications): that is, his election of derived rhyme with alternation of absence and presence of "feminine" -*a*.

But are Aimeric's editors justified in assuming that *motz* means "rhyme words?" That it can have this sense has been shown—for instance, by Mölk; but it is not a technical term.[9] Moreover to gloss it so narrowly in the excerpt from Aimeric de Peguilhan is to impute to him the indefensible claim that "masculine" rhymes might be expected to occur solely in *vers* and "feminine" ones (i.e., rhymes in -*a*?) in *cansos*. His meaning might be less specific: "topic, preoccupation, diction." Similarly, Gavaudan's use of *rim/rima* may be less technical than we have so far supposed.[10] Could he be referrring to the dramatization in his poem, and by the rhyme-scheme, of the opposition between the deceptive female and the foolish male victim?[11]

As we saw, derived rhyme in the troubadours overwhelmingly takes the form of pairing forms with and without final -*a*. Whether they were aware of it or not, then, they were giving preference to a technique which embodies the principal formal gender distinction of the language and also expresses other morphological oppositions (first person/third person, indicative/subjunctive) which ideally lend themselves to their chief subject matter, the imaginary charting of the relations between the sexes. Derived rhyme, then, has the facility of mediating between form and content, its formal properties enabling it to function simultaneously as metaphor and metonym for textual meaning.[12]

That two of the few trobairitz use derived rhyme may not be significant, since the technique seems to have been particularly in vogue at the turn of the twelfth and thirteenth centuries when they were writing (see Appendix 1); it is, however, an unusually elaborate technique in a body of poetry which elsewhere cultivates an air of unaffected simplicity. Did it recommend itself to them because of its suitability to expressing themes of reciprocation? Could the possible association of its commonest form with gender distinctions have appealed to writers so preoccupied by the difficulty of finding a space for self-expression in an ethos and tradition dominated by men? These questions are too ambitious to admit of definitive answers, but I hope that a close examination of the use made of derived rhyme in these two texts might throw some light on how two poetesses wielded a semantically highly-charged technique forged by their male predecessors.

Before discussing the Comtessa de Dia's song "Ab joi et ab joven m'apais," it would be helpful to comment on the version of the song offered in Appendix 2 to this essay, the text of which follows Kussler-Ratyé's except for the interversion of stanzas III and IV.[13] The core of the problem, to which this interversion is proposed as a solution, is the opacity of verses 13–16. The proverb in verses 15–16, whose general meaning is that hurtful intentions often miscarry against the person who entertains them, could be seen as reflecting on any of the individuals referred to in this stanza—the Comtessa, the lover, their intermediary or some slanderer; but its most likely target is the lover, for this makes the best sense of the Comtessa's injunction to the intermediary in verse 14 not to believe ill of her *cavallier* "except that which I retail," which seems to preface some criticism on her part of the lover's conduct.[14] The other most likely possibility is that the proverb refers to the Comtessa's own ill-judged behavior: complaining of one's lover rebounds against one-self.[15] But why should she ask to have her, and only her, criticisms believed (vv. 13–14), if she then intends—at least by implication—to re-tract them? Stanza II, then, combines the following ideas: praise of the lover and gratitude for having met him (vv. 9–12); anxiety about slanderers (vv. 13–14); oblique and muted criticism of the lover by herself (vv. 15–16).

Stanza IV* in the standard text (= stanza III in mine) parallels this movement very closely. The element of eulogy is more emphatic than previously (vv. 24*–28*). Then fear is expressed about slanderers—this time lest the lover believe evil reports of her (vv. 25*–27*). The final line assures of her unfailing love for him, yet makes it dependent on his toward her, thus hinting again at the possibility of criticism by allowing his desertion to be conceivable. (This sentiment also echoes verses 5–8.) The idea that his *faillimen* might rebound against him balances the proverb of verses 15–16, where castigation in fact harms the person trying to inflict it.

Stanzas II and IV* are not only parallel in content; the second helps to develop and clarify the extremely opaque narrative of the first. The publicly acknowledged worth of her lover is in both cases set against the fear that the course of their love may be upset by slander of either his behavior, or hers, or both. If she ventures to criticize him (vv. 15–16), it is so reticently as to be almost unintelligible; yet even so the Comtessa is alarmed lest he be alerted to her misgivings (vv. 30*–31*), and teasingly reassures him of her fidelity—which, with a slightly anxious reference back to verses 5–8, she makes conditional only upon his.

Once juxtaposed, the verbal echoes between the two stanzas generate poetic effect instead of becoming lost over the intervening text. Note especially the chiasmus in the ordering of the ideas "He should not believe anyone else" (A) and "He should believe me" (B):

> no·l creza (A) fors so qu'ie·l retrais (B) (v.14)

> (prec li que) m'aia crezenssa (B) (v. 21) ni hom no·l puosca far crezen (A) (v. 22).

Further parallels between the new final stanza and the *tornada* immediately spring into prominence:

> . . . deu ben pausar s'entendenssa
> en un pro cavallier *valen*
> pois ill conois *sa valenssa* . . .

Floris, *la vostra valenssa*
saben li pro e *li valen* . . .

The rhetoric of this conclusion is now very like that of "A chantar m'er de so qu'eu no volria," in which the vocabulary and narrative situation of the last stanza are likewise reiterated in a *tornada* appealing directly to the lover to moderate his behavior toward her:[16]

> . . . per qu'ieu vos mand lai on es vostr' estatges
> esta chansson que me sia *messatges:*
> e voill saber, lo mieus bels amics gens,
> per que vos m'etz tant fers ni tant salvatges,
> non sai si s'es *orguoills* o mals talens.
>
> Mas aitan plus vos diga lo *messages*
> q'en trop d'*orguoill* ant gran dan maintas gens. (vv. 32–37)
>
> [. . . And so I send to you, where you are staying, this *canso* to be my messenger; and I want to know, my handsome, noble friend, why you are so fierce and so savage to me—I don't know if it's pride or ill will.
>
> But all the more may the messenger tell you that many people suffer greatly as a result of too much pride.]

In "Ab joi et ab joven m'apais," the appeal in the *tornada* is a *requête d'amour* and stems from the Comtessa's decision in the preceding stanza to love openly. The structure that results from interverting stanzas III* and IV* is thus at once more comprehensible and more rhetorically effective. Henceforth, quotations from the text will use the line numbers of this revised ordering.

The rhyme words help to guide the listener through the song's meanings. The first stanza foregrounds inner responses. *Apais-apaia* must mean "satisfy" rather than "nourish": forms derived from Latin *pascor* could not produce the third person singular of verse 2.[17] The "satisfaction" of *joi* and *joven* actualizes itself in the rhymes *gais-gaia* and *verais-veraia*. The last two rhymes of stanza I initiate a series of verb forms translating movement of inclination and of speech; the (technically deficient) pairing *que val mais-que m'aia* offers an interesting encapsulation of what Shapiro has described as "the capsized situation in which desire must express itself as the wish to be possessed" (562). The third stanza is organized around rhymes suggesting, respectively, values (*gen-genssa*), cognition (*conoissen-conoissenssa-crezensa-crezen*), and failure (*faillimen-faillensa;* again, the rhymes are imperfect). The final stanza then reiterates the idea of cognition (*s'enten-entendenssa*) to conclude the song with an effusive celebration of public values.

This chain of meaning, which arises out of what I called the metonymic function of rhyme, is supported by the types of derivation used, and which constitute its metaphorical dimension. All the rhymes manifest an alternation between presence and absence of -*a*.[18] Many of them illustrate two of the characteristic relations discerned above: alternation of masculine and feminine, expressing concern with reciprocity (notably verses 3–6, although the same theme is conveyed as a relation between the trobairitz and her values by the first/third person verb forms of verses 1–2); and alternation of adjective and noun, imaging the relation between an exponent of a quality and the abstract conceptualization of that quality (notably verses 27–28, 31–32, 33–34). Each of these two semantic relations dominates one of each pair of *coblas doblas*—the outer stanza of each pair in the reordered text. Together these preoccupations of individual aspiration to a mutual love, and recognition of the power invested in public opinion and values, are an admission of the ideologically exposed position of a woman troubadour, an admission which becomes explicit in stanza IV's carefully lodged appeal for social approval of her declaration.

The transition between a celebration of reciprocal—but otherwise private—emotion in stanza I, and the exuberant conviction that such emotion is sanctioned by public standards in stanza IV, is effected by stanzas II and III, whose rhymes do not, for the most part, correspond with either of the two patterns just discussed. In stanza II, the related verbal forms do not continue, as one might have expected, the I/he alternation of stanza I, verses 3–6. New subjects are God, the lovers' go-between, and potential *lauzengiers;* there is an opening into a wider context from that of the first stanza, but one accompanied by an anxiety translated by the alternation of indicative and subjunctive that we have seen to be associated, in some poets' works, with oscillation between reality and possibility. Confronted by this wider context, the Comtessa tries at the beginning of stanza III to placate it, and disarm its criticisms, by establishing a connection between her *cavallier*'s value in its eyes and in her own (vv. 17–20). This prepares for her affirmation, in the final stanza, that she is unexceptionable to society (vv. 25–28). In the *tornada* she goes further, writing herself out of her own text by subordinating her own perception of "Floris" to that of others, and by using a metaphor derived from the male-dominated structure of feudalism in which to cast her *requête d'amour.*

From a post-Romantic perspective, then, this song is self-undermining in that it licenses the expression of individual desire and self-determination only at the moment when the individual becomes indistinguishable from society at large. To a medieval mentality, however, with its far less radical disjunction between individual and collective experience, this irony may not exist. But what of a second possible irony: that the cost of merging with society, for the woman troubadour, is the abandonment of her gender and the placing of her personal gaity and devotion (*gaia, veraia*, vv. 5, 6) under the authority of *li avinen* (v. 31) and *li valen* (v. 34)—the male arbiters of *avinenssa* and architects of *mantenensa?* The morphological oppositions at the rhyme in the first and second stanzas bring the trobairitz into relation with individual men; those of the last, for the most part relating adjectives to nouns, forsake *real* for *vocal* gender, placing the abstractions within a masculine domain. The result is that the Comtessa's declaration, in the final stanza, of her freedom to choose as a woman whom she should love is undermined by a rhyme scheme that grounds values ultimately in men. Unable to gain control of a traditional poetic language, the Comtessa de Dia finds it ironizing the content of her song.[19]

The text of the *coblas* exchanged between Bernart Arnaut d'Armagnac and Lombarda, which is included in Appendix 2, is essentially that of Boutière and Schutz,[20] but with slight differences of interpretation which need briefly to be outlined. Bernart opens with a flattering expression of solidarity with his addressee. A similar sentiment is voiced by Peire Bremon Ricas Novas in "Rics pres" (Appendix 1, no. 32):

> Mais n'amera Catalans
> si vos fosses Catalana;
> pero, car es Castelana
> volgr'ieu esser Castellans . . .
> . . . .
> e servira·i Surianz
> si vos fossetz Suriana. (vv. 31–34, 39–40)

[I would love the Catalans more if you were Catalan, but, since you are Castilian, I wish I were Castilian . . . and I would serve the Syrians there if you were a Syrian.]

Bernart Arnaut's preparedness to become a Lombard is perhaps less extreme than Peire Bremon's to serve the Syrians, but it may nonetheless represent a major concession if the anti-Italian stance of the near-contemporary *partimen* between Tostemps and a Raimon (probably de la Salas) is to be believed.[21]

Having through the wordplay of the opening line blurred the identity of his interlocutor with the (purported) "meaning" of her name, Bernart proceeds to compare her with an Alamanda, identified by Boutière and Schutz with Giraut de Bornelh's lady, and a Guiscarda, whom they take to be the wife of the viscount of Comborn referred to by Bertran de Born.[22] Whoever these ladies may be, Lombarda is preferred for her greater allure, which, in the best tradition, signals love but simultaneously withholds it.

Dejeanne,[23] followed by Boutière and Schutz, sees the Seigner Jordan of the next stanza as a rival for Lombarda's love, and identifies him with the *vila* of verse 19. Certainly Bernart is offering Jordan terrritories in which to make his conquests, and retaining for himself the land he (humorously) associates with his lady: Lombardy.[24] What of Liverno (some editors read Liverna) and Lomagna? The latter is generally agreed to be Lomagne, part of the territory of the counts of Armagnac; Liverno is diversely recognized as northern Italian Livorno or the southern French village of Livernon, formerly in the dependence of the viscounty of Lomagne.[25] The manuscript spelling makes the latter more likely (particularly as it is an Italian manuscript that could have been quick to record an Italian toponym). Rather than jealous rivalry, it seems we have here an amiable and jocular proposal whereby vast, but distant, tracts of land are offered to Seigner Jordan by the younger brother of the count of Armagnac[26] in return for the unhampered enjoyment of his lady (here *Lombardia*) in his own back yard. Hence the amused observation of verse 11: How could Jordan quibble at a partition so favorable to himself? (True, the beginnings of the Albigensian crusade may have made the offer difficult to translate into reality . . .) If this stanza in fact cements an alliance between the two men, defensive with respect to each other and offensive in regard to their female prey, then *vila* in verse 19 is merely a reference to any possible *lauzengier*.

The inclusion of Alamagna among Seigner Jordan's "territories" might imply that the Alamanda of verse 2 falls to his share. If she is Giraut de Bornelh's lady, the association with Germany is certainly humorous, since Alamanda d'Estanc came from near Condom—that is, in Armagnac! Verses 15–16 are variously edited in attempts to resolve the unsatisfactory "q'es stragna / des tot avol prez" of the sole manuscript. Is *es(s) tragna* an adjective or a verb? The play on personal names and toponyms could be a reason for taking it adjectivally, with a jocularly "literal" backward reference to Alamanda (= "foreign") and a "courtly metaphorical" reference brought out by the subsequent content of verse 16 (= "far-removed").[27]

There can be little doubt that *Mirail-de-prez* is a *senhal* for Lombarda, though she will affect not to recognize it as such (see below). It is also used, though doubtless for other *domnas,* by Bertran de Born and Elias Cairel.

Meg Bogin's edition of the *coblas* introduced a significant alteration to the first line of Lombarda's reply (numbered v. 21 for ease of reference), by printing *Nom* as *No·m* (114). In the context of her note that "Provençal women often took their husbands' names," this suggested a spirited independence in Lombarda, seen as declining the honor of becoming Bernart Arnaut's wife. Bogin's interpretation is not, however, borne out by the initial *e* of verse 22 (after *no,* one would expect *ni*) nor by the *gran merses* of verse 23 unless these are rather crassly ironic. Moreover, Bogin cites no authority in support of her observation about names. The adoption of feminine forms of masculine names is, in fact, much more common within the lineage than as a result of marriage, where it is extremely rare for names—other than titles—to be passed from husband to wife.[28] Verses 21–24 are, then, more likely to be a gracious acknowledgment and reciprocation of Bernart's fanciful opening line: if he would accept translation from his native Armagnac to furthest Lombardy for her, she, for her part, will abandon her "foreignness" and try to assimilate to his lineage. Her opening quatrain having thus responded to his, her next four lines engage with verses 5–8 of his *coblas:* there she was inaccessible; now he is insufficiently explicit in his declarations. (This fencing between the protagonists is reminiscent of Jean Renart's *Lai de l'Ombre.*)[29] Boutière and Schutz are surely right to see the *e* of verse 28 as "and" and not, as previous editors had done, as a contracted *en,* "in."

Lombarda's final stanza (the *tornada* is lost, a blank space in the manuscript revealing the assumption, at least on the scribe's part, that it existed) has been stigmatized for its pretentious obscurity (e.g., by Dejeanne). I think she is rather commenting on the unclarity of Bernart's text. *Mirailz* (v. 29) is plainly a quotation from his *coblas* that she has already asked to have clarified (vv. 25–28). It has been generally assumed that *no veser* should be construed in relation to this mirror (Dejeanne: "car parler de miroir et ne pas vouloir s'y regarder"; Bogin: "for the mirror with no image") but it too can be viewed as a quotation from Bernart's text, verse 5, where he complains that her fair look (*bel veser*) is withheld from him. *Bel Veser* is of course, like *Mirail,* a *senhal* used by other poets (Bernart de Ventadorn, Arnaut de Maruelh). She could be drawing attention to the ambiguity of such *senhals,* which blur the distinction between reference (<a paragon> for *Mirail,* <fair looks> for *Bel Veser*) and a specific referent (herself or another lady) in a haze of ill-directed or even specious flattery; she could merely be protesting at the confusing number of poetic *domnas* (Alamanda and Guiscarda among them) crowding her out of the text. His poetry, she contends, disturbs (*descorda*) her understanding (*acord*) to the point almost of destroying (*des-acorda*) it. The only point in his verses that is intelligible to her is the use he makes of her name: "but when I remember (*record*) what my name signifies (*recorda*) all my concern resolves itself (*s'acorda*) into a good resolve (or: harmoniously, *en bon acord*)."[30] Her name recalls an identity distinct from the other *domnas,* an ancestry separate from Bernart Arnaut's, and perhaps also a gender not disguised like those of the masculine *senhals.*

The wordplay of this passage may be a response to verses 1 and 12 of the opening *coblas,* but it also introduces a new, self-reflexive pun on poetic composition, since the term *acort,* and some of its cognates, belongs in literary as well as in reflective discourse.[31] Many of the *tensos* or *partimens* between a male and female protagonist involve removal, or slipping, of the mask of "courtly love." Is Lombarda mocking, as Bogin suggests, the phraseology and technique of her interlocutor? Although the derived rhymes themselves are not based on a distinction of gender, they use masculine and feminine gender markers (absence and presence of -*a*) in a way that might furnish a commentary on the derivational wordplay of verses 1 and 21–22 where both morphological and *real* gender are clearly at stake, as well as commenting on the artificiality and obscurity of the conventions of male lyric poetry.

Her point emerges most forcefully in the last four lines that survive of her text, where the profusion of derivatives of the root -*cord*- yields to produce *cor,* and the wide-ranging geographical reference of verses 9–12 shrinks down to *maiso* and *borda.* Heart and hearth are the "feminine" answer to the male trobadour's technical display. The fencing is over; now Lombarda insists on knowing if Bernart loves her. To confront him in this way she has had to fight through the language of her model, and his tradition, and win.

The cultural construction of gender difference is very clearly echoed in the morphology of medieval Occitan, and in the poetic technique of derived rhyme. The women troubadours probably do not realise how powerful and cohesive are these parallel social, linguistic, and poetic structures. The Comtessa sees the need to defend her right to court her *cavallier* in relation to her gender, and to social norms, but cannot prevent her text from seeming to allow the latter to undermine the former. Although the simple language she finally elects to use marks a triumph of female rhetoric, Lombarda appears unruffled by the casual deconstruction of her identity into a display of (not very witty) wit, while the easy identification of a woman with her territory (such a regular occurrence on the marriage market) concerns her less than insufficiently explicit declarations by her admirer. But they chose the difficult medium of derived rhyme with its ritualization of male–female boundaries, and transgressed those boundaries while respecting the medium. That tension alone makes their texts more interesting than those of many of their male counterparts.

APPENDIX I *Derived Rhyme in the Poetry of the Troubadours*

	Troubadour[a]	Dates[b]	Song	P-C	Frank[c]	Brief account[d]
1.	Marcabru	...1130–49...	Contra l'ivern	293,14	864,6	±a retro 1/3 2/4 5/6
2.	B de Vent	...1147–70...	Ara no vei	70,7	753,1	±a 1/4 2/5 3/6 7/8
3.			Bel m'es quan	70,9	295,11	±(C)a capfin 1/2 etc.
4.	Raim d'Aur	...1147–73...	Ar s'esplan	389,16	859,1	e/a ±s rhyme words
5.			Cars, douz	389,22	884,1	±a e/a 2/14 ; 3/13 8/12 10/11
6.	Gir de Born	...1162–99...	En aital	389,26	879,12	±a 1/2 3/5 4/6 7/8
7.			A be chantar	242,1	826,1	±s 1/2 refrain words
8.			Amors	242,9	452,1	±a 10/11
9.	Guilh de S-D	...1165–95...	Belh m'es	234,5	879,10	±a retro
10.			Pois tant	234,16	3,4	prefix 1/2/3/4/5/6
11.	Gc Fdit	...1172–1203....	Una dolors	167,64	29,6	±(C)a 3/6 4/5 7/8
12.	G Gausmar	3rd quarter 12 c	Lanquan	190,1	879,13	±(C)a retro 1/3 2/4 5/7 6/8
13.	A d Peg	...1190–1221....	En amor	10,25	32,1	±(C)a rhyme roots 1/8 2/7 3/6 4/5
14.			Ses mon aplec	10,47	436,1	±a ±re ±er rhyme V
15.	E d Barj	...1191–1230	Car compri	132,7	624,74	±e 5/6 or 7/8
16.	Gavaudan	...1195–1211	A la plus	174,1	416,1	±a 5/8 or 7/8
17.			Ieu no sui	174,5	837,1	s/a 1/13
18.			Lo mes	174,7	762,1	±a rhyme words 1/9 2/7 3/6 4/5
19.			Lo vers	174,8	882,2	±a 1/2. . . 7/8
20.	G Ademar	...1195–1217....	Al prim	9,5	882,1	±a ±atge ±ansa retro rhyme words
21.	C de Dia	end 12-early 13 c	Ab joi	46,1	295,8	±a 1/2 etc.
22.	E Fonsalada	end 12-early 13 c (ed.)	En cor ai	134,2	230,1	±a alter 1/2 etc. rhyme words
23.	Guir de Cal	...1202–12...	Ara s'es	243,4	225,4	a/s ±(C)a ar/ada 1/2 etc.
24.	El Cairel	...1204–22...	Abril	133,1	863,1	±a 4/12
25.	Lombarda	...1206–17... (BS)	Nom volgr'	288,1	29,2	prefix 1/2 3/4 (st II)
26.	Rost de Merg	?	La douss' amor	428,1	174,1	±(C)a 1/2/3/4 5/6/7/8 9/10/11/12...
27.	Peire Milon	1st half 13 c (?)	Pois l'us	349,5	877,1	±a ar/aire 1/5 2/6 3/7
28.	D Pradas	...1214–82...	De lai on	124,7	407,17	±a 1/2 etc.

No. / Name	Dates[b]	Proper Name		Frank[c]	Rhyme scheme[d]
29. Uc de S C	. . . 1217–53 . . .	Pei Ramonz	457,27	436,2	±a
30. Guil P de Ca	1st half 13c (J)	A trop gran	227,5	721,1	±a 1/4 10/11
31. Uc de Muret	1st half 13c (ed.)	Ges si tot	455,1	302,10	±a a/s 1/2 etc.
32. P B Ric Nov	. . . 1230–41 . . .	Rics pretz	330,15a	558,1	s/a 1/2 etc.
33.		Tut van	330,19	214,1	10/11 12/13
34. Peire de Bl	?	En est son	328,1	403,1	±a 1/2 3/4 etc.
35. Raim Bist	. . . 1221/23 . . . (ed.)	Aissi com	416,2	233,4	±(C)a 1/2 . . . 15/16
36. F de Lun	. . . 1244–84 . . .	Si com	154,6	187,1	±a 5/6 retro
37.		Tan fin' amors	154,7	302,1	il/ila 1/2 etc.
38. Guir d'Esp	. . . 1245–65 . . .	Dona, si tot	244,1	407,23	±a 1/2 etc.
39.		Si la belha	244,14	407,14	±a I 3/4 5/6 II 1/2 7/8 III 1/2 3/4
40.		Si-l dous	244,15	256,1	±a 1/2 3/4
41. G Riquier	. . . 1254–92 . . .	Lo mons par	248,52	134,2	prefix 1/2 3/4 5/6 7/10 8/9
42. C de Gir	. . . 1259–85 . . .	Entre-ls reis	434a,22	644,6	±s 15/II8 18/II5 III5/IV8 III8/IV5 etc. rhyme words
43.		Pois amors	434a,49	descant	±(C)a in I II III
44.		Si per amar	434a,61	823,1	rhyme roots 1/2/3/8/9/10/11
45. P de Mars	. . . 1262–68	Belha domna	319,4	179,1	±a 9/12 10/11
46. J Esteve	. . . 1270–88 . . .	El dous temps	266,5	97,1	±a 10/14 11/13
47. Guil An de T	last third 13 c (J)	Vera merces	204,4	32,2	±a rhyme roots

[a] The editions of troubadours consulted are as in Chambers, *Proper Names*, with the following exceptions: (no. 1) ed. P.T. Ricketts, "*Contra l'ivern qui s'enansa de Marcabru*," paper read at the Fourth British Occitan Conference, Royal Holloway College, 1986 (I am grateful to Professor Ricketts for making a copy of this paper available to me); (no. 5) ed. Paterson in *Troubadours and Eloquence* 147; (no. 12) ed. de Riquer, *Los trovadores* 1:273; (nos. 16–19) ed. Guida, *Il trovatore Gavaudan*; (nos. 21 and 25) see Appendix 2; (no. 22) ed. Raupach, "Elias Fonsalada" 169; (no. 24) ed. de Riquer, *Los trovadores* 2:1147; (no. 34) ed. Rochegude, *Le Parnasse occitanien* 393; (no. 38) Hill and Bergin, *Anthology* 1:235. I have not been able to consult Hoby, *Die Lieder des Trobadors Guiraut d'Espanha*; information about songs nos. 39 and 40 is derived from Frank.

[b] Unless otherwise indicated these dates are taken from de Riquer, *Los trovadores*. BS = Jean Boutière and A.H. Schutz, *Biographies des troubadours*; ed. = edition consulted (see n. a, above).J = Alfred Jeanroy, *La poésie lyrique*; "Liste bio-bibliographique des troubadours" (1:326ff.). Peire de Blai (no. 34), for whom I have found no dates, is placed after Peire Bremon Ricas Novas, who uses a very similar form of repetition in the first stanza of "Pois lo bels temps renovella." Similarly, Rostanh de Mergas' accumulation of words derived from the same root is reminiscent of Guilhem de Saint-Didier (no. 10). Aimeric de Peguilhan (nos. 13 and 14), and Lombarda (no. 25), and he has therefore been listed as no. 26.

[c] Entries in Frank, *Répertoire métrique*. No. 43 is *descort* no. 28 in Frank, 1:128; no. 29 is a *contrafactum* of no. 14, and no. 47 of no. 13; no. 18 is an imitation of no. 5. Frank has minor errors in his entries for nos. 15, 16, 23, and 30; I propose a different analysis of no. 26.

[d] This column gives a brief account of the nature and extent of derived rhyme in each song. "±(C)a" means that a consonant may be inserted in this operation, e.g., in the pair *man-manda*. "E/a," "a/s," and the like indicate derivation by alternation. Arabic numerals are used for line numbers within any stanza, and the notation here follows Frank. "1/2" etc." indicates that derivational rhyme links lines 1 and 2, 3 and 4, 5 and 6, and so on to the end of the stanza; "1/3 2/4," etc., that the linked forms are found on alternating lines to the end of each stanza; "1/2 . . . 5/6," that the derived rhymes operate in pairs of consecutive lines up to verse 6. Roman numerals are used for stanza numbers. "Prefix" indicates that the rhymes are derived by prefixation instead of suffixation. "v" indicates a vowel. "Retro" indicates retrograded rhymes; "alter" indicates alternating rhymes; "capfin" indicates *coblas capfinidas*.

APPENDIX II   Texts

1. Comtessa de Dia, *Canso* (P–C 46,1)

I   Ab joi et ab joven m'apais
        e jois e jovens m'apaia,
        car mos amics es lo plus gais
4   per qu'ieu sui coindet' e gaia;
        e pois eu li sui veraia
        be·is taing q'el me sia verais
        c'anc de lui amar no m'estrais,
8   ni ai cor que m'en estraia.

II   Mout mi plai car sai que val mais
        sel q'ieu plus desir que m'aia,
        e cel que primiers lo m'atrais
12   Dieu prec que gran joi l'atraia;
        e qui que mal l'en retraia
        no·l creza, fors so qu'ie·l retrais:
        c'om cuoill maintas vetz los balais
16   ab q'el mezeis se balaia.

III   Q'ieu n'ai chausit un pro e gen   IV*
        per cui pretz meillur' e genssa,
        larc et adreig e conoissen,
20   on es sens e conoissenssa;   28*
        prec li que m'aia crezenssa,
        ni hom no·l puosca far crezen
        q'ieu fassa vas lui faillimen
24   sol non trob en lui faillensa.   32*

IV   E dompna q'en bon pretz s'enten   III*
        deu ben pausar s'entendenssa
        en un pro cavallier valen
28   pois ill conois sa valenssa,   20*
        que l'aus amar a presenssa;
        e dompna, pois am' a presen,
        ja pois li pro ni·ll avinen
32   no·n dirant mais avinenssa.   24*

V   Floris, la vostra valenssa
        saben li pro e li valen,
        per q'ieu vos qier de mantenenen,
36   si·us plai, vostre mantenensa.

[I   I content myself with joy and youth and joy and youth content me, for my lover is the merriest, and so I am attractive and merry; and since I am true to him, it is fitting he should be true to me, for I never strayed from loving him, nor do I wish to do so.

II   I'm delighted to know that the one by whom I most desire to be possessed is the worthiest, and I pray God to bring great joy to the man who first led me to him; and whoever speaks ill of my lover to this intermediary, let him not believe it, unless it is I who say it: for one often makes a rod for one's own back.

III   For my choice has lit on one who is noble and handsome, through whom merit improves and is enhanced, generous, skillful, and discerning, with wisdom and discernment; I entreat him to have faith in me, and not to be persuaded that I might leave him provided he does not fail me.

IV   And a lady who devotes herself to merit should indeed set her sights on a worthy, courageous knight once she knows his worth, so that she should dare to love him openly. And provided a lady loves openly, people (men) of worth and seemliness will never say anything but compliments about it.

V   Floris, people of worth and courage know your value, and therefore I straightway ask for your protection.]

2. Exchange of *coblas* between Bernart Arnaut d'Armagnac and Lombarda (P-C 54,1 and 288,1). Rejected Readings in Manuscript *H*: 8 no·ls] nols ne. 16 es de tot] des tot. 29 descorda] desacorda. 36 las] lui.

I   [L]ombards volgr'eu es[s]er per na Lonbarda,
     qu'Alamanda no·m plaz tan ni Giscarda,
     qar ab sos oiltz plaisenz tan jen mi garda,
4   qe par qe·m don s'amor; mas trop me tarda,
         Qar bel vezer
         e mon plaiser
         ten e bel ris en garda,
8   c'om no·ls ne pod mover.

II   Seigner Jordan, se vos lais Alamagna
     Fransa e Piteus, Normandia e Bertagna,
     be me devez laisar senes mesclagna
12   Lonbardia, Liverno e Lomagna.
         E si·m valez
         eu per un dez
         valdre·us ab leis q'es(s)tragna
16   es de tot avol prez.

III   Mirail de prez,
             conort avez:

ges per vila no·m tenez

20   l'amor en que·m tenez!

I   [N]om volgr'aver per Berna(r)d na Berna(r)da
e per n'Arnaut Arnauda apellada,
e gran merses, seigner, car vos agrada

24   c'ab tal[s] doas domnas m'aves nomnada;
voil qe·m digaz
cal mais vos plaz,
ses cuberta selada,

28   e·l mirail on miratz.

II   Car lo Mirailz e no Veser descorda
tan mon acord c'ab pauc no·l desacorda;
mes can record so qe·l meus noms recorda

32   en bon acord totz mons pensars s'acorda.
Mas del cor pes:
on l'aves mes,
que sa maiso ni borda

36   no vei, que las taisses?

[I   For my lady Lombarda's sake, I wish I were a Lombard, for Alamanda and Guiscarda do not please me so much—she looks at me so pleasingly with her lovely eyes that it appears that she is granting me her love; whereas in fact she is holding out on me, for she keeps under guard her fair look, my pleasure, and her fair smile, so that one can't get them out of her.

II   My lord Jordan, if I leave you Alamagna, France and Poitou, Normandy and Britanny, then you should certainly cede to me without a struggle Lombardy, Livernon, and Lomagne. And if you help me in this way, I'll do so tenfold with her who is foreign to/far removed from all base repute.

III   Mirror of worth, you have this comfort: never let our love be broken by an uncourtly man!

I   I should be glad to have the name Bernarda, for Bernard's sake, and be called Arnauda, for the sake of Arnaut, and I thank you, lord, for being so good as to name me alongside two such fine ladies (as Alamanda and Guiscarda). I'd be glad if you'd tell me, without concealment, which you like best, and what is the mirror (paragon) you gaze at.

II   For this "Paragon" and the not "Looking" disturbs my understanding to the point of almost destroying it. Yet when I remember what my name signifies, all my concern resolves itself in a good resolve (harmoniously). But I am concerned about your heart: where have you put it, for I cannot see its house or home, since you are silent about them?]

Notes

1. Lote is disparaging of derivative rhyme (2:148–50). Dragonetti gives an account of derivation in Northern French *trouvères* (407ff.). For scholarship in the field of medieval Occitan, see Smith 130 and references, and 174–81.

2. Anglade, ed., *Las Leys d'amors* 2:112–14; Gatien-Arnoult 2:184–88.

3. Guida, *Gavaudan,* song IX, note to v. 2, quotes with approval the remarks of Jeanroy, *Poésie lyrique* 2:64–66, who likewise translates "rimes masculines" and "féminines." This translation is adopted without question by Köhler, "Zum Verhaltnis von *vers* und *canso*" 209.

4. Anglade, ed., *Las Leys d'amors* 2:53–62; Gatien-Arnoult 1:56ff., 100–02 where the terms *accen greu* (feminine) and *accen agut* (masculine) are introduced. Rhyme is also defined by *accen* in the treatises assembled in Marshall, *The 'Razos de trobar' of Raimon Vidal: Regles de Trobar,* ms. *H,* pp. 60 and 62; ms. *R,* pp. 61 and 63; *Ripoll Treatises,* p. 104; the *Doctrina d'Acort,* vv. 774–75, further uses the terms *accens greus* and *agutz.*

5. Anglade, ed., *Leys* 3:37 ff.; cf. Gatien-Arnoult 2:64ff. and Marshall, ed., *Razos de Trobar* ms. *B,* p. 8 ff. (also at less length in ms. *H*). The *Doctrina d'Acort,* vv. 105–64, abridges this teaching. In ms. *H* of the *Regles de Trobar,* the term *linatges* is used for the concept of gender, followed by a passing reference to the distinction between *masculis* and *femenis* (58).

6. See Anglade 3:37; Gatien-Arnoult 2:64. The distinction between *real* and *vocal* gender is not found in the treatises edited by Marshall, but the association of *-a* with the feminine is well established: e.g., *Razos de Trobar,* ms. *B,* p. 8: "Las paraolas substantivas femininas son *belezza, bonezza, dompna, poma,* et totas las autas qe demostran substantia feminina"; and *Doctrina d'Acort,* v. 238ff.: "Parladura feminina tals en *-a* fenis e·s declina, Aysi con *domna, blanca, bella, Gaya, poma e isnella'* (feminine endings in *-s* are dealt with subsequently).

7. Anglade lists "*taula, porta, cadiera, ayga, poma, naus, claus*" (3:37).

8. Gatien-Arnoult 2:66.

9. Mölk, *Trobar clus, trobar leu* 77–80, 86–97, 103, etc. In many of his examples *motz* seems to refer both to the rhyme words and, more generally, to the topics they encapsulate. For a non-technical use of *motz,* see the introductory section of the *Leys* ed. Gatien-Arnoult (1:8): "Aytals dictatz deu hom far am bels motz. e plazens. clars. acordans. am bona et am certa sentensa. oz am belas e am plazens methaforas. don hom puesca trayre bo sen" (Such compositions should be composed with beautiful and pleasing *motz,* clear, harmonious, with a good and certain meaning, or with beautiful and pleasing metaphors from which good sense may be drawn out), which seems a recommendation to use a diction both edifying and poetic.

10. See the remarks of P. Zumthor, *Langue, texte, énigme* 131–32, quoted by Guida, n. to v. 2 of Gavaudan, *Lo vers.*

11. For the idea of texts having gender, see the anecdote in one of the *vidas* of Bertran de Born: "E·l reis d'Arago donet per moiller las chansos d'En Giraut

de Borneill a sos sirventes" (And the king of Aragon gave the *cansos* of Sir Giraut de Borneill as wife to his *sirventes*) (ed. Gouiran 1:3). Could Aimeric de Peguilhan be rejecting an analogous conception of *cansos* being "female" or engaging "feminine" subject matter, and *vers* being correspondingly male?

12. A possible corroboration of this view is the fact that several of the texts using derived rhyme play on the corresponding masculine and feminine forms of certain common names. The earliest such pair, Costans and Costanza, may occur in Marcabru though not in *Contra l'ivern* (see Dejeanne no. 37, v. 53). They are perhaps revived, alongside an uncontroversial Domerc/Domerga, by Raimbaut d'Aurenga in the difficult "Cars, douz" in a stanza which has been the object of much emendation. Gavaudan imitates Raimbaut (though his names seem clearly not to refer to couples), and there is a return of Costans/Costanza later in the tradition with Raimon Bistort d'Arles (see Appendix 1, no. 35). The significance of this play on names will be discussed below in relation to the *coblas* of Lombarda. It is, of course, attested outside the corpus of songs using derived rhyme, but its frequency there may give weight to our suggestion that the use of derived rhyme, in particular with ± -*a,* can be intended to dramatize relations between individuals of different sexes.

13. Kussler-Ratyé 161 ff. None of the 8 manuscripts preserving this song deviates from the stanza order that she prints, but many show disturbance (mainly omissions) at the end of stanza II, and at verse 23 all the manuscripts but *D* are at fault: see Kussler-Ratyé's note. It does not seem too outrageous to postulate an error common to all the manuscripts.

14. The proverb occurs in other troubadours' work as a rueful recognition of having miscalculated in their behavior towards their lady: e.g., Peire Vidal, "Plus que·l paubres," ed. Anglade no. 18, vv. 12–15 (the poet has made presumptuous advances to the lady); Bernart de Ventadorn, "Can vei la flor," ed. Lazar no. 7, vv. 29–32 (the poet is guilty of infidelity).

15. In that case, the initial *c'* of v. 15 must be interpreted as "for," not "that": "Let him not believe ill spoken by anyone except myself—for one often makes a rod for one's own back."

16. Text cited from Kussler-Ratyé 165.

17. Raynouard 4:456; cf. Kussler-Ratyé, who translates "je me complais . . . me satisfont," and *pace* de Riquer, *Los trovadores* 2: 794.

18. Though in the first pair of *coblas doblas* the rhyme is *entrechada* (in the terminology of the treatises), while in the second pair it is *derivada.*

19. The marginality of female judgment in the male world is clearly illustrated by Bertran de Born's "Rassa tan creis" (ed. Gouiran no. 1), in which the qualities discerned in his "ideal" lady are in harmony with the male values of *joven,* and are properly esteemed by men (vv. 7–9), but provoke jealousy and dislike among other women (vv. 3–6) whose judgment is thereby disqualified by the poet and for his public.

20. *Biographies* 416 ff. Their list of previous editions omits De Lollis 161 ff. and Desazars 57–59. The latter is referred to by Almqvist, *Guilhem Adémar* 224, note to v. 47 of song IX; I have not been able to consult it.

21. See Topsfield, *Raimon de Miraval,* song no. LI, p. 372; for discussion of attribution and date, see pp. 54–55. Such virtues as are ascribed to the Lombards by Tostemps are austere: they are efficient in war and above the vices of courtly love.

22. See Gouiran 1:73 ff. and 123. If these identifications are correct, the date of composition of the *coblas* should perhaps be brought back to the later twelfth century. The possibility that Guiscarda is a poetess none of whose works have survived but whose name is associated with the history of chansonnier *H* (the manuscript that also contains the Bernart-Lombarda *coblas*) means that Alamanda should perhaps be identified with the participant in the *tenso* with Giraut, distinguished from his lady of the same name in the accompanying *razo.* The name Guiscarda figures in the contents of the *libro slegato* used by Barbieri, which seems to have had much in common with *H:* see Gauchat and Kehrli 346.

23. "Les coblas." The sexual attitudes informing Dejeanne's gloss of the *coblas* and *razo* are a true period piece.

24. Association, or identification, of a lady with her land is to be found in numerous troubadour songs. E.g., Raimbaut de Vaqueiras, "Domna tant" (ed. Linskill no. 3), prefers to have the Genoesa than the combined wealth of the Genoese; Guiraut Riquier's *partimen* with three friends (ed. Mahn, *Werke* 4:233) has the poet ask (presumably a different) Senh' En Jorda ostensibly about Livernon and Lautrec, but obtain answers about the ladies associated with these localities.

25. Proponents of the former include Dejeanne, Boutière and Schutz, and Chambers (*Proper Names* s.v. Liverna); of the latter, De Lollis ("Appunti"), and Wiacek, (s.v. Liverna).

26. Identification going back to Chabaneau, *Biographies des troubadours* 1219: see Boutière and Schutz. For more speculation about the historical Bernart Arnaut and Lombarda, see Almqvist.

27. Was Peire Bremon Ricas Novas similarly punning on *Castelan,* meaning either "Castilian" or "castellan"?

28. See, e.g., Pattison, *Raimbaut d'Orange* 29: Isoard, count of Die, had a daughter Isoarda who, as daughter of a count, was entitled to style herself countess. Pattison has further examples of titles transmitted to women by male relatives. The Guiscarda celebrated by Bertran de Born was the sister of En Giscard de Beljoc according to the *razo* (Gouiran 1:73), his cousin according to Stronski (quoted by Gouiran 1:70). Uc de Baux's wife Barrale was the daughter of Raimon Jaufré Barral, viscount of Marseille 1178–1192 (Jeanroy, *Poésie lyrique* 1:172). According to Chambers, *Proper Names,* the senhal Berenguiera (q.v.) was an "allusion to the fact that she was the daughter of Raimond Berengier of Provence" and Raimonda de Rocafoill (q.v.) was the daughter of Raymond II de Roquefeuil. The taking of a husband's name is more difficult to illustrate. Guilhem Adémar (Almqvist no. 9) suggests the existence of a fictional couple Bertran—Bertranda; Guillem de Berguedan refers to Peire de Berga and his wife as Mon Sogre—Ma Sogra, and Bertran de Born calls the wife of Henry of Saxony La Saisne, but are the latter examples really names? See also the references in n. 12 above, very few of which are demonstrably couples, married or not.

29. See Kay, "Two Readings of the *Lai de l'Ombre*," e.g., 523–25.

30. Raynouard 2:484, *descordar* "désaccorder, déranger"; Levy, *SWB* s.v. *acort* (2) "Entschluss, Willen, Meinung," cf. Godefroy, s.v. (1) *acort* "volonté, sentiment, avis, résolution"; Levy *SWB* s.v. *dezacordar* (1) "in Nicht-übereinstimmung versetzen"; s.v. *acordar* (2) *se* "mit sich eins werden, beschliessen"; for "harmoniously," cf. the gloss in the *Donatz Proensals* cited in the *SWB*, *acort* "concordia."

31. Levy *SWB* sv. *dezacordar* (1), citation from Raimbaut de Vaqueiras: *acort* (4), "Bezeichnung einer Dichtungsart."

9　Lombarda's Reluctant Mirror: Speculum of Another Poet

"Mais si l'objet se mettait à parler?"

Luce Irigaray

In her book *Speculum de l'autre femme,* the French feminist psychoanalyst Luce Irigaray deconstructs such textual mainstays of Western thought as Plato and Freud to demonstrate that these authors situate woman only in the male perspective of the *homo* (the same, i.e., male sameness and presence) rather than in that of the *hetero* (the Other, i.e., an awareness of female difference and specificity). Traditionally relegated to the role of confirming man's male identity, of being his mirror, "fidèle, poli et vacant de réflexions altérantes" (168), women can, however, use the speculum—no longer a passively reflecting mirror, but an active instrument of female self-discovery—to assert their Otherness against "a world structured by man-centered concepts [in which they] had no way of knowing or representing themselves" (Jones 364).

From Luce Irigaray backward to the trobairitz . . . a big, maybe an improbable leap? Two notions make it eminently possible: first that of self-discovery and self-representation, for are not the trobairitz among the first women in western Europe to speak, not in Latin, but in their own tongue, of feelings and emotions, of despair and desire (Dronke, *Women Writers* 97 ff.)? The second notion, that of speculum, resounds with medieval echoes and presences. Indeed, the image of the mirror shines everywhere in the literature and the iconography of the Middle Ages. The Latin name of the august journal of medieval studies, *Speculum,* was chosen because of its power to evoke the interests and preoccupations of an era, suggesting, as it did, "the multitudinous mirrors in which people of the Middle Ages liked to gaze at themselves and other folk—mirrors of history and doctrine and morals, mirrors of princes and lovers and fools" (Rand). Antique as well as patristic in origin, the image of the mirror is markedly present in the Latin as well as in the vernacular literature of the Middle Ages, where it presents a figure of multiple and changing meanings and implications (Bradley).

In literature of love the mirror often becomes the mirror of Narcissus, and this is not surprising since the Ovidian tale of the young man enamored of his reflection enjoyed great popularity and received the tribute of several medieval adaptations (Goldin). In the poetry of the troubadours and the ideology of *fin'amors,* the presence of Narcissus hovers constantly even when not explicitly evoked, so constantly that Narcissus's exclamation upon perceiving himself in the water of the fountain, "Iste ego sum" (Ovid, *Metamorphoses* 3:463), might well serve as a lapidary formulation of the troubadours' self-referential erotic quest for beauty and perfection. When Julia Kristeva points out that "Eros est homosexuel" (63), she uses the adjective not in its most commonly accepted sense but rather to render and describe the lover's need for homologation with the Other, for circumscribing and imprisoning the Other in the homo-sphere denounced by Luce Irigaray. Kristeva elucidates by stating that "Tout désir pour l'autre est une manie de jouir d'un semblable sous le mirage d'un supérieur" (63), and, speaking now specifically about the troubadours, remarks that "la chanson courtoise ne décrit ni ne raconte. Elle est essentiellement image d'elle-même, signe de l'intensité amoureuse, . . . incantation" (268). *Intensity, incantation . . .* Kristeva's choice of vocabulary to describe the courtly expression stresses the *in*voluted, *in*ward looking character of the typical *canso* in which the poet, reacting to the tensions within himself—tensions between desire and submission, between *voler* and *amar,* between confidence and hesitation—looks in the mirror of the *domna,* imagined and fashioned by him, to seek there the solution to his dilemmas: his own actual or potential perfection. Imagined and desired, imagined because desired, this perfection either of joy or of despair allows him the transformation effected by poetry's incantatory power: the transformation of life's ordinary banality and fragmentation into the extraordinary prestige, merit, and beauty of *fin'amors.* Arnaut Daniel's *sestina* "Lo ferm voler q'el cor m'intra" (P-C 29,14) is a good example of the *canso* in which the poet works his way painfully through the labyrinthine complexities of his desires and fears to the *cambra,* the woman's paradisiacal inner chamber with its sexual and spiritual implications, where he will be united through her mediating presence with the *joi* which is the supreme confirmation of his merit and excellence. Throughout the poem, the woman functions as the goal toward which the poet strives and the mirror of his progressive accomplishments. While the other key words in the poem, the *sestina*'s important rhyme-words, have shifting meanings and applications, *cambra* is always indicative of the woman and therefore of the poet, since the term refers not to the *domna*'s intimate Otherness but to the poet's wish to penetrate into his own perfection's space.

By exalting the *domna* as superior to him, the lover fills his mirror with an image of superiority which, since he gazes in it at his reflection, is also an image of himself. He sees himself, "semblable" but better, "supérieur," as the *domna*-mirage sends back to him a flattering likeness of his virtues, chiefly of his capacity for self-perfection, which may lead to enhanced life or to heroic death as in Bernart de Ventadorn's "Can vei la lauzeta mover" (P-C 70,43), and which leads in any case to the all-important self-expression of *cantar*. Whether destined for ecstasies of joy or for paroxysms of suffering, in the mirror the lover is always the hero, the sole player on a mirrored stage. "Dans l'univers de Narcisse il n'y a pas d'autre" (Kristeva 110), and *domna* is man-lover-poet enhanced, enlarged, enthroned. She is indispensable as Narcissus's well was to him, a serviceable and necessary object, "miralhs de mi" (mirror of me) as Aimeric de Peguilhan calls her (P-C 10,50 line 31).[1] Bertran de Born addresses a woman as "mos Bels Miraills" (my Fair Mirror) and describes her as one who "no s'en cambia ni·s muda" (neither alters nor changes) (P-C 80,12, lines 56, 60). Even a poet as protean as Bertran may find in the woman-mirror the consoling if illusory image of his identity as an unbroken, untouched, beautifully coherent whole.[2] But, Luce Irigaray asks, "si l'objet se mettait à parler?" (167). What if woman decided "to create rather than to be created?" (Gubar 81). What if the mirror, reluctant to go on reflecting, became opaque?

When the *domna* turns trobairitz this is what does occur, since the sung will now sing, the looked-into will look at, the muted will speak. Do we then witness a perfect volte-face, an exact reversal of roles and procedures? Do we see another homologation, where now the male lover is reduced to being woman's exalting self-reflection? Does the idealization of the subject (the poet) through the idealization of its reflecting object (the beloved) take place in the works of the trobairitz as it does in the male poetry? Scholars who have examined the poems of the trobairitz— still an exhilaratingly pioneering enterprise—agree that differences exist between the male and the female poets, but they are not always capable of pinpointing them as precisely as we might, maybe unrealistically, wish. What these studies suggest, however, is interesting and rewarding. So, for example, Marianne Shapiro, in an article in which she analyzes significant instances of what she calls "unconventionality" in the works of the trobairitz, states in answer to my last question that "in none of the women's poems . . . does the masculine beloved appear to incarnate or substitute, as she (i.e., the *domna*) had, for a total scheme of ideals" (564).

While it is undoubtedly true that "the woman writer can express her difference only through a posture critical of prevailing discourse" (Abel 3), it is also true that this is a particularly arduous task to accomplish in a culture where each acceptable (i.e., culturally valuable and identifiable) experience is provided with a suitable corresponding vocabulary which is its only possible, comprehensible, mode of expression. *Fin'amors* becomes such an accepted cultural experience and artifact when it is launched by the troubadours as a topos complete with its own coherent rhetoric and ideology (Zumthor, "Héloïse"). To renounce that ready-made scheme, to reject that rhetoric, that "prevailing discourse," is not an easy matter. Yet "unconventionalities," deviations from that discourse and from its ideological foundation, have been identified and explored in the poetry of the trobairitz. In a detailed examination of Castelloza's four extant poems, Paden and his collaborators demonstrate how this trobairitz' quasi-masochistic and almost exclusive insistence on pain and suffering separates her from the prevailing troubadour model, exemplified by Bernart de Ventadorn and based on a recurrent *joi-dolor* antithesis. Marianne Shapiro, in the above-mentioned article, suggests that the women poets ignore the principle of *mezura* (i.e., moderation, patience, discretion) frequently mentioned and observed in the male texts out of a "preference for depicting love only in terms of its most dramatic emotions" (556). Deborah Perkal-Balinsky notes that the woman-lover in several *tensos* between male and female poets seems more willing to manipulate the principles of *fin'amors* than her male respondent, and at times even transgresses its prescriptions ("Introduction").

As we have seen, for Luce Irigaray the mirror is an emblematic image of woman's submission to man. In the *fin'amors* construction, the mirror also assumes that emblematic significance, since "nowhere else do we see so plainly that courtly love begins with the lover's image of his own perfection, an image which later takes on the form of an honored lady in whom the ideal is considered to be realized" (Goldin 104–05). We will therefore turn now to a *tenso* between Lombarda and Bernart Arnaut (P-C 288,1) which consists of two juxtaposed texts, one by a male, the other by a female author, both structured around the significant image of the mirror. Study of the *tenso* will allow us to consider gender-based differences in discourse while focusing on the treatment of a particular central figure, and to describe these differences in a more precise way than is often possible.[3]

Bernart Arnaut

I   Lombards volgr'eu eser per na Lonbarda,
q'Alamanda no·m plas tan ni Giscarda,
qar ab sos oiltz plaisenz tan jen me garda
qe par qe·m don s'amor; mas trop me tarda,   4
      qar bel veser
      e mon plaiser
     ten e bel ris en garda,
     c'om no·ls ne pod mover.   8

II   Segner Jordan, se vos lais Alamagna,
Fransa e Piteus, Normandia e Bretagna,
be me devez laisar senes mesclagna
Lonbardia, Liverno e Lomagna.   12
      E si·m valez,
      eu per un dez
     valdre'us ab leis q'esstragna
     de sse tot avol prez.   16

III   Miral de Pres,
      conort avez;
     ges per vilha no·s fragna
     l'amor en qe·m tenez.   20

Lombarda

I   Nom volgr'aver per Bernard na Bernada
e per n'Arnaut n'Arnauda apellada;
e grans merses, seigner, car vos agrada
c'ab tals doas domnas m'aves nomnada;   24
      voil qe·m digaz
      cal mais vos plaz
     ses cuberta selada,
     e·l mirail on miraz.   28

II   Car lo mirailz e no veser descorda
tan mon acord c'ab pauc no·l desacorda;

mas can record so qe·l meus noms recorda
en bon acord totz mons pensars s'acorda.   32
    Mas del cor pes,
    on l'aves mes,
    qe sa maiso ni borda
    no vei, qe lui taises.   36

[*Bernart Arnaut* I I should like to be Lombard for Lombarda, for Alamanda does not please me as much, nor Giscarda, for with her pleasing eyes she looks at me so gently that she seems to give me her love; but she delays me too long, for she keeps to herself the beautiful sight, and my pleasure and beautiful smile, so that a man cannot get them from her.

II Lord Jordan, if I leave you Germany, France and Poitou, Normandy and Brittany, you really should leave me undisputed Lombardy, Leghorn and Lomagna. And if you help me, I will, ten times more, help you with her who thrusts away from herself all baseness.

III Mirror of Merit, you offer comfort; surely the love in which you keep me should not shatter because of a lout.

Lombarda I I should like to have for Bernart the name Lady Bernada and for Sir Arnaut the name Lady Arnauda; and thank you very much, lord, that it should please you to name me with two such ladies; I want you to tell me which one pleases you most without any secret dissimulation, and the mirror in which you look.

II For your mirror without sight so upsets my harmony that it almost destroys it; but when I recall that what my name recalls all my thoughts agree in total harmony. But I wonder about your heart, where you have put it, for its house and hut I do not see, since you keep it silent.]

Two images, two vessels of identity, dominate both Bernart's and Lombarda's *coblas:* that of the mirror and that of the proper name, which may be seen as a form of mirror. In the Middle Ages, the etymological significance of proper names endows them with symbolic value and meaning, renders them capable of expressing and reflecting the deep reality, the intimate, revealing truth of a person. As the dictum cited by Dante states it, "Nomina sunt consequentia rerum" (Names are the consequences of things) (Curtius 499), or, in the words of François Rigolot, "le sens profond des choses se trouve dans la sève originelle des mots" (15). So when Bernart claims that "Lombards volgr'eu eser per na Lombarda," he asserts his uniquely close relationship with the *domna* through the etymological link he creates between their names. Supposedly, the etymological chain descends from Lombardia to Lombarda to Lombard, with the poet-lover, under this assumed name, occupying the conventionally humble position: he is owned, rather than he owns. His name is the *consequens* of his belonging and submission to Lombarda. The second stanza reveals that this claim is false, however, when Bernart enumerates in line 12 a list of properties he wants to keep in his bargain with Lord Jordan: "Lonbardia, Liverno e Lomagna." The nonpoetic joker here is the last term. The region of Lomagna, situated in Gascony between the rivers Gers and Garoupe, was indeed the property of the house of Armagnac to which Bernart belonged and over which he ruled as Count of Armagnac from 1217 to 1226. While Lombardy and Leghorn belong to the realm of property—Lombardy maintaining the flattering fiction of the proprietary woman, Leghorn chosen maybe for its alliterative linking power, maybe for its reputation as a *locus amoenus* on the shores of the Tyrrhenian Sea[4]—Lomagna recalls the importance and reality of possessions, and of Bernart's possessing status. He may pretend to be owned by Lombarda, but he is, in truth, an owner, and the fact that he mentions Lomagna indicates that he does not want this to be forgotten or neglected. But even before line 12, line 2 has given us a glimpse of Bertran's proprietary reality. When he compares Lombarda to Giscarda and Alamanda, he portrays himself, not as one inevitably, fatefully, possessed, but as one judiciously shopping for a possession. When, therefore, he adopts the name Lombard, he does not obliterate his identity in passionate abandon to another's being but rather invests that name with his status as natural owner—natural, that is, by male birthright, as well as by virtue of his belonging to the landowning class. "Lombard" then means "who owns Lombarda," and not vice versa, and his dominance is mirrored in her name. It is only a logical consequence that all of her should be his mirror. In lines 3–8 he first evokes the mirror ("sos oiltz") which assures him that he is loved ("par qe·m don s'amor"). The verb *gardar,* used in lines 3 and 7, takes here its two meanings: to look and to keep. His reflection in the *domna's* eyes keeps his identity intact, complete with his assurance of being loved, of having access to beauty ("bel vezer") and pleasure ("mon plaiser"), and to a deep sense of contentment and satisfaction ("bel ris"), all reflected back at him approvingly from the mirror, which, moreover, offers him a guarantee of stability and perpetuity: "om no·ls pot mover."

After the second *cobla*—an unabashed, overt, almost comical haggling scene between two men—he reiterates the mirror image in the *senhal* "Miral de Pres," used to indicate Lombarda. She is the mirror of his "Pres" (i.e., his value, worth, merit, as well as prestige and good name:

personal as well as social excellence), and, naturally enough, the source for him of all comfort. The last two lines seem at first to hint at the possibility that the mirror of love and approbation might break, thus dissevering the lover from his profound self-satisfaction, but then they reaffirm the security implied in the verb *tener* (to hold, to keep, to contain), an echo of line 7.

Bernart's *coblas* begin and end with the notion of the significant name, thanks to etymology and *senhal*. The function of the *senhal* appears here in all its possible ambiguity: while it guarantees discretion, it also signifies appropriation, as it occults the *domna's* identity and absorbs it. In line 1, the *domna's* name is invaded; in the *tornada* it is effectively effaced and replaced. In line 1 her name is reduced to mirroring the male name—it is like a mirror; in the *tornada* her name is Mirror.

However, in the second part of the *tenso* that mirror speaks, and speaks in terms of subversive imitation (to use a felicitous expression of current feminist criticism) as Lombarda adopts Bernart's vocabulary of name and mirror, but only to subvert in a first movement the name-as-mirror ploy, and then in a second movement to fracture the mirror once and for all and to recuperate, from the shards, her name.

Line 21 is read by some editors (e.g., Bogin) as "no·m volgr'aver" (I do not wish to be). While this punctuation would make Lombarda's rejection of the naming ploy/play immediately and perfectly clear, it would do so at the price of strained syntax in the following line (where "e" would need to be replaced by "ni"), and it would efface the parallel structures in "nom . . . na Bernada" and "n'Arnauda apellada" (where *apellada* is a noun). The line as punctuated more straightforwardly by Perkal-Balinsky obtains the same effect in a more subtle, more delicately sarcastic way. Lombarda subverts the ploy she imitates by exaggerating and literalizing it. One name will not do, she will have two, and does so by splitting Bernart Arnaut in two, using his full name as a pretext, and by becoming "two" herself (lines 21, 22). Then, also taking his mention of Alamanda and Giscarda literally, she confronts him, not with one mirror, but with three ("doas domnas" and herself) or even four ("doas domnas" and her two selves), and summons him to disclose what is truly "·l mirail on miraz." She thus transports him into a house of mirrors, the antithesis, in its shimmering confusion, of the one, faithful, unchanging mirror.

In her second *cobla* she once again takes Bernart literally: he has called her Mirror, so mirror she is. But since Bernart is wavering between mirrors and refuses to say where he is reflected, she is a mirror in which nothing appears and therefore no better than a useless void, since a mirror's function is indeed to reflect. This frightening possibility might threaten her "acord," her sense of self, of inner harmony, were she not able to look upon and into herself. Thus the mirror-figure now becomes a speculum,[5] a recording instrument of her self-examination, allowing her access to her own being and awareness (thanks to self-memory) of her identity as reflected in her proper name—symbol not of belonging but of being, not of dependency but of autonomy, not of homologation but of differentiation. Her etymon may be Lombardia—earth, birth, genesis, belonging[6]—but it is certainly not Lombard, the facetiously adopted sobriquet of a gamester. It is situated in her reality, not in another's frivolous illusion. With that realization, the rescue and affirmation of her identity are complete. Her "pensar," the totality of her inner intellectual and emotional being, recovers a blissful harmony and security, gained not from being reflected in another, but from having reflected upon itself. The play on "acord"—"record" and their derivatives in lines 29–32 allows Lombarda to express, strongly and concisely, the importance of self-memory, that is, of a deeply rooted awareness of the self as a continuous and inalienable core of identity, reflected and recorded by one's proper name.

In the last four lines, Lombarda turns back from that safe center to her interlocutor, who is now nothing but a dwindling, insubstantial ghost. His house—his center—and even his hut, its attenuated, pitiful shadow, are nowhere to be seen, as no mirror reflects them any more. Bernart, stuck in the solipsistic little world in which Lombarda's scenario sardonically situates him, is unable even to speak and so break the silence of his sterile self-absorption. Already in line 25 Lombarda seems to propose speaking as a salutory alternative to mirror-gazing for Bernart: if he could only speak, that is, engage in communication, not with himself before a mirror but with another being apprehended truly as Other, then he could situate, define, and affirm himself. As it is, he is locked in silence and absence, the final lot of the doomed Narcissus.

After this last *cobla* there is a blank space in the manuscript, and it has been suggested that this space, the equivalent of a few lines, might have been intended for Lombarda's *tornada*. But we may also consider that the last lines of the second *cobla* function as a *tornada*, counterbalancing Bernart's *tornada* to Lombarda. The fear he signalled with the mention of the verb *franher* (line 19) has become a reality—not because of a

hostile outsider (*vilha,* line 19) but because of the mirror's insubordina-
tion. It has indeed shattered, shattering his self-image, destroying his
wholeness, which depended on the mirror's hold and frame. "Mais si
l'objet se mettait à parler?" Luce Irigaray's already-quoted question is
followed by another one: "Quelle désagrégation du 'sujet' s'amorcerait
par là?" (167). At the end of Lombarda's *coblas* we see a disaggregation
indeed, not only of Bernart's image, but of a certain discourse. Where we
most frequently see the troubadours, and also at least to some extent (an
extent which is increasingly being investigated) the trobairitz, as "prison-
niers de la topique et de la rhétorique courtoises" (Zumthor, "Héloïse"
315), Lombarda frees herself, goes through the looking-glass, and so introduces us to the other side, the Other's side.

In this *tenso* we do not see a reversal of roles between male and female
poets; we see a total rejection by Lombarda of the reflecting role Bernart
would have imposed on her, but which she refuses either to accept for
herself, or to impose upon him. She does not appropriate to herself a
traditionally male privilege, but rather demonstrates, by her de(con)struc-
tion of the mirror and the name figures, the ultimate vacuity and dangers
of these topoi when they are used conventionally. They are dangerous
because, as Lombarda shows, they may finally lead not to *cantar* but to
silence. Jacques Derrida remarks that "the speculary dispossession which
at the same time institutes and deconstitutes me is also a law of language.
It operates as a power of death in the heart of living speech . . . " (*Of
Grammatology* 141). Lombarda shows Bernart as dispossessed of himself
when his efforts toward self-institution in the mirror have led him to a
self-deconstitution which leaves him deprived of language as well. The
blank at the end of the *tenso* is the blank space which swallows Bernart's
speech. Specularity has become poetic death.

It is possible, however, to redeem the mirror and name figures by
altering them, and turning them into instruments not of assimilation but
of authentic self-perception: speculum and the *proper* name, "qui donne
ses lettres de créance à l'individu" (Rigolot 17). This is what the poet
Lombarda is able to do, and the result is this insight implicit in her *coblas:*
when woman, who has traditionally been muted, goes in search of her
poetic voice, she must avoid the danger of that other muteness, of the
trap of Narcissus, and turn, bypassing the treacherous mirror, to the
truth of her being as a source not of flattering illusion but of autonomous
self-knowledge and of independent, nondependent, self-representation.

This is Lombarda's contribution to a female poetics of difference acclaimed and identity reclaimed, the poetics, indeed, of another poet.

In his article "Aristotle's Sister: A Poetics of Abandonment," Lawrence Lipking remarks that though there has not been an established, "officially" recognized, what he calls "classic" (62) woman's poetics, such a poetics has in fact been elaborated "across the centuries by thousands of women, in the innumerable acts of response and commentary on which every poetics depends" (63). The female *coblas* of this *tenso* constitute a response to the preceding male ones and a commentary on them. While it is impossible to use them as the basis for generalizations about all trobairitz poetry and poetics, they encourage us to look further into these still enigmatic texts for evidence of ideological and rhetorical differentiation from the dominant male poetry of the troubadours.

Notes

1. For a penetrating and subtle analysis of Aimeric de Peguilhan's poem as well as other troubadour lyrics which use the mirror image, see Goldin 69 ff.

2. It is ironic that in Ezra Pound's poem "Near Perigord" (151), a meditation on Bertran de Born's art and on the poem "Dompna, puois de mi no·us cal" in particular (P-C 80,12), he ends with the image of ". . . a shifting change,/ A broken bundle of mirrors . . . ," thus denying Bertran his illusion of wholeness.

3. Text from Perkal-Balinsky. For the translation and for the explanatory notes to the text, I have consulted both Perkal-Balinsky and Boutière-Schutz.

4. The earliest reference to Leghorn occurred in 891, and mentioned a church. In 1071 it was called a "castellum," and c. 1100 its ruler, Countess Matilda di Canossa, erected there a cylindrical tower, the "mastio di Matilda," famous for its magnificence and elegance as well as for its enduring strength (Guarnieri 107).

5. In medical terms, a speculum is defined as "an instrument for rendering a part accessible to observation" (*The Random House Dictionary of the English Language*).

6. The *vida* accompanying the *tenso* describes Lombarda as a "lady from Toulouse." In Boutière-Schutz (419) she is identified with a Lombarda mentioned in a Toulouse charter of 1206. No further identification is possible. I have speculated that this *Toulousaine* may originally have been from Lombardy. Raimon de Miraval similarly designates a woman from Lombardy as Lombarda (P-C 406,16, see Chambers 170).

III Reception

10 The Troubled Existence of Three Women Poets

Among some modern scholars, at least, it has been believed that three women wrote poetry in Italian during the thirteenth century. It would seem to be an enticing project to write about the poems of these counterparts of the trobairitz, because the comparison of similar phenomena in two cultures which are closely related and yet so different could be expected to yield stimulating results. The task, however, proves not to be very rewarding—not to say downright impossible. Two major difficulties stand against it. The first is the meagerness of the corpus of thirteenth-century Italian poetry that may be attributed to women, no more than four sonnets in all. The second difficulty, of still greater consequence, is that only one of the three women considered over the years to have been active poets during the thirteenth century is still so considered today, and even her existence has been seriously questioned. For these reasons, I shall renounce any attempt at reading the sonnets looking for their possible feminine qualities, since it is not at all certain that their authors were women. But the reader may be interested in another facet of the history of these women poets. They did exist for a while, but only in the imagination of historians of Italian literature, who, especially during the Romantic period, seemed to cherish the characteristic of "spontaneity" in their poetic voice and the supposed unconventionality of their lives. The arguments for and against the existence of such women poets have involved some of the best philologists in heated debates. Thus, rather than speculating about the role of women poets in the thirteenth century on the basis of the few sonnets we have, it may be much more interesting to trace the history of how these women poets came into existence and how they later vanished from the history of Italian literature. This essay, therefore, will survey the critical history of the creation and the demise, or difficult survival, of the thirteenth-century women poets, Gaia da Camino, Nina Siciliana, and La Compiuta Donzella, all of whom, at one time or another, have had the honor of being considered "the first Italian woman poet."

« » Gaia da Camino

The name of Gaia da Camino is known to all readers of the *Divine Comedy*, for she is mentioned in canto XVI of *Purgatory* (lines 139–41) as the daughter of Gherardo, whose courtly virtues are renowned the world over. Dante's allusion to Gaia is open to opposite interpretations, which may be why some commentators on the *Comedy* portray her as given to licentious living while others make of her a model of courtly gentility. Benvenuto da Imola, for instance, tells us that she was "mulier quidam vere gaia et vana; et ut breviter dicam, tarvisana tota amorosa; quae dicebat domino Rizardo fratri suo: Procura tantum mihi iuvenes procos amorosos et ego procurabo tibi puellas formosas" (a certain very gay and vain woman; and to speak briefly, a thoroughly licentious woman of Treviso, who said to Master Richard her brother, "Just bring me licentious young noblemen, and I shall bring you pretty girls"). A different picture is conveyed by the commentaries of Buti, the Anonimo, and others who praise Gaia's fine character (see Biagi et al., 326–27). Giovanni da Seravalle, a fifteenth-century commentator on Dante, adds something new to her qualities: "De ista Gaja filia boni Gerardi possent dici multae laudae, quia fuit prudens domina, literata, magni consilii, et magnae prudentiae, maximae pulchritudinis, quae scivit bene loqui rythmatice in vulgari" (Of this Gaia, daughter of the good Gerardo, many praises may be said, since she was a prudent woman, well-read, of great common sense, and of great prudence, of greatest beauty, who knew well how to speak rhythmically in the vernacular). So Gaia was a poet; however, this information comes to us in a document written roughly two centuries after her death. Francesco Maria Barbieri in his *Dell'origine della poesia rimata* (169), which was written by the end of the sixteenth century, accepts the statement of Giovanni da Seravalle, and so includes a woman among the poets of the "origini." G. Tiraboschi, who edited Barbieri's work, in his own monumental *Storia della letteratura italiana* (book 3, chap. 3; vol. 4, pt. 2, p. 411) places Gaia among the early Italian poets, and even claims for her the title of "first lady poet of Italy," a title previously held by Nina di Dante. Tiraboschi perhaps trusted his sources because what they told him fit with the notion that Gherardo da Camino was an important Maecenas of Provençal poetry and poets; it would seem, then, not improbable that Gaia learned the art of composing poetry at her father's court.

But for Gaia to number surely among Italian poets one needs some evidence of her writing, and no poem has ever come to light. Her fame as a poet has depended on the authority of a commentary on Dante which was published only at the end of the last century, on the few words found in an erudite work of the sixteenth century, which also remained unpublished for a long time, and on a footnote in a prestigious history of Italian literature. More recently, positivist scholars, who have unearthed a great deal of biographic data concerning Gaia—especially Pio Rajna ("Gaia da Camino")—have resolutely silenced the myth of her poetic activity.

«» *Nina Siciliana*

Quite different for its vitality, and far more fantastic, is the case of Nina Siciliana, who appeared for the first time on the scene of Italian poetry in 1527 when the so-called *Giuntina di Rime Antiche* was published by the Giunta Press in Florence. Among the poems collected in this important anthology are those by Dante da Maiano, another author unknown until 1527. Two of his poems are addressed to a Monna Nina, and between these two sonnets in the collection there is another one by Monna Nina herself responding to her admirer. In this exchange of sonnets, Dante says he has heard marvelous things about Monna Nina, whom he has never seen; he confesses his love for her and offers her his service. Monna Nina expresses pleasure at his offer and invites him to write to her again and to let his pen speak his heart. Dante replies, expressing his love once more and revealing his name through an acrostic.

Since no one questioned the authority of the *Giuntina*, and since women poets were a historical reality in sixteenth-century Italy, it was not difficult to accept Nina's real existence. She was quoted as an authority in the Tuscan language by the *Dizionario della Crusca*, and Alessandro Tassoni relied on the "purity" of her language in his *Considerazioni sopra le Rime del Petrarca* (Crescimbeni 3:84). But this Tuscan authority soon became . . . Sicilian. The transformation occurred in 1661, thanks to Leone Allacci, who wrote in his *Poeti antichi* as follows:

> Non mancarò di notare, che siccome li primi rimatori tra gl'Italiani furono Siciliani, s'ordinò da Dio, che tra le donne quella che prima rimasse fosse Siciliana. E questa fu Madonna Nina come scrive Alessandro Zilioli nell' Historia de' Poeti: "Donna dotata di buone qualità, che i poeti capricciosi nella scielta delle donne a gara s'innamoravano di lei; tra' quali fu Dante da Maiano, che per sola fama innamoratosi di lei, le scrisse un sonetto, ricercandola del suo amore, al quale ella rispose in questa maniera tutta dolce et amorevole: 'Qual sete voi si cara proferenza' etc." E se è vero quello che m'ha detto un bell'ingegno, e delle cose di Sicilia molto pratico, questa deve essere Messinese, poiché in niuno altro luogo di Sicilia pratticasi questo nome se non in Messina. So bene che qualche altro la fa Fiorentina.[1]

> [I will not fail to notice that, since the first poets among Italians were Sicilians, God also planned that the first woman poet was a Sicilian. And this was Madonna Nina, as Alessandro Zilioli writes in his *Historia de' Poeti:* "She was a lady gifted with good qualities so that poets, who are capricious in choosing their ladies, competed with each other to fall in love with her. Among them there was Dante da Maiano who, having fallen in love with her only because of her fame, wrote a sonnet to her requesting her love; she replied in this manner all sweet and loving: 'Qual sete voi si cara proferenza' etc." And if it is true what I was told by a good mind who is also very expert on Sicilian matters, she must have been from Messina, since this name is used in no other place of Sicily except Messina. I know very well that others consider her to be from Florence.]

Thus through the authority of God and the suggestion of a friend, Nina's destiny changed: not only did she become a Sicilian (I cannot determine whether this change had already taken place in Zilioli's work and if so on what basis, since the *Historia de' Poeti* is still unpublished), but it was even ascertained that she was from Messina. The distance between Maiano and Messina made this "amor de lonh" more dramatic!

The warp was set for weaving a biography which could rival that of Jaufre Rudel and for creating a legendary lady. G. M. Crescimbeni, one of the first historians of Italian poetry, was also the first one to fantasize about Nina.

> Questa gentile e leggiadra donna, bellissima e sopra tutte le altre del suo tempo e della sua nazione, non solamente fu la prima femmina, che s'abbia notizia, che poetasse in nostra lingua; ma non volle che niuno si vantasse dell'amor suo fuorchè un poeta. Fu questo Dante da Maiano . . . il quale appena la richiese d'amore con un sonetto che le scrisse, che alla quantunque

non l'avesse mai veduto, si dispose a compiacerlo rispondendogli . . . e l'amò poi tanto che si faceva chiamare Nina di Dante . . . Pochissime sue rime sono arrivate a' nostri tempi, dalle quali ben si conosce quanto virtuosa e spiritosa fra i fondatori della Toscana favella. (3:84)

[This gentle and poised lady, the most beautiful one of her time and her country, was not only the first lady known to have written in our language, but also she did not want anyone to boast about her love except for one poet. This was Dante da Maiano. . . . As soon as he requested her love with a sonnet that he wrote to her, she, although never having seen him, pleased him by answering . . . and loved him so much that she called herself Nina of Dante. . . . Very few of her poems have come down to us; from them one realizes how virtuous and gifted she was among the founders of the Tuscan language.]

Crescimbeni embellishes Nina's story. From him we learn for the first time about Nina's extraordinary beauty as well as about her total devotion to a man whom she was never to see but who nonetheless was to change her name. How an historian of Crescimbeni's rigor could be tempted to embroider these elements of legend is not difficult to understand. He was writing at a moment when, after the parenthesis of the Baroque, the appeal of "ewige Weiblichkeit," the myth of Woman sung by Renaissance poets, was undergoing a revival. Crescimbeni's Nina, with her beauty and her devotion, seems a forerunner of the many ladies sung by Arcadian poets, or of the heroines of Metastasio's theater. Crescimbeni was blinded by Nina's beauty to the point of overlooking the incongruity of the claim that a Sicilian lady was founder of the Tuscan language. Nina's legend, as elaborated by Crescimbeni, appealed to eighteenth-century scholars either for patriotic reasons or because of the revival of the ideals mentioned above. As an example of these two attitudes, it suffices to remember that Crescimbeni's brief article, translated into Latin and only slightly altered, became an entry in the *Bibliotheca Sicula* of A. Mongitore (2:104); and it represented a source for Quadrio (1:165).

But the appeal of Nina's legend was even stronger in the pre-Romantic and Romantic periods. The reasons are plain: Nina's love from afar, her beauty, and her distinction as the "first Italian poetess" in a century when women were not allowed to climb Mount Parnassus met many of the requirements of a Romantic heroine. Sponsored by the masters of eighteenth-century erudition, Nina Siciliana or Nina di Dante appears in all the encyclopedias of illustrious Sicilians or illustrious women, in all the histories of Italian literature, be it that of Ginguené or that of Settembrini, of Emiliani Giudici[2] or even the most celebrated one, that of F. De Sanctis. The last closes the first chapter of his *Storia* commenting on a sonnet ("Tapina mia che amava uno sparviero") which a few years earlier had been cautiously attributed to Nina by F. Trucchi (53).[3] This sonnet is for De Sanctis an indication of the linguistic excellence achieved by the vernacular (1:16). On another occasion, he mentions Nina but he does not exalt her poetry: she belongs with the "dilettanti convenzionali," and yet the fact that she was a woman would have made her look like a miracle to her contemporaries (1:12).

But suddenly, at the height of her popularity, Nina's life came to an end. In 1878, Adolfo Borgognoni, a positivist philologist, pronounced her death sentence in an article entitled "La condanna capitale d'una bella signora." The only element which could extenuate the cruelty of this sentence was the fact that, in the critic's opinion, Nina had never lived. According to Borgognoni, the whole legend of Nina was based exclusively on the title of a sonnet by Dante da Maiano. No other document proves that she ever existed. Moreover, Borgognoni questions the authenticity of Dante da Maiano's poetry, since there are no documents that concern him dated before 1527, the year in which his poems were first published. For Borgognoni, these poems are a fabrication perpetrated by the partisans of the Tuscan origins of Italian poetry. As for the correspondence between Dante and Nina (a name, by the way, amply recorded in Tuscan onomastics), it is nothing more than a conventional exchange between a poet and a fictitious woman.

Borgognoni's article gave rise to a *cause célèbre*. Some of the best names of Italian philology from Novati down to Barbi and Debenedetti were able to ascertain, against Borgognoni, that Dante da Maiano really did exist and flourish at the time of the other Dante, Dante Alighieri, with whom he exchanged several sonnets.[4] The "caso maianese" has long been closed, and Dante da Maiano is strongly entrenched as a legitimate Italian poet. But in the debate on Dante de Maiano's case, Nina, the beautiful lady, was irrevocably sacrificed.[5] Borgognoni's idea that Nina is the embodiment of a literary convention is universally accepted today. Dante da Maiano, like his master Guittone d'Arezzo, fictionalized an interlocutor with a feminine name and this name was Monna Nina.

Although philologists have killed Nina, her legend was too beautiful to die. Indeed, in areas far removed from the ruthless realm of philology Nina has survived. Her name still appears in semipopular biographical dictionaries, and her memory is kept alive by a column dedicated to her in the city gardens of Palermo; she is remembered by a monument in the church of Saint Dominic in Palermo and by a portrait in the public library of the Sicilian capital. It is not improbable that a tourist in Palermo who asks a guide to tell him something about this Nina will hear yet another fantastic story about this lady poet. She is supposed to have asked Frederick II to pardon Pier delle Vigne, and she was able to obtain this pardon through the intervention of Beatrice of Savoy, wife of Thomas I; but Nina reached the jail where Piero was detained just minutes after he had committed suicide, and she fainted over his dead body.[6]

«» La Compiuta Donzella

Better suited for survival was La Compiuta Donzella. Her extant works, which amount to three sonnets, are transmitted by an authoritative manuscript (Vatican Latino 3793). Her name is not accompanied by glamorous legends which could arouse the suspicions of fastidious philologists. Moreover, no biographical data concerning her have ever been unearthed (contrary to the case of Gaia), so that the verification of her identity and the authentication of her supposed works is impossible. La Compiuta Donzella's major, perhaps fatal problem has been and still is her name, which literally translated means "The accomplished young lady." F. S. Quadrio, who was familiar with the manuscript tradition of Italian poetry, was the first to introduce La Compiuta Donzella into the history of literature. He considers her a "poetessa di valore per li tempi suoi" (2:157), but it is not clear whether "li tempi" denote the difficulty for a woman to be a poet or just the mediocre quality of Italian poetry in its earliest times. Compiuta's poems were not published until the following century. First to appear were two sonnets with religious overtones; they were published by F. Massi in 1840 (9). A third sonnet, on a secular theme and contained in a "tenzone con anonimo," was published in 1846 by F. Trucchi (135). The fact that she was a woman and that the themes of her poetry were a little unusual was enough to attract the attention of historians like C. Cantù (3:1292) and literary critics like De Sanctis. The latter quotes a sonnet by La Compiuta as a stupendous example of simplicity and compares it with a sonnet by Bondie Dietaiuti, concluding, "A me piace più la perfetta semplicità del sonetto femminile, con movenza più vivace, più immediata e più naturale" (I am more pleased by the perfect simplicity of the feminine sonnet, with its more lively, more immediate, and more natural movement) (1:22–23). For De Sanctis, "semplicità" was synonymous, in this case, with "femminile." His judgment is a positive one but it implies that La Compiuta Donzella had a lesser degree of learning than Bondie. Compiuta was "a miracle" like Nina: two women who were gifted with poetic genius which found its expression despite society.

When the fame of La Compiuta Donzella seemed fairly well established, A. Borgognoni, as implacable as he had been with Nina, attempted to demolish it ("Rimatrici italiane," 164–70). Again he questioned the historical reality of such a woman poet. Her name was highly unusual and would have been more appropriate as a *senhal* than as a proper name. The manuscript containing her poems mentioned only once that she was from Florence, and there were indications that other Tuscan poets addressed a few of their poems to a "compiuta donzella." If her name was to be taken as an antonomasia, as a name indicating a really special young woman, it seemed strange that Florentine history had left no record of her. The sonnet "Esser donzella di trovar dotta" by Maestro Torreggiano, supposedly addressed to her, in fact supported Borgognoni's thesis, since Maestro Toreggiano likened "a young lady learned in composing poetry" to "a great marvel." Had such a marvel appeared, Borgognoni continues, history would have left some record of it. This was not the case; hence Borgognoni concluded that La Compiuta Donzella never existed. The two religious sonnets attributed to her seemed too autobiographical to be authentic. Borgognoni was convinced that they were written by a man who used a feminine voice and who hid himself under the assumed name of La Compiuta Donzella.

But La Compiuta Donzella found a champion in Liborio Azzolina, who, in a long article, undertook the task of refuting Borgognoni's thesis point by point. The first point of disagreement concerned medieval Italian culture, which, in Borgognoni's view, prevented women from participating in literary activity. In an ample excursus, Azzolina listed several women who distinguished themselves: some wrote verses in Provençal, as is the case with the Isabella who had a *tenso* with Elias Cairel, identified as Isabella Pallavicini by Azzolini and others;[7] some in Italian, like Saint Catherine of Siena; some in French, like Christine de Pisan; and some were great literary figures like Accorsa, the daughter of the illustrious Accursio. Azzolina also drew several passages from Francesco da Barberino's *Costumi e reggimenti di donna,* which describe poetic activities as most becoming for a woman, and added that these passages testified to current practice. Thus no cultural bias could be adduced to disprove the existence of La Compiuta Donzella. Maestro Torregiano of Florence had confirmed it by addressing her as "donzella di trova dotta" (a young lady learned in composition), and by adding that to be such a lady caused "grande meraviglia." This statement implied that the case was unusual rather than impossible, as Borgognoni had maintained. But Maestro Torregiano, adds Azzolina, had not been the only admirer of La Compiuta Donzella. The anonymous author of the *tenzone* with Compiuta was Chiaro Davanzati, who indeed, argued Azzolina, addressed La Compiuta Donzella with several poems of his vast *canzoniere* and, specifically, with a series of sonnets. To account for the difference in subject and tone between the religious and the love poetry, Azzolina hypothesized two periods in La Compiuta Donzella's life: one which must have been intensely religious and another which must have been more given to the pleasures of this world. Fortunately, Azzolina refrained from speculating which came first and what role Chiaro had in this dramatic life. Azzolina, in any case, had taken a definite step toward bringing to life a sentimental world for La Compiuta Donzella, and he did so in the simplest way, namely, by reading her sonnets as if they were autobiographical.

Azzolina was to a certain extent successful. He proved, at least, that La Compiuta Donzella could not be dismissed like Nina as a legendary creature. M. Pelaez accepted the general lines of Azzolina's thesis, but found several points unconvincing; he especially objected to the documentation concerning the poet Chiaro Davanzati. Since Chiaro addressed his poems to a "donna" or "madonna" but never to a "compiuta donzella," it was more likely that we were dealing with the usual "convenzionalismo della poesia lirica d'amore" (249). In this situation of uncertainty, any new evidence in favor of either thesis was welcome. A new document supporting Azzolina was presented by S. Santangelo in 1907 (289–90). He had noticed that letter number five of Guittone d'Arezzo was addressed to a Compiuta Donzella. Guittone's *intitulatio* reads: "Soprapiacente Donna, di tutto compiuto savere, degna mia Donna compiuta, Guittone . . . " (Surpassingly pleasing lady with all accomplished wisdom, my worthy, accomplished lady, Guittone . . .). Also, the content of the letter seems fitting for the poet called La Compiuta Donzella: Guittone exhorts her to finish her life as well as she has begun it. Azzolina's study suggested that La Compiuta Donzella had gone through two phases of love, and this would explain why Guittone exhorts her to abandon love of this world and return to her love for God. Given that

Guittone's letter can be dated after 1260, Santangelo inferred that La Compiuta Donzella flourished around the years 1270 to 1280. At last all the pieces seemed to fit! Santangelo, however, was aware that Guittone never mentions the poetic activity of La Compiuta Donzella; he only talks about her beauty and her "compiuto savere," which are things "che fanno al caso nostro" (which support our case). Santangelo was also aware that his was just a hypothesis. This hypothesis, in any case, allowed La Compiuta Donzella to survive. G. Bertoni, in a survey (*Il Duecento*) which was meant to represent a synthesis of the studies on thirteenth-century Italian literature, expressed no doubt about the historical figure of La Compiuta Donzella. She left us "tre gioielli di sonetti, pieni di grazia e di amabilità femminile. C'è nei suoi versi una nota di sincerità, che attrae, e insieme un senso di scetticismo che sorprende in una giovinetta" (Three jewels of sonnets, full of grace and feminine charm. There is in her verses a note of sincerity which is attractive, along with a sense of scepticism which is surprising in a young girl) (101). Bertoni saw no reason to doubt the attribution given by the manuscript, nor could he accept the idea that behind that feminine voice there was that of a man, since he found it had an authentic feminine quality; at the most, he would allow that "La Compiuta Donzella" was a *senhal* behind which there hid a real lady. Bertoni's assessment has been repeated now and again by historians of Italian literature, and through these repetitions La Compiuta Donzella has slowly emerged from the limbo of uncertainty to live with the dignity of a real poet.

But alas, as we have seen happen before, well-established women poets of the Duecento can vanish into nothing. La Compiuta Donzella disappeared, at least for a moment, into the realm of pure . . . allegory! It all came about because of a book by L. Valli published in 1928 entitled *Il linguaggio segreto di Dante e dei 'fedeli d'amore.'* Valli's main thesis is that from the twelfth through the fourteenth centuries there was a thriving religious-political sect whose acolytes (Dante, Petrarch, and Boccaccio, among others) used a clandestine and cryptic language to attack the corruption of the church and to promote religious reform. One of his chapters is devoted to Francesco da Barberino's *Documenti d'amore,* in which there is a series of fourteen miniatures distributed in thirteen frames; each one of them is accompanied by a few verses explaining the meaning of the picture. Above all of them is a representation of Love crossing the sky on a white horse. From left to right these pictures portray (1) a religious man, (2) a religious woman, (3) a girl, (4) a "compiuta donzella,"

(5) a married woman, (6) a widow, (7–8) a wife and a husband, (9) a knight, (10) a commoner, (11) a carefree young man, (12) a boy, (13) a dead man, (14) a dead woman. Leaving aside the conclusions Valli drew from this group of images, let us look only at what he made of the allusion to a "compiuta donzella." Valli devoted a footnote to this figure just to say that the Florentine poet, "la compiuta donzella," was the cryptic symbol of the sect itself (249). The poems written under her name, he claimed, were "in gergo" (in code), and a key to decoding them is the figure of her father, who should be understood as the Pope.

Valli's hint turned into a major thesis in the hands of F. Egidi. This eminent philologist, editor (among other things) of the work by Francesco da Barberino which had caught Valli's attention, wrote an article in which he attempts to decode the cryptic language of the two religious sonnets by La Compiuta Donzella. To follow his argument, it will be useful to paraphrase the two sonnets. The first: "When in the spring lovers are fond of gardens where birds sing of love, and everyone is full of joy, I feel very sad and have reason only for crying. My father is determined to give me a husband, but I don't want him at all. Thus, in this season made beautiful by leaves and flowers, I live in pain." The second sonnet: "I would like to become a nun in order to serve God rather than the vanities of this world. Folly, villainy, and falsehood become stronger by the day, while wisdom, courtesy, and virtue decay. Thus, if I were free to do what I want, I would not stay among those evil people and would rather devote myself to God. I know who Christ is; I don't know the man whom my father wants to give me." Following the allegorical reading given to "compiuta donzella" by Francesco da Barberino, Egidi interprets the imagery of these sonnets in the following way: the father of whom the girl complains is the Pope; the leaves and the flowers are Holy Wisdom; the gardens are the places where the acolytes of the sect gather; these acolytes are represented by the birds; the joy refers to the sect; the cries mean the hypocrisy imposed on the "fedeli d'amore." The general message is this: the sect wants to leave this world and devote itself to God, but the Pope opposes it and wants it to marry an unknown rather than Christ, who is the known one. And, of course, "compiuta donzella" is the sect itself.

Later, good sense disputed Egidi's overreading. And good sense came from Francesco Mazzoni, who wisely chose not to discuss the sect, and kept his objections to Egidi on strictly philological grounds. He did not see, for instance, any allegorical dimension to the verses which Francesco da Barberino had placed under the picture of the "compiuta don-zella," nor did he see any relation between this "compiuta donzella" and the other who lived at least thirty years before the composition of the *Documenti*. According to Mazzoni, the name "compiuta donzella" is as strange a name as would be, for example, "La Beatrice donzella." For Mazzoni, it was a sort of proverbial name which perhaps reflected the story of a girl who opposed her father's plans for her marriage; the girl's opposition showed her to be an "accomplished young woman" and she was proverbially remembered as La Compiuta Donzella. The poems at-tributed to her were in reality written by a man who chose the autobio-graphic mode of composing poems which plainly belong to the genre of the "mal maritata," in which a woman complains of her boorish hus-band, and often sets about to cuckold him. Thus Mazzoni demoted La Compiuta Donzella from her rank of poet to that of a semi-legendary character whose actions became the subject of poetry. Perhaps his good sense went too far.

The impossibility of establishing anything concrete about the his-torical existence of this accomplished young lady was considered a great advantage by A. Chiari. At last, he said, it is possible to enjoy a few poems without having to look for a real face behind them but rather for an authentic soul embodied in them. Unfortunately, Chiari failed to see much of either one. His approach was purely impressionistic, a bit Crocean. The key words with which he attempted to characterize this poetry were "sincere," "original," "new," "spontaneous"; and he saw everywhere a "grazia espressiva" which he never really analyzed. All of the seductive power of these poems lay, for Chiari, in the name of their author, which evokes an ideal of beauty; their enchantment was all in those few lines which succeed in revealing a real person.

Despite its shortcomings, Chiari's essay is a meaningful contribution insofar as it shows boredom and even intolerance with biographical problems which, even if they could be resolved, would be of question-able value for reading poetry. But Chiari did not pay any attention to the cultural context of La Compiuta Donzella, and he overvalued her poems as a manifestation of "sincerity." A reader of the stature of G. Contini,[8] who is distrustful of impressionistic approaches to medieval poetry, finds Compiuta's poetry quite mediocre. Contini gives a new focus to the whole problem of La Compiuta Donzella and supports a reasonable ap-proach to the question. For Contini, problems of authenticity and of autobiography are not as compelling as they used to be. He finds no serious reason to reject Compiuta's historical reality, even though her name seems to be a pseudonym. In any case, our knowledge of the conventions governing medieval lyrics would exclude the presence of autobiographic elements in the poems of this elusive young lady, and therefore one cannot find the real Compiuta Donzella by looking there.

Contini's is the most reasonable conclusion one can reach after evaluating all the data and all the critical discussion to date. It would seem that La Compiuta Donzella has now found firm ground and a *modus vivendi*. But one never knows; considering the critical vicissitudes of the earliest Italian women poets, it is not improbable that some day in the not so distant future a critic may maintain that, for example, La Compiuta Donzella was actually married to Chiaro Davanzati and that she is the real author of his poems. And her case would be opened anew.

Notes

1. The fact that this work was dedicated to an Academy in Messina makes it more understandable that Allacci was eager to make Nina a poet from Messina. The quotation is taken from the introduction on an unnumbered page.

2. In an amusing footnote (85), Emiliani Giudici mocks Tiraboschi for his attempt to steal Nina's place as the first Italian woman poet for Gaia da Camino!

3. This sonnet was very likely written by a man (see Croce 289).

4. An accurate bibliography on this subject is provided by Bettarini.

5. A last weak defense of Nina was made by Bertacchi (67–71).

6. This legend is mentioned in the *Enciclopedia biografica e bibliografica italiana,* series VI: *Poetesse e scrittrici,* 2:77–79.

7. The identification as Isabella Pallavicini is regarded as improbable by Bertoni, *I trovatori d'Italia* 130–31.

8. *Poeti del Duecento* 1:433–38. Contini's anthology includes all the texts mentioned in this essay.

11 Images of Women and Imagined Trobairitz in the Béziers Chansonnier

"Aujourd'hui, comme hier, la féminité de l'écriture des 'trobairitz' . . . fait mirage aux yeux et écran à la lecture. . . . Les 'trobairitz' sortent aujourd'hui de l'oubli," as the critic Jean-Charles Huchet states (59). And Antoine Tavera evokes "la remarquable compagnie de ces poétesses (sans équivalent chez les trouvères)" (139). Recently Angelica Rieger devoted a study ("Ins e·l cor") to the illustrations found in Provençal chansonniers depicting these women whose preserved work numbers around twenty-five pieces, one percent as compared to the 2,500 poems in the corpus of the troubadours. Throughout the centuries, the perception of their image has been modified, of course, but according to precise criteria which vary from period to period, bearing witness to their long-term reception (see Meneghetti). A later and as yet little known anthology of troubadour songs in manuscript form presents three striking examples of this phenomenon.

The Béziers chansonnier, acquired in 1983 by the Centre International de Documentation Occitane, was the subject of a paper I delivered at the *Colloque de l'Association Internationale d'Etudes Occitanes* in 1984 in Southampton, the *Actes* of which were published in 1987. Since this earlier paper contains all the relevant detail concerning the history of the manuscript, I shall simply summarize its conclusions here.

The chansonnier preserved in Béziers is a manuscript from the end of the seventeenth or the beginning of the eighteenth century. It presents an abridged copy of the Provençal chansonnier *I* (Paris, Bibl. nat., fr. 854), ordered by Hubert de Chasteuil-Gallaup, the *avocat général* in the Parlement at Aix-en-Provence and brother of Pierre de Chasteuil-Gallaup (1644–1727), who first spoke of it in 1701.[1] Supposedly "perdu ou égaré," the manuscript was the subject of a discussion between Camille Chabaneau and Paul Meyer about a century ago, and has resurfaced only recently. The interest of the find lies as much in the resolution of this small problem of Provençal historiography as in the chansonnier's construction and particularly its decoration.

The Béziers chansonnier is an abbreviated copy of ms. *I,* and like it contains a series of illuminations. Whereas *I* has 91 historiated initials—or 92 if one counts f. 154, which is entered twice (see Anglade, "Les miniatures" 597)—the Béziers copy contains twenty-three, depicting twenty troubadours and three trobairitz: Castelloza, Azalais de Porcairagues, and the Comtessa de Dia, the same ladies as in *I.* However, the particular interest of the illustrations in the Béziers chansonnier results from the manner of their fabrication and from the idea that they transmit of the poet represented, whether man or woman. The illustrator employed a process discussed by Pierre de Chasteuil-Gallaup in one of the letters published by Chabaneau (106). In connection with the printing of portrait miniatures in his work on the troubadours, Pierre de Chasteuil-Gallaup notes that in the manuscripts that he consulted at the Bibliothèque du Roi, the poets "etoient peinds a miniature, qu'il y avoit trois de ces manuscrits ecrits sur le velin, que le duc qui avoit eu celui [qui] est le mieux conditionné avoit coupe avec des cizeaux les portraits de nos trouvaires" (were painted with miniatures, that there were three of these manuscripts written on vellum, that the duke who had had the one in the best condition had cut out the portraits of our troubadours with scissors). In the Béziers chansonnier, we see the results of an inversion of such an operation: of twenty depictions of troubadours, nineteen, all representing armed men on horseback, are seventeenth-century engravings cut out of a printed book and enhanced with colors. One notable exception is the picture of Bertran del Pojet (p. 145), illustrated with a pen drawing that has been colored. Without going into further detail (I gave the complete list of the illustrations in my earlier communication), I shall return to the subject of the three trobairitz.

The three ladies mentioned are presented in an even more curious manner, the character of which merits close examination. How was the woman troubadour understood at the end of the seventeenth century in Provence, the place of origin of this copy? In thirteenth-century Italian chansonniers such as manuscript *I,* the illustrations are not true portraits of the characters represented, but serve a largely ornamental role in the context of an initial. Only occasionally are our poets depicted in the more

Ab las vostras quar pres penet batailla
gira bon
e plus jabon
fair per com mas vailla
bona guarsa
sens narsa
que ria gazailla
que to jota
que non permeta
non podra me tailla
ans asaia
com deschaza
son drut en vailla

Ara non fai come chapteira
Si me lais damar o non teingna
del dos afars, el ols, quel meillor preingna
chatia e cela, non me deingna

Que non del camp se conveingna
e si me destreing plus que suoi non fai
Leuigna
men sui saus
que granmasi
fuelle ia manteigna
d'ieu non laise, ni no la bais
son pres el manteingna
e luganda
A gazanda
per el mon e lenpeingna
Si que la via
fosa gens tezena
d'ieu menagua
Si noui logua
Totes e non peingna
Si tal nova
non auh muoua
don ca lei noit veingna

Ma Castelosa

Na castelosa si fo daluexne gentil
domna, moillier del crue de Meuxona
e ama naxman de txxon e fess de
lui sas cansos e era domna mout gaia
e mout enseignada e mout bella

nostradamus nen a rien escrit

Chanson ou elle se plaint de l'absence de son ami

Mout aues faich lonc estaie
amics pois de mi us partits
l'es me greu e saluaie
car me iurets e me plevits
que els iorns de vostra uida
non ac dompna mes me
e si bautra uos parte
mi aues mort e traida
car los ma esperanssa
que manatets sens doptansa

Bels amics de fin coratge
vos ai amat pos ma valor
e sai que faill a i follatye
que plus menes escarits
can non fit vos gan chiela
e sin feres mal per be
beus a me nimen reire
que benananssa
puesc auer sos vostra manssa

Béziers, Centre International de Documentation Occitane, Provençal Chansonnier, p. 149: Castelloza. Reprinted by permission

Béziers, Centre International de Documentation Occitane, Provençal Chanson-nier, p. 171: Azalais de Porcairagues. Reprinted by permission

Béziers, Centre International de Documentation Occitane, Provençal Chansonnier, p. 174: la Comtessa de Dia. Reprinted by permission noble, framed miniature (rather than in an initial), as in manuscript *H* (Vatican, lat. 3207), which moreover has the particularity, significant for our topic, of including only representations of trobairitz.[2] In the Béziers chansonnier, the illustrations of the three ladies are executed on small pieces of paper glued in at the beginning of the texts that they were supposed to illustrate. The distinctive feature to be pointed out in these three illustrations, in contrast to the nineteen engravings of the troubadours, is that they are pen drawings, each one different in style but nonetheless to be examined as a series. Only the Provençal chansonniers *A* (Vatican, lat. 5232), *H* (Vatican, lat. 3207), *I* (Paris, Bibl. nat., fr. 854), and *K* (Paris, Bibl. nat., fr. 12473) include miniatures of the trobairitz in question:

Comtessa de Dia	Na Castelloza	Azalais de Porcairagues
(P-C 46)	(P-C 109)	(P-C 43)
A f. 167v°	*A* f. 168v°[3]	---
H f. 49v°	---	---
I f. 141	*I* f. 125	*I* f. 140
K f. 126v°	*K* f. 110v°	*K* f. 125v°

I shall discuss the image and the text of each trobairitz in the Béziers chansonnier in relation to their source, following the order of the manuscript (see the Appendix to this essay). One general remark is necessary: the Béziers copy, although corrupt, is in no way original; it reproduces exactly the readings of *I*.

The *vida* of Na Castelloza, found on page 149 of the Béziers chansonnier, is quite close to the text published by Boutière and Schutz (333–34):

> Na Castelosa si fo d'Alverne, gentil domna, moiller del Truc de Maurona: e ama n'Arman de Breon e fets de lui sas cansos. E era domna mout gaia e mout enseignada e mout bella.[4]

> [Lady Castelloza was from Auvergne, a noble lady, wife of The Truc de Maurona; and she loved Sir Arman de Breon and made for (and about) him her love-songs. And she was a very gay lady, and very learned and very beautiful.]

Following this is the "chanson ou elle se plaint de l'absence de son ami" beginning "Mout aves faich lonc estaie. . . ."[5] This is a *canso* of five *coblas unissonans,* each consisting of ten heptasyllabic lines with masculine and feminine rhymes; the text fills pages 149 and 150 of the chansonnier. The illustration that was glued into the blank space left between the name and the *vida* represents a standing lady, "Castelosa," bare head slightly bowed as in prayer, her hands joined. At her feet a lamb (a symbol of Christ, purity, faithfulness?) lies on a cross placed on the ground. In the original chansonnier *I* (f. 125), Na Castelloza stands singing in a red gown inside of the initial.

On page 171 of the Béziers chansonnier, beneath the name "Nasalais de Porcairagues," we read the following *vida* (cf. Boutière-Schutz 341–42):

> Nasalais de Porcarages si fo de l'encontrada de Monspeilier, gentils dona e enseignada, et enamoret se d'En Guy Guereiat qu'era fraire d'En Guillen de Monspeilier; et la donna si sabia trobar, e fets de lui mantas bonas cansos.

> [Lady Asalais de Porcarages was from the region of Montpellier, a noble lady and learned, and she fell in love with Sir Guy Guereiat, who was brother of Sir Guillem de Montpellier; and the lady knew how to write poetry, and made for (and about) him many good love-songs.]

The only song by Azalais that has been preserved, "Ara eme el freg tems vengut," includes six *coblas doblas* of eight heptasyllabic lines and one *tornada* of four lines, and follows a scheme that Aimo Sakari called an "unicum métrique" ("A propos" 527, cf. Frank item 382:107).

Azalais is represented as a standing frontal figure dressed in a long low-cut gown with a high lace collar, her hair drawn back in a chignon. The costume could be from the sixteenth century. Lifting her full skirt to the knees, the courtesan reveals her pink-sheathed legs and the amazingly high, stilted shoes of a prostitute.[6] Chansonnier *I* represents Azalais frontally, standing and singing in a long blue gown and green mantle that reach the ground (f. 140).

Finally, on page 174 of the Béziers chansonnier, we find the *vida* of the "Comtessa de Dia" (cf. Boutière-Schutz 445–46):

> La Comtessa di Dia si fo mouilier d'En Guillen de Peitieus, bella domna e bona; si s'ennamouret se d'En Rambaut d'Aurenga, et fets de lui mantas bonas cansos.

[The Countess of Dia was the wife of Sir Guillem de Peitieus, a beautiful lady and good; and she fell in love with Sir Raimbaut d'Aurenga, and made for (and about) him many good love-songs.]

The copyist then inserted a passage from the romantic love story of Guilhem Adémar and the Comtessa de Dia, created by Jean de Nostredame, that clever forger who belonged to the sixteenth century Provençal nobility.[7] The text reads as follows:

Nostradamus dist que ceste comtesse de Die estoit une dame fort sage et verteuse, de grande beaute, docte en la rithme provensale; qu'elle fust amoureuse de Guillen Adhemar, a la louange duquel elle a escrit plusieurs belles chansons, ainsy qu'il a este dit en la vie dudit Adhemar, apres la mort duquel elle se fit religieuse au monastere de St Honore de Tarascon, ou elle mit par escrit plusieurs belles euvres, et entre autres lo Tractat de la Tarasca et qu'elle y mourut de doleir, l'an 1193.[8]

Following this, there is a copy of "la Chanson ou elle fait des sohets de pouvoir poseder son ami a son gre" (the song where she expresses the wish to be able to possess her lover according to her whim). This well-known *canso* is made up of three eight-line *coblas doblas,* and begins "Estat ai en consirer" (Frank item 624:57).

The large illustration chosen for the Comtessa de Dia shows her frontally, standing in a grandiloquent pose that may be considered theatrical. Set off against a conventional pastoral landscape, she wears a classical toga that is drawn up over the right shoulder, and which, with her rhetorical gestures, suggests a feminized version of a Roman orator. In chansonnier *I,* f. 141, the Comtessa de Dia is shown more soberly as a frontal standing figure attired in a green gown and a red mantle. As Angelica Rieger rightly points out, "Les attributs accordés à la Comtesse de Die par [*I* et *K*], tels que le manteau pourpre doublé d'hermine . . . la désignent nettement comme la plus noble et la plus distinguée de toutes" (393). She retains this same high status in the Béziers chansonnier.

How do these illustrations contribute to an understanding of the trobairitz?

First, as others before me have pointed out,[9] the word *trobairitz* is not mentioned in Provençal lyric poetry, in the thirteenth- and fourteenth-century Occitano-Catalan treatises, nor in the *vidas.* The term does appear, however, around 1250 in the romance *Flamenca* (ed. Gschwind, v. 4577), in the text of the poem written by Flamenca and her two maid-servants, when one of them, Margarida, composes [*troba*] an answer to the message from Guillaume de Nevers, "Mor mi" ("I die"). From her enforced seclusion Flamenca in turn answers Guillaume, who has become a cleric and troubadour for her, by inventing lyrics with three female voices. Thus the trobairitz speaks out clearly in a world in which writing is essentially masculine. Her answers not only respond to Guillaume's complaint, "Ailas," but also sustain the debate until she grants the final agreement, "Plas mi."

As Huchet correctly shows, woman "est le moteur, le principe de l'é-criture troubadouresque" (67). Moreover, it is as if the lady could not be satisfied to be the poet's muse. The "grandes dames" in rhetoric, *enseigna-das,* as the *vidas* of the trobairitz say, left significant traces of the lyrical "authenticité" discussed by Tavera (144–45). Nonetheless, this feminine writing could not be conceived independently from the masculine system upon which it was grafted, and which it parrots and parodies. This is the source of the "dimension critique" analyzed by Huchet, this "dialogue intérieur qu'on décline au féminin et attribue aux 'trobairitz' " (79).

Yet it remains true, despite the results of Tavera's close analyses, that the mystery lingers on in this literary game between fiction and reality, between "une féminité génétique"—to use Pierre Bec's expression—"(avec un auteur dont on sait pertinemment qu'il est une femme), et une féminité textuelle, à savoir une pièce, dans la très grande majorité des cas amoureuse, et dont le 'je' lyrique est une femme (l'auteur pouvant être assez fréquemment un homme)" (" 'Trobairitz' et chansons" 235). The latter case is illustrated by the French *chansons de femme* and the Portu-guese *cantigas de amigo.*

Let us grant that the *cansos* and *tensos* attributed to the trobairitz were written by women,[10] and ask ourselves about the milieu which produced them. As Bec states, "Les trobairitz participaient du même monde cour-tois et aristocratique que les troubadours" (" 'Trobairitz' et chansons" 239–40). They are *domnas* graced by the *vidas* with qualities such as *gen-tils* or *ensenhadas,* but rather than benefiting from the ritual of *fin'amors,* in which the poet-lover puts them on a pedestal and begs their favors, the system is reversed. In the three texts chosen for the Béziers chansonnier, we clearly find the model of the "troubadour mal-aimé" with the usual topoi (desire to possess the loved object, suffering in its absence, fear of abandonment), but reversed. The trobairitz are unhappily married—Na Castelloza and the Comtessa de Dia say so themselves.

However, to a woman in Provence, the world of their day (between 1180 and 1230) seems to have offered "une parenthèse dorée," to use the expression of Martí Aurell i Cardona, after the degradation of aristocratic women's status in the south, which had followed a favored period around the year 1000, and immediately before what has been called the "feudal crisis." During this "parenthèse dorée," about 1180–1230, "les chants des troubadours, qui inversent les rapports de fidélité en faveur de la dame, battent leur plein dans les cours du Comté" (22). According to the study of the Catalan historian, this was a period characterized by marriages in which the rank of the wife was superior to that of the husband (hypergamy)—a point in history rapidly eclipsed by the much longer lasting patriarchal system in which aristocrats married women of a lesser social rank than their own (hypogamy).[11] For this brief period, the privileged status of the aristocratic woman in Provence must have been marked by *fin'amors* and have allowed (why not?) the magnificent and singular blossoming of trobairitz songs in which the superiority of the woman is expressed in another manner. She has become active once again, in love as in writing. As Michel Zink observes, "Il y a confusion entre 'j'aime' et 'je chante' " (228), and the literary game reserved for men comes under the power of women, with all of the playful ambiguity of courtly lyricism creating a subtle dialectic between the register of the *grand chant courtois* and the popularizing one (Bec, " 'Trobairitz' et chansons" 261). A violent distortion can thus take place, which is clearly represented by our three illustrations of women and which tends either toward the pious or the burlesque. In the Béziers chansonnier, Na Castelloza brings to mind the former, whereas Azalais portrays the latter— on one hand the trobairitz is shown as being intensely devout, and on the other she appears as a prostitute. Between the "Bonne Dame," for whom the ideal model is the Virgin Mary and to whom homage with folded hands is due as to the one and only Lord, and the "mauvaise dame," lustful and venal, corruptor of youth (Rouillan-Castex 310–11), there stands the image of beautiful language, of the rhetoric of years gone by—an allegory of one of the seven liberal arts, of the verbal game that characterizes *fin'amors* and of which the high point is *joi*.

Our illustrations are the reflection of a break between the different modes of a unique and complex reality. After the thirteenth century, as Julia Kristeva remarks, *fin'amors* lost "cette ambiguité propre au jeu et à la joie" (269). The Béziers chansonnier gives us back a shattered image in which the three sides of the luminous prism have fallen flat, so much so that instead of a mysterious and captivating volume, nothing is left but three two-dimensional illustrations, disfigured but touching witnesses of a brilliant past. However, this caricatured past did bear other fruits in feminine writing—I see sufficient proof of this in the magnificent text that another aristocratic woman from Provence, probably Philippa de Porcelet, devoted to the famous Beguine nun Douceline de Digne, the sister of the Franciscan Hugues de Digne, who preached to Saint Louis.[12] One woman writing the mystical love story of another: such a *vida* is unequaled in the northern vernacular.

The critical voice will never again be silent. "L'amour provençal peut disparaître," concludes Sylvette Rouillan-Castex (329), but feminine writing of love has endured, more or less confined, hidden, to such an extent that these near-mythical names, transmitted by tradition, have been given an imagined and caricatured bodily form. From the idealized image carried by the chansonnier initials of the thirteenth century, we have come to the deformed portrait: the female poet still goes forth masked. In the history of their reception, the Béziers chansonnier is a privileged witness of the trobairitz.

APPENDIX: *Synoptic Transcription of Trobairitz Texts in the Béziers Chansonnier and in Manuscript I*

Na Castelloza (P-C 109,3)

Béziers, pp. 149–50		*I, fols. 125–125v*
Mout aves faich lonc estaie		Mout avez faig lonc estaie
amics pos de mi·us partits		amics pos de mi·us partitz
E es me greu e salvaie		Et es me greu e salvaie
Car me iurets e me plevits		car me iuretz e·m plevitz
Que als jorns de vostra vida	5	Que als iorn⌣ de vostra vida
Non ac dompna mes me		Non acses dompna mes me
E si d'autra vos parte		Et si d'autra vos perte
Mi aves mort'e traida		mi avetz e mort'e traida
car los [*sic*] ma esperansa		Cam los [*sic*] ma speransa
que m'amasets sens doptansa	10	que m'amassetz ses doptansa
Bels amics de fin coratge		Bels amics de fin coratge
vos ai amat pos m'abellitz		vos ai amat pos m'abellitz

e sai que faitz ai follatge
que plus m'en es escaritz
Can non fis vos ganchida   15

e si·n fezes mal per be
be·us am e no m'en recre
. . . .
. . . que benanansa
puesc'aver sos vostr'amansa   20

[*p. 150*]

Mout aurai mes mal usage
A las autras amairits
C'om sol trametre message
Ei nos [*sic*] triats a chausits
E s'ieu tenc me per guerida   25
Amics a la mia fe
Canc vos prec c'aissi·m conve
que plus pros n'es enrigida
S'ai de vos calc'aondansa
de baisar o de coindansa   30

Mal agr'eu son cor volage
Vas vos mos fui camiairitz
ni druts de alcun paratge
per mi non fon encobits
Ans son pensiv'e marida   35
Car de m'amor non sove
E si de vos ioi non ve
Tost me trobaras fenida
Car petit de malanansa
Mor domna s'on no tal lansa.   40

Tot lo maltrag e·l damnage
Que per vos m'es escarits
vos fas grasir mon lignange [*sic*]
E sobre tots mos marrits
E s'anc fes ves mi s faillida   45
perdon la.us per bona fe
E prec que aurets ausida
Ma chanson qu.us fas fiansa
Sai trobets bella semblansa.

E sai que faitz ai follatge
que plus m'en es escaritz
Can non fis ves [*fol. 125v*] vos
     ganchida
e si·n fezez mal per be
be·us am e no m'en recre
. . . .
. . . que benanansa
puosc'aver ses vostr'amensa.

Mout aurai mes mal usage
A las autras amairitz
C'om sol trametre message
E moz triatz a chauzitz
E s'ieu tenc me per guerida
Amics a la mia fe
Canc vos prec'aissi·m conve
que plus pros n'es enriqida
S'ai de vos calc'aondansa
de baisar o de coindansa

Mal agr'eu son cor volage
Vas vos mos fui camiairitz
Ni drutz de algun paratge
per mi non fon encobitz
Anz son pensiv'e marida
Car de m'amor non sove
E si de vos ioi no·m ve
Totz me trobaretz fenida
Car petit de malanansa
Mor domna s'on no tal lansa.

Tot lo maltrag e·l damnage
Que per vos m'es escaritz
Vos fatz grasir mon lignage
E sobre totz mos marritz.
E s'anc fes ves mi s faillida
perdon la·us per bona fe
E prec que auretz ausida
Ma chanson que·us fatz fiansa
Sai trobetz bella senblansa.

[One verse of the final stanza is missing.]

Azalais de Porcairagues (P-C 43,1)

Béziers, pp. 171–72

Ara eme el freg tems vengut
Quel gel, el neus et la faingna
e ill auselet estan mut
c'us de cantar s'afraingna
e son sec li rams per plais   5
que flors ni foilla non nais
ni rosignols non i crida
que lame e mai me resida

Tant ai lo cors deseubut
Per qu'eus suis a tots
      estraengna   10
E sai que l'om a perdut
Molt plus tot que non
      gasaigna
Et s'ieu fail ab mots verais
d'aurenga me moc l'esglais
Per que n'estauc esbaïda   15
En pert solats e partida

Domna met moult mal s'amor
Que ab ric home plaideia
Ab plus haut de vavasor
et s'il o fai il foleia   20
Quar lo dison en velai
que ges per ricor non vai
e domna que n'es chausida
en tenc per envilanida

Amic ai de gran valor   25
Que sobre tots segnoreia
e non a cor trichador
Vas me que s'amor m'autreia
Eu dic que m'amor l'eschai
E cel que dis que non fai   30
Dieus li don mal escarida
Que m'en tenc fort per garida

[*p. 172*]

Bels amics de bon talan
son ab vos tots iorns en gatge
cortesa e de bel semblan   35

I, fol. 140

Ar em al freg temps vengut
Quel gels el neus e la faingna
e ill ausellet estan mut
C'us de chantar s'afraingna
e son sec li rams pels plais
Que flors ni fuoilla noi nais
ni rossignols noi crida
que lam e mai me ressida

Tant ai lo cors deseubut

Per qu'ieu sui a totz estraingna
E sai que l'om a perdut
mot plus tost que non
      gasaingna
E s'ieu faill ab motz verais
D'aurenga me moc l'esglais
per qu'ieu n'estauc esbaïda
E'n pert solatz e partida

Domna met mout mal s'amor
Que ab ric home plaideia
ab plus aut de vavasor
E s'il o fai il foleia
Quar so dison en velai
Que ges per ricor non vai
E domna que n'es chausida
Entenc per envilanida

Amic ai de gran valor
Que sobre totz seingnoreia
E non a cor trichador
Vas me que s'amor m'autreia
Eu dic que m'amors l'eschai
E cel que dis que non fai
Dieus li don mal escarida
Qu'ieu m'en teing fort per
      guerrida.

Bels amics de bon talan
son ab vos totz jorn en gatge
cortesa e de bel senblan

sol non demandes outrage
tot enveiren el assai
qu'en vostra merce me metrai
vos m'aves la fe plevida
que non demandes faillida   40

A Dieu coman bel Esgar
E plus la ciutat d'aurenga
E gloriet'e·l cailar
el seignor de proensa
e tot quant vol mon ben lai   45
E larc en son faig l'assai
celui perdei c'a ma vida
E'n sarai tots iorns marida

Ioglars que aves cors gai
vers narbona portats lai   50
Ma chanson ab la fenida
lei cui iois e iovens guida.

sol non demandes outrage.
Tost enveirem al assai
qu'en vostra merce·m metrai
vos m'avez la fe plevida
Que non demandes faillida

A Dieu coman bel esgar
E plus la ciutat d'aurenga
E gloriet'e·l caslar
El seingnor de proenssa
E tot quant vol mon ben lai
E larc on son faig l'assai
cellui perdei c'a ma vida
E'n serai totz iorns marrida

Ioglars que avetz cors gai
ves narbona portatz lai
ma chanson ab la fenida
lei cui iois e iovenz guida.

Comtessa de Dia (P-C 46,4)

Béziers, pp. 174–75

Estat ai en consirer
per un cavalier qu'ai agut
et voil sia tots temps saubut
come eu l'ai amat a sobrier
Ara vei que sui trahida   5
car eu non li donei m'amor
on ai estat en grant error
en leit et quant sui vestida

[*p. 175*]

Ben volria mon cavaillier
Tener un ser en meis bras nut   10
qu'el s'en tengra per errebut
sol cal ni fes conseillier
quar plus m'en sui abellida
non fis floris de blansaflor
Mon cor l'autrei e m'amor   15
mon sen mos oills e ma vida

Bels amics avinens et bos
quora·us tenrai en mon poder
et que iaguese un ser ab vos
et que·us dese un bais amoros   20

I, fol. 141

Estat ai en conssirer
per un cavallier qu'ai agut
E voill sia totz temps saubut
Cum eu l'ai amat a sobrier
Ara vei qu'ieu sui traida
Quar eu no li donei m'amor
on ai estat en grant error
en leit e quant sui vestida

Ben volria mon cavallier
Tener un ser en mos bratz nut
Qu'el s'en tengra per errebut
sol c'a lui fesse coseillier
Quar plus m'en sui abellida
non fis floris de blansaflor
mon cor l'autrei e m'amor
mon sen mos oillz e ma vida

Bels amics avinens e bos
Quora·us tenrai en mon poder
E que iagues ab vos un ser
E que·us des un bais amoros

Sapchats que grant talent n'auria
que·us tenguese en loc de
    marit
ab so que m'agueses pleuvit
de far tot so que volria.

Sapchatz grant talent n'auria
Que·us tengues en loc del
    marrit
Ab so que m'aguesses plevit
De far tot so qu'*ieu* volria.

Notes

1. In his *Discours sur les Arcs Triomphaux dressés en la Ville d'Aix, à l'heureuse arrivée de Mgr le duc de Bourgogne et de Mgr le duc de Berry* (Aix, 1701), 21, quoted by Chabaneau 31.

2. See Anglade 595–96 for *H.* Na Castelloza and Azalais de Porcairagues do not appear in *H,* whereas the Comtessa de Dia seems to be represented by two miniatures on fol. 49 v°. See also A. Rieger, "'Ins e·l cor' " 389–92.

3. The miniature represents a lady and a knight seated face to face; see A. Rieger, "Ins e·l cor" fig. I.

4. See Paden et al., "Castelloza," especially 159–62, on the characters named in the *vida* and the mysterious troubadour Pons de Mérindol, probably invented by Pierre de Chasteuil-Gallaup; also my communication at Southampton, and Dronke, "Castelloza," especially 140–41 for this song.

5. See the Checklist for editions. Paden edits the texts from ms. *N,* in which all the poems of Castelloza are anonymous.

6. See the Musée de la Chaussure in Romans.

7. Ed. Chabaneau-Anglade 31–32. On the use made of Jean de Nostredame in our manuscript and in the milieu of Pierre de Chasteuil-Gallaup, see my communication at Southampton.

8. [Nostradamus said that this countess of Die was a very prudent and virtuous lady, of great beauty, learned in Occitan poetry; that she was in love with Guillem Adhemar, in praise of whom she wrote several beautiful songs, as it is said in the *vida* of the said Adhemar, after whose death she became a nun in the monastery of Saint-Honoré in Tarascon, where she wrote several beautiful works, among others the *Tractat de la Tarasca,* and that she died there of grief in the year 1193.] See Riquer 2:791–93.

9. Notably Bec, "Trobairitz occitanes" 60.

10. Dronke does not doubt it as for Castelloza (131–45).

11. On this question, see also Paden et al., "The Troubadour's Lady."

12. Text preserved in a single manuscript, Paris, Bibl. nat., fr. 13503; Brunel item 184. See the dissertation by Aurell i Cardona, "La famille de Porcelet et l'aristocratie provençale (972-1320)," revised and condensed as *Une famille de la noblesse provençale au moyen âge: Les Porcelet.*

Checklist of Poems by the Trobairitz

This checklist attempts to include the name of every known trobairitz, whether she has been considered a historical or a fictional woman, and the first line of every poem by a trobairitz which has been preserved. It gives biographical references, the genre of each poem, the manuscripts which contain it, and the principal editions (with the best generally available edition in **boldface**).

For explanation of the sigla used here for manuscripts see P–C.

Alais and Iselda (or Alaisina Iselda)

The names should probably be read *N'Alais i na Iselda*, "Lady Alais and Lady Iselda," in P–C 12,1 v. 21, and not as a single name, *N'Alaisina Iselda*, as some scholars read it. Alais and Iselda are identified within the text (v. 2) as two sisters. The objections raised by Bec, *Mittelalterstudien* 24–25 and *Burlesque* 204, do not withstand scrutiny: (1) the conjunction *e*, "and," is well attested in the form *i* in *S–W* 2.311, including several thirteenth–century sources; (2) the name Alais, though it represents a syncopation of Azalais, scans in two syllables, as here, in all the other passages where I have found it: Sordello, P–C 437,38 v. 70; Uc de Saint Circ, P–C 457,36 v. 1; and the response by Nicol de Turin, P–C 310,3 v. 2. Iselda is a form of Occitan Iseut, as in Iseut de Capio; in English, Isolde. Nothing further is known about the life of these women or this woman. Jeanroy 1:332; Bogin 178–79.

Na Carenza al bel cors avinen (P–C 12,1)

Cobla answered by Carenza (P–C 108,1). 1 ms.: Q.

Editions: Schultz-Gora 28. Véran 112–14. Bogin 144–45. Nelli 256–59. Bec, *Mittelalterstudien* 22–23. **Bec**, *Burlesque* 201–05. Perkal-Balinsky 133–37.

Alamanda

For discussion of the fictionality or historicity of Alamanda see Chambers, item 8. Guiraut de Bornelh was active 1162–99 (Riquer 1:463–66). Jeanroy 1:333; Bogin 170.

S'ie·us quier conseill, bel'amig'Alamanda (P-C 12a,1)

> *Tenso* with Guiraut de Bornelh (= P-C 242,69). 14 mss.: *ABCDGHIKNQRS*^{g}*Va*. *Razo* in Boutière-Schutz 43–46.
>
> Editions: Schultz-Gora 19–20. Kolsen, *Sämtliche Lieder* 366–73. Véran 95–100. **Riquer** 1: 506–10. Bogin 102–07. Perkal-Balinsky 47–59.

Almuc de Castelnou

Beginning of the 13th c.; identified as Almodis, the wife of Guigue de Châteauneuf-de-Randon (arrondissement of Mende, Lozère), by Brunel, "Almois de Châteauneuf." Jeanroy 1:336; Bogin 165–66.

Domna n'Iseutz, s'ieu saubes (P-C 20,2)

> *Cobla* answering Iseut de Capio (P-C 253,1). 1 ms.: *H* + κ. *Razo* in Boutière-Schutz 422–24.
>
> Editions: Schultz-Gora 25. Véran 72–74. **Boutière-Schutz** 422–24. Bogin 92–93. Nelli 247–49. Perkal-Balinsky 129–32.

Azalais d'Altier

Addressed in a *canso* by Uc de Saint-Circ (P-C 457,4; Uc fl. "1217–53 env.," Jeanroy 1:434). Altier in the canton of Villefort, arrondissement of Mende (Lozère), according to Crescini. About 47 kilometers from Anduze (Gard); see Clara d'Anduza.

Tanz salutz e tantas amors (P-C 42a,1)

> Letter to a certain Clara, possibly Clara d'Anduza. 1 ms.: *V*.
>
> Editions: **Crescini**. Perkal-Balinsky 213–22. Partial ed. by Rieger in this volume. Ed. by **Poe** forthcoming.

Azalais de Porcairagues

Addressed in poems by Raimbaut d'Aurenga, who died in 1173; Portiragnes (canton and arrondissement of Béziers, Hérault) according to Riquer 1:459. *Vida* in Boutière-Schutz 341–42. Jeanroy 1:341; Bogin 166–67.

> Ar em al freg temps vengut (P–C 43,1)
>
>> *Canso.* 8 ms. transcriptions: *CDªH¹H²IKNd.*
>>
>> Editions: Schultz-Gora 16–17. Véran 116–21. Sakari, "Le Joglar" 184–97. **Riquer** 1: 460–62. Bogin 94–97. Sansone 248–51. Perkal-Balinsky 145–52. Béziers ms. ed. by Brunel-Lobrichon in this volume.
>
> See also the note on a lost manuscript, below.

Beatritz de Dia (P-C 46). See Comtessa de Dia

Beatritz de Romans

On the attribution of P–C 93,1 see Zufferey, item I.5, and the essay by Rieger. Romans (arrondissement of Valence, Drôme). Jeanroy 1:333; Bogin 176–77.

> Na Maria, pretz e fina valors (P–C 93,1)
>
>> *Canso* ("mas coblas") sometimes attributed to Alberico da Romano (P–C 16a,2). 1 ms.: *T.*
>>
>> Editions: Schultz-Gora 28. Bertoni, *I trovatori d'Italia* 265–66. Bogin 132–33. Roubaud 326. Nelli 302–05. Bec, *Burlesque* 197–200. Perkal-Balinsky 157–60. **Rieger** in this volume.

Carenza

Unknown; cf. Alais and Iselda.

> N'Alais i n'Iselda, ensenhamen (P–C 108,1)
>
>> *Cobla* answering Alais and Iselda (P–C 12,1). 1 ms.: Q.
>>
>> Editions: Schultz-Gora 28. Véran 112–14. Bogin 144–45. Nelli 256–59. Bec, *Mittelalterstudien* 22–23. **Bec**, *Burlesque* 201–05. Perkal-Balinsky 133–37.

Castelloza

Early 13th c., Auvergne. Addressed Almuc de Castelnou in P-C 109,2. *Vida* in Boutière-Schutz 333–34. Jeanroy 1:355–56; Riquer 3:1325; Bogin 175; Paden et al., ed., 158–63.

> Amics, s'ie·us trobes avinen (P-C 109,1)
>
>> *Canso.* 5 mss.: *AIKNd.*
>>
>> Editions: Schultz-Gora 23. Lavaud 2: 496–503, 3: 87. Véran 128–31. Bogin 118–21. **Paden**, "Castelloza" 170–73. Trans. Dronke, "The Provençal *Trobairitz*: Castelloza" 146–47.

> Ja de chantar non degr'aver talan (P-C 109,2)
>
>> *Canso.* 5 mss.: *AIKNd.*
>>
>> Editions: Schultz-Gora 23–24. Lavaud 2: 502–09, 3: 87–88. Véran 123–27. Riquer 3: 1328–30. Bogin 122–27. **Paden**, "Castelloza" 173–77. Trans. Dronke, "The Provençal *Trobairitz*: Castelloza" 147–49.

> Mout aurez fag lonc estage (P-C 109,3)
>
>> *Canso.* 5 mss.: *AIKNd.*
>>
>> Editions: Schultz-Gora 24. Lavaud 2:510–15, 3:88–89. Véran 132–35. Bogin 126–29. Riquer 3:1325–30. **Paden**, "Castelloza" 177–79. Trans. Dronke, "The Provençal *Trobairitz*: Castelloza" 149–50. Béziers ms. edited by Brunel-Lobrichon in this volume.

> Per joi que d'amor m'avegna (P-C 461,191)
>
>> *Canso,* anonymous in ms. 1 ms.: *N.*
>>
>> Editions: Lavaud 2: 516–21, 3: 89. **Paden**, "Castelloza" 180–82. Trans. Dronke, "The Provençal *Trobairitz*: Castelloza" 150–51.

Clara d'Anduza

Anduze in the arrondissement of Alais (Gard); see Azalais d'Altier. Perhaps Clara d'Anduza is the *dompna d'Andutz* mentioned in a *razo* to a poem by Uc de Saint-Circ (Boutière-Schutz 244–47). Jeanroy 1:357; Bogin 176.

> En greu esmay et en greu pessamen (P-C 115,1)
>
>> *Canso.* 1 ms.: *C.*
>>
>> Editions: Schultz-Gora 26. Véran 159–62. Bogin 130–31. **Bec**, *Burlesque* 193–96. Perkal-Balinsky 153–56.

Comtessa de Dia

Attested in a charter of 1212 (Monier); "fines del siglo XII o principios del XIII" (Riquer 2:791–93). Die (Drôme). *Vida* in Boutière-Schutz 445–46. Jeanroy 1:360; Bogin 163–64.

Ab joi et ab joven m'apais (P-C 46,1)

> *Canso*. 8 mss.: *ABDHIKTa*.
>
> > Editions: Schultz-Gora 17–18. Kussler-Ratyé 161–64. Véran 169–71. **Riquer** 2:794–95. Bogin 82–85. **Kay** in this volume.

A chantar m'er de so qu'eu no volria (P-C 46,2)

> *Canso*. 14 mss.: *ABCDGIKLMNRWab* + κ.
>
> > Editions: Schultz-Gora 18. Kussler-Ratyé 164. Véran 172–74. **Riquer** 2:800–02. Bogin 84–87.

Amics, en gran consirier (P-C 46,3)

> See **Anonymous Trobairitz**

Estat ai en greu consirier (P-C 46,4)

> *Canso*. 4 mss.: *ADIK*.
>
> > Editions: Schultz-Gora 18–19. Kussler-Ratyé 173–74. Véran 167–68. **Riquer** 2:798–99. Bogin 88–89. Béziers ms. edited by Brunel-Lobrichon in this volume.

Fin joi me don'alegransa (P-C 46,5)

> *Canso*. 1 ms.: *D*.
>
> > Editions: Schultz-Gora 19. Kussler-Ratyé 174–75. Véran 175–76. **Riquer** 2:796–97. Bogin 90–91.

On the attribution of further works to the Comtessa de Dia by the seventeenth-century scholar Francesco Redi, see P-C pp. 42–43 and Monier 273.

See also the note on a lost manuscript, below.

Comtessa de Proensa

Identified by S. Stronski ("Garsende") as Garsenda de Forcalquier, daughter of Guillaume IV de Forcalquier, countess of Provence by her marriage in 1193 to Count Alfonso II; widowed in 1209, she entered a religious order in 1225. Mentioned in the *vidas* of Elias de Barjols and Gui de Cavaillo (Boutière-Schutz 215–16, 505–07). Jeanroy 1:369; Bogin 170–73.

Vos que·m semblatz dels corals amadors (P-C 187,1)
> *Cobla* answered by Gui de Cavaillon (P-C 192,6). 2 mss.: *FT*.
> Editions: Schultz-Gora 21. Véran 85–87. **Riquer** 3:1191–92.
> Bogin 108–09. Nelli 244–45. Perkal-Balinsky 68–71.

Garsenda. See Comtessa de Proensa

Gaudairenca

P-C 169. The wife of Raimon de Miraval (Raimon fl.1191–1229, Riquer 2:983), from Miraval-Cabardès (canton of Mas-Cabardès, arrondissement of Carcassonne, Aude). According to a *razo* Gaudairenca "sabia ben trobar coblas e dansas" (Boutière-Schutz 380), but no poems are attributed to her.

Gormonda de Monpeslier

P-C 177,1 is dated 1229 by Städtler in this volume; about 1228 by Rieger, "Un *sirventes* féminin." Montpellier (Hérault). Jeanroy 1:372.
> Greu m'es a durar (P-C 177,1)
>> *Sirventes* answering Guilhem Figueira (P-C 217,2). 2 mss.: *CR*.
>> Editions: **Levy** 74–78. Véran 196–205. Perkal-Balinsky 185–207. **Städtler** in this volume. A. **Rieger,** "Un *sirventes* féminin."

Gräfin von Provence (P-C 187). See Comtessa de Proensa

Guillelma de Rosers

Her partner in the *partimen,* Lanfranc Cigala, flourished around 1235–57 according to Riquer 3:1359. She left Provence to go to Genoa according to an anonymous song (P-C 461,204, ed. Schultz[-Gora], *Die provenzalischen Dichterinnen* 31). Rougiers, canton of Saint-Maximin, arrondissement of Brignoles (Var). Jeanroy 1:374; Bogin 177–78.
> Na Guillelma, maint cavalher aratge (P-C 200,1)
>> *Partimen* with Lanfranc Cigala (= P-C 282,14). 6 mss.: *IKMOPa¹*. *Razo* in Boutière-Schutz 571–75.

Editions: Schultz–Gora 27. Véran 144–48. **Branciforti** 172–80. Bogin 134–37. Perkal-Balinsky 96–104.

See also the note on a lost manuscript, below.

H. (Domna)

Fl. 1220–40 according to Schultz[-Gora], *Die provenzalischen Dichterin-nen* 15. Cf. Chambers, item 18. Bogin 178.

Rofin, digatz m'ades de cors (P-C 249a,1)

Partimen with Rofin (= P-C 426,1). 5 mss.: *IKOa¹d*.

Editions: **Schultz–Gora** 25–26. Véran 101–06. Bogin 138–43. Nelli 262–69. Perkal-Balinsky 80–88.

Isabella

First third of the 13th c. according to Jeanroy 1:386; cf. Bertoni, *I trova-tori d'Italia* 130–31. Bogin 173–74.

N'Elias Cairel, de l'amor (P-C 252,1)

Tenso with Elias Cairel (= P-C 133,7). 2 mss.: *Oa¹*.

Editions: Schultz–Gora 22–23. **Bertoni** 471–72. Véran 153–57. Bogin 110–13. Perkal-Balinsky 72–79.

Iselda. See Alais and Iselda

Iseut de Capio

On the date see Almuc de Castelnou; Chapieu, commune of Lanuéjols, arrondissement of Mende (Lozère), according to Jeanroy 1:386. Bogin 165–66.

Domna n'Almucs, si·us plagues (P-C 253,1)

Cobla answered by Almuc de Castelnou (P-C 20,2). 1 ms.: *H +* κ. *Razo* in Boutière-Schutz 422–24.

Editions: Schultz–Gora 25. Véran 72–73. **Boutière-Schutz** 422–24. Bogin 92–93. Nelli 247–49. Perkal-Balinsky 129–32.

Lombarda

Attested in a charter of 1206 (Chabaneau, *Biographies* 279 n. 4); ex-changed *coblas* with Bernart Arnaut, Count of Armagnac 1219–26 (Jeanroy 1:343). The *vida* says she was from Toulouse (Boutière-Schutz 416–19). Jeanroy 1:394; Bogin 174–75.

> Nom volgr'aver per Bernard Na Bernarda (P-C 288,1)
>
>> *Coblas* answering Bernart Arnaut (P-C 54,1). 1 ms.: $H + \kappa$.
>>
>> Editions: Schultz-Gora 22. Véran 90–92. Boutière-Schutz 416–19. Bogin 114–17. Perkal-Balinsky 89–95. **Perkal-Balinsky**'s text trans. by **Sankovitch** in this volume. **Kay** in this volume.
>
> See also the note on a lost manuscript, below.

Maria de Ventadorn

Wife of Eble V, Count of Ventadorn; died shortly after 1225 according to Jeanroy 1:396. Ruins of the castle of Ventadorn are near Moustier-Ventadour (canton of Egletons, arrondissement of Tulle, Corrèze). Stronski, *Légende amoureuse* 41–44; Bogin 168–69.

> Gui d'Uisel, be·m peza de vos (P-C 295,1)
>
>> *Partimen* with Gui d'Ussel (= P-C 194,9). 9 mss.: *ACDEHPRTa¹* + κ. *Razo* in Boutière-Schutz 212–14.
>>
>> Editions: Schultz-Gora 21. **Audiau** 73–75. Véran 138–402. Bogin 98–101. Perkal-Balinsky 60–67.

Tibors

First half of the 13th c. according to Jeanroy 1:430. Her *vida* (Boutière-Schutz 498–99) says she was from *Sarenom,* that is Séranon, canton of Saint-Auban, arrondissement of Grasse (Alpes-Maritimes). Tibors is named as the judge of a *partimen* (P-C 449,1, ed. Mahn, *Werke* 3:213), and again by Guiraut d'Espanha (P-C 244,12, ed. Hoby). Bogin 162–63.

> Bels dous amics, ben vos puosc en ver dir (P-C 440,1)
>
>> Fragmentary *canso*. 1 ms.: $H + \kappa$.
>>
>> Editions: Schultz-Gora 25. Véran 76–77. **Boutière-Schutz** 498–99. Bogin 80–81. Perkal-Balinsky 161–63.

Anonymous Trobairitz

> A l'entrade del tens clar (P-C 461,12)
>
>> *Balada.* 1 ms.: *X*.
>>
>> Edition: **Appel**, *Chrestomathie* 86.

Ab lo cor trist environat d'esmay (P-C 461,2)

> *Planh*. 2 mss.: *a;* Barcelona, Bibl. Centr., 1744 (fol. 6v).
>
> Edition: **Stengel** vii.

Amics, en gran consirier (P-C 46,3)

> *Tenso* with Raimbaut d'Aurenga (P-C 389,6), sometimes attributed without sufficient grounds to the Comtessa de Dia. 3 mss.: *CDM*.
>
> Editions: Schultz-Gora 28–29. Kussler-Ratyé 169–74. Véran 177–81. Pattison 155–58. **Riquer** 1: 452–54. Bogin 146–51. Perkal-Balinsky 105–13.

Auzir cugei lo chant e·l crit e·l glat (P-C 231,1)

> *Tenso* with Guillem Rainol d'At. 4 mss.: *D^aHIK*.
>
> Edition: **Kolsen**, *Trobadorgedichte* 37–40.

Bela domna, si·us platz (P-C 15a,1)

> *Tenso* with Albert de Saint Bonet; only the first line is preserved. 1 ms.: *B*.
>
> Edition: P-C.

Bella, tant vos ai prejada (P-C 392,7)

> See below: Domna, tant vos ai preiada.

Bona domna, d'una re que·us deman (P-C 87,1)

> *Tenso* with Bertran del Pojet. 8 mss.: *CDIKOSTa¹*.
>
> Edition: **De Lollis** 708–10.

Bona domna, tan vos ai fin coratge (P-C 461,56)

> *Tenso* by two Anonymous Trobairitz. 1 ms.: *R*.
>
> Editions: Selbach, *Streitgedicht* 102. **Schultz-Gora** 29–30. Véran 107–11. Bogin 152–55. Perkal-Balinsky 138–44.

Bona domna, un conseill vos deman (P-C 372,4)

> *Tenso* with Pistoleta. 8 mss.: *D^aIKLORS^gT*.
>
> Editions: **Niestroy** 65. Véran 79–84. Perkal-Balinsky 114–22.

Coindeta sui, si cum n'ai greu cossire (P-C 461,69)

> *Balada*. 1 ms.: *Q*.
>
> Editions: **Appel**, *Chrestomathie* 86. Véran 61–64. Perkal-Balinsky 180–84.

Dieus sal la terra e·l pa[is] (P-C 461,81)

> *Cobla*. 1 ms.: *H*.
>
> Editions: Kolsen, "25" 289, 303–04. **Zufferey** in this volume.

Domna, a vos me coman (P-C 296,1a)

> *Tenso* with Marques. 1 ms.: *R*.

Edition: **Bertoni** 469–70.

Domna, per vos estauc en greu tormen (P-C 10,23)

> *Tenso* with Aimeric de Peguilhan. 10 mss.: *CDIKLMNRfα*.

Edition: **Shepard/Chambers** 133–36.

Domna, quar conoissens'e sens (P-C 409,3)

> *Tenso* with Raimon de las Salas. 5 mss.: *DᵃIKLd*.

Edition: **Chambers** 37–40.

Domna, tant vos ai preiada (P-C 392,7)

> *Tenso* of a Genoese lady with Raimbaut de Vaqueiras. 4 mss.: *DᵃIKa¹*.

Edition: Linskill 98–107. **Riquer** 2:816–19.

En un vergier sotz fuella d'albespi (P-C 461,113)

> *Alba*. 1 ms.: *C*.

Editions: Appel, *Chrestomathie* 90. Véran 68–70. **Riquer** 3: 1695–96. Hamlin 117–18. Perkal-Balinsky 176–79.

Eu veing vas vos, segner, fauda levada (P-C 306,2)

> *Tenso* with Montan. 2 mss.: *IT*.

Edition: Cluzel 160–62. Nelli 200–03. **Bec**, *Burlesque* 161–64.

No·m pois mudar, bels amics, q'en chantanz (P-C 451,2)

> *Cobla* answered by Uc Catola (?). 1 ms.: *Dᵃ*.

Editions: Bartsch, *Chrestomathie* 59–60. **Dejeanne** 219–20.

No·m puesc mudar no digua mon veiaire (P-C 404,5)

> *Sirventes* attributed in ms. to Raimon Jordan. 1 ms.: *C + α¹α²*.

Editions: Kjellman 61–63. **Riquer** 1:576–77. Perkal-Balinsky 208–12.

Per joi que d'amor m'avegna (P-C 461,191)

> See **Castelloza**.

Quan vei les praz verdesir (P-C 461,206)

> *Canso*. 1 ms.: *W*.

Editions: **Bartsch**, *Chrestomathie* 249–52. Véran 64–67. Perkal-Balinsky 170–75.

Quant aug chantar lo gal sus en l'erbos (P-C 231,4)

> *Tenso* with Guilhem Rainol d'At. 4 mss.: *DᵃHIK*.

Editions: Kolsen, *Dichtungen* 61–66. **Riquer** 3:1240–42.

Quant lo gilos er fora (P–C 461,201)

> *Balada*. 1 ms.: Q.

Edition: **Appel**, *Chrestomathie* 85.

Si·m fos grazitz mos chans, eu m'esforsera (P–C 409,5)

> *Tenso* with Raimon de las Salas. 4 mss.: D*ª*IKd.

> Editions: Schultz-Gora 30. **Chambers,** "Raimon de las Salas" 43–46. Bogin 156–59. Perkal-Balinsky 123–28.

Un guerrier, per alegrar (P–C 269,1)

> *Tenso* with Joan de Pennas. 1 ms.: *f*.

Edition: **Bartsch**, *Chrestomathie* 353–56.

NOTE ON A LOST MANUSCRIPT

In 1836 Félix Torres Amat, bishop of Astorga, included the following entry among the anonymous works catalogued in his *Memorias para ayudar a formar un diccionario crítico de los escritores catalanes,* published in Barcelona by J. Verdaguer (p. 711):

> RECULL *de trobadóras provenzals:* "Nadalayda de Porcaragues, Na-Lombarda, Na-Guilleuma de Rosen, la Comptesa de dia." MS. en fol. de la bib. real.

This entry was reproduced by Riquer, *Trovadores* 1:14, note 5.

Unfortunately no such manuscript was included by J. Massó Torrents, *Manuscritos catalanes de la biblioteca de S[u] M[ajestad]* (Barcelona: Verdaguer, 1888), or by J. Domínguez Bordona, *Catálogo de los manuscritos catalanes de la Biblioteca Nacional* (Madrid: Blass, 1931). In response to my inquiries, representatives of the Biblioteca Nacional (Teresa Simarro Martinez, letter of 1 November 1987) and of the Biblioteca de Palacio (Consolación Morales, letter of 28 October 1987) have been unable to report any further trace of such a collection.

In a personal letter of 29 April 1988, Martín de Riquer has informed me that he is convinced that the manuscript exists, but that it is not, today, in the Biblioteca del Rey de España, del Palacio de Oriente de Madrid. It may be among the uncatalogued manuscripts of the Biblioteca Universitaria de Salamanca, to which certain holdings of the Biblioteca del Rey were transferred in 1954, or among those of the Biblioteca Nacional.

Bibliography

Abbreviations

FEW: Wartburg, Walther von. *Französisches Etymologisches Wörterbuch.* Bonn: Klopp, etc., 1928—.

LR: Raynouard, François-Just-Marie. *Lexique roman ou dictionnaire de la langue des troubadours.* 6 vols. Paris: Silvestre, 1844.

P-C: Pillet, Alfred, and Henry Carstens. *Bibliographie der Troubadours.* Halle: Niemeyer, 1933.

PD: Levy, Emil. *Petit dictionnaire provençal-français.* Heidelberg: Winter, 1909.

SW: Levy, Emil, and Carl Appel. *Provenzalisches Supplement-Wörterbuch.* 8 vols. Leipzig: Reisland, 1894–1924.

Studies of the Trobairitz

Albert-Birot, Arlette. "Du côté de Clara d'Anduze." *Mélanges de littérature du moyen âge et du XXe siècle offerts à Mademoiselle Jeanne Lods.* 2 vols. Paris: Ecole Normale Supérieure de Jeunes Filles, 1978. 1:19–27.

Bec, Pierre. "'Trobairitz' et chansons de femme: Contribution à la connaissance du lyrisme féminin au Moyen Age." *Cahiers de civilisation médiévale* 22 (1979): 235–62.

———. "Trobairitz occitanes et chansons de femme françaises." *Perspectives médiévales* 5 (1979): 59–76.

Bénétrix, Paul. *Les femmes troubadours: Notes d'histoire littéraire.* Agen: Lenthéric, 1889.

Bertoni, Giulio. "Il vestito della trovatrice Castelloza." *Archivum romanicum* 1 (1917): 228–30.

Blakeslee, Merritt R. "La chanson de femme, les *Héroïdes,* et la *canso* occitane à voix de femme: Considérations sur l'originalité des *trobairitz.*" Forthcoming in *"Farai chansoneta nueva . . .": Essais sur la liberté créatrice (XIIe–XIIIe s.). Mélanges . . . Jean Charles Payen.* Ed. Jean-Louis Backès et al.

Bruckner, Matilda Tomaryn. "Na Castelloza, *Trobairitz,* and the Troubadour Lyric." *Romance Notes* 25 (1985): 239–53.

Brunel, Clovis. "Almois de Châteauneuf et Iseut de Chapieu." *Annales du Midi* 28 (1916): 462–71.

Chabaneau, Camille. "Sur un vers de Na Gormonda." *Revue des langues romanes* 19 (1881): 303–04.

Desazars, Baron. "Les premières femmes lettrées à Toulouse." *Revue des Pyrénées* 23 (1911): 56–91.

Dronke, Peter. "The Provençal *Trobairitz:* Castelloza." In *Medieval Women Writers.* Ed. Katharina M. Wilson. Athens: University of Georgia Press, 1984. 131–52.

Faucheux, Christian. "Etude sémantique et syntaxique de l'oeuvre de la Comtesse de Die." *Signum* 1.1 (1974): 1–17 and 1.2 (1974): 5–16.

Gégou, Fabienne. "En lisant les *vidas* . . . Lumière nouvelle sur les *trobairitz.*" *Marche romane* 33 (1983): 101–07.

———. "*Trobairitz* et amorces romanesques dans les 'Biographies' des troubadours." In *Studia occitanica in memoriam Paul Remy.* Ed. Hans-Erich Keller. Vol. 2. Kalamazoo, Michigan: Medieval Institute Publications, 1986. 43–51.

Giraudon, Liliane, and Jacques Roubaud, eds. *Les trobairitz: Les femmes dans la lyrique occitane. Action poétique* 75 (1978).

Hölzle, Peter. "Der abenteuerliche Umgang der Irmtraud Morgner mit der Trobairitz Beatriz de Dia." In *Mittelalter-Rezeption: Gesammelte Vorträge des Salzburger Symposions 'Die Rezeption mittelalterlicher Dichter und ihrer Werke in Literatur, bildender Kunst und Musik des 19. und 20. Jahrhunderts.'* Ed. Jürgen Kühnel, Hans-Dieter Mück, Ulrich Müller. Göppinger Arbeiten zur Germanistik, 286. Göppingen: Kümmerle, 1979. 430–45.

Huchet, Jean-Charles. "Les femmes troubadours ou la voix critique." *Littérature* 51 (1983): 59–90.

Jeanroy, Alfred. "Les femmes poètes dans la littérature provençale aux XIIe et XIIIe siècles." In *Mélanges de philologie offerts à Jean-Jacques Salverda de Grave.* Groningen: Wolters, 1933. 186–91.

———. *La poésie lyrique des troubadours.* 2 vols. Toulouse: Privat, and Paris: Didier, 1934. New York: AMS, 1974. 1:311–17.

Kasten, Ingrid. "Weibliches Rollenverständnis in den Frauenliedern Reinmars und der Comtessa de Dia." *Gallo-Romanisches Monatsschrift* 37 no. 2 (1987): 131–46.

Kristeva, Julia. *Histoires d'amour.* Paris: Denoël, 1983.

Kussler-Ratyé, G. "Sur un passage de Alaisina Iselda et Carenza." *Archivum romanicum* 1 (1917): 227.

Malinowski, J. "Dormunda, dame quercynoise, poète du XIIIe siècle." *Bulletin de la Société des études littéraires, scientifiques et artistiques du Lot* 6 (1880): 5–19.

Monier, Janine. "Essai d'identification de la comtesse de Die." *Bulletin de la Société d'archéologie et de statistique de la Drôme* 75 (1962): 265–78.

Paden, William D. "*Utrum copularentur:* Of *cors.*" *Esprit créateur* 19.4 (1979): 70–83.

Poe, Elizabeth Wilson. "Another *salut d'amor?* Another *trobairitz?* In Defense of *Tanz salutz et tantas amors*" [P–C 42a,1]. Forthcoming in *Zeitschrift für romanische Philologie* 105 (1989).

Rieger, Angelica. "'Ins e·l cor port, dona, vostra faisso.' Image et imaginaire de la femme à travers l'enluminure dans les chansonniers de troubadours." *Cahiers de civilisation médiévale* 28 (1985): 385–415.

———. "Un *sirventes* féminin: la *trobairitz* Gormonda de Monpeslier." *Actes du premier congrès international de l'Association Internationale d'Etudes Occitanes.* Ed. Peter T. Ricketts. London: A.I.E.O., 1987. 423–55.

Rieger, Dietmar. "Die französische Dichterin im Mittelalter: Marie de France— die 'trobairitz'—Christine de Pisan." In *Die Französische Autorin vom Mittelalter bis zur Gegenwart.* Ed. Renate Baader and Dietmar Fricke. Wiesbaden: Akademische Verlagsgesellschaft Athenaion, 1979. 29–48.

———. "Die *trobairitz* in Italien: Zu den altprovenzalischen Dichterinnen." *Cultura neolatina* 31 (1971): 205–23.

Robbins, Kittye Delle. "Woman/Poet: Problem and Promise in Studying the 'Trobairitz' and Their Friends." *Encomia* 1.3 (1977): 12–14.

Sakari, Aimo. "A propos d'Azalaïs de Porcairagues." *Mélanges de philologie romane dédiés à la mémoire de Jean Boutière.* 2 vols. Liège: Soledi, 1971. 1:517–28.

Santy, Sernin. *La Comtesse de Die: Sa vie, ses oeuvres complètes, les fêtes données en son honneur, avec tous les documents.* Paris: Picard, 1893.

Schultz[-Gora], Oscar. "Nabieiris de roman." *Zeitschrift für romanische Philologie* 15 (1891): 234–35.

Shapiro, Marianne. "The Provençal *Trobairitz* and the Limits of Courtly Love." *Signs* 3 (1978): 560–71.

Städtler, Katharina. "Altprovenzalische Frauendichtung: Sozialhistorische Untersuchungen und Interpretationen." Diss. Universität Augsburg 1986. Forthcoming from Heidelberg: Winter, 1989.

Stronski, Stanislaw. "Garsende, comtesse de Provence, trobairitz." *Revue des langues romanes* 50 (1907): 22–27.

———. *La légende amoureuse de Bertran de Born.* Paris: Champion, 1914.

Tavera, Antoine. "A la recherche des troubadours maudits." *Senefiance* 5 (1978): 135–62.

Editions of the Trobairitz

Bec, Pierre, ed. "Avoir des enfants ou rester vierge? Une tenson occitane du XIIIe siècle entre femmes" [P–C 12,1]. *Mittelalterstudien: Erich Köhler zum Gedenken.* Heidelberg: Winter, 1984. 21–30.

Bogin, Meg. *The Women Troubadours*. New York: Paddington Press, 1976. New York: Norton, 1980. French translation by Jeanne Faure-Cousin with the collaboration of Anne Richou. *Les femmes troubadours*. Paris: Denoël/Gonthier, 1978. Catalan trans. Montserrat Abelló and Alfred Badia. *Les trobairitz: Poetes occitanes del segle XII*. Col.lecció Clàssiques Catalanes 3–4. Barcelona: LaSal, 1983.

Camproux, Charles. Review of Bogin, *The Women Troubadours*. *Revue des langues romanes* 83 (1977): 417–26.

Crescini, Vincenzo. "Azalais d'Altier." *Zeitschrift für romanische Philologie* 14 (1890): 128–32.

Dejeanne, Jean-Marie-Lucien. "Les coblas de Bernart-Arnaut d'Armagnac et de Dame Lombarda." *Annales du Midi* 18 (1906): 63–68.

Kussler-Ratyé, Gabrielle. "Les chansons de la Comtesse Béatrix de Dia." *Archivum romanicum* 1 (1917): 161–82.

Levy, Emil. Review of Schultz[-Gora], *Die provenzalischen Dichterinnen*. *Literaturblatt für germanische und romanische Philologie* 5 (1889): 178–84.

Lore, Priscilla Metz. "Carnival and Contradiction: The Poetry of the Women Troubadors." *DAI* 47 (1987): 2577A. University of California, San Diego, 1986.

Paden, William D., with Julia C. Hayes, Georgina M. Mahoney, Barbara J. O'Neill, Edward J. Samuelson, Jeri L. Snyder, Edwina Spodark, Julie A. Storme, and Scott D. Westrem, eds. "The Poems of the *Trobairitz* Na Castelloza." *Romance Philology* 35 (1981): 158–82.

Perkal-Balinsky, Deborah. "The Minor *Trobairitz:* An Edition with Translation and Commentary." *DAI* 47 (1987): 2577A. Northwestern University, 1986.

Rieger, Angelica. *Die liebende Frau als lyrisches Ich in der altokzitanischen höfischen Lyrik: Edition des Gesamtkorpus*. To appear 1989.

Sakari, Aimo. "Azalais de Porcairagues, le Joglar de Raimbaut d'Orange." *Neuphilologische Mitteilungen* 50 (1949): 23–43, 56–87, 174–98.

Schultz[-Gora], Oscar, ed. *Die provenzalischen Dichterinnen. Biographien und Texte nebst Anmerkungen und einer Einleitung*. Leipzig: Fock, 1888. Genève: Slatkine, 1975. Also published in *Einundachtzigste Nachricht von dem Friedrichs-Gymnasium zu Altenburg*. Altenburg: Oskar Bonde, 1888. 1–36.

Stanton, Domna C., ed. *The Defiant Muse: French Feminist Poems from the Middle Ages to the Present*. New York: Feminist Press, 1986.

Véran, Jules, ed. *Les poétesses provençales du moyen âge et de nos jours*. Paris: A. Quillet, [1946].

Selected Studies of Women in Medieval Literature and Society

Allen, Sister Prudence, R.S.M. *The Concept of Woman: The Aristotelian Revolution, 750 BC–AD 1250*. Montréal: Eden Press, 1985.

Alverny, Marie-Thérèse d'. "Comment les théologiens et les philosophes voient la femme." *Cahiers de civilisation médiévale* 20 (1977): 105–29.

Aurell i Cardona, Martí. "La détérioration du statut de la femme aristocratique en Provence (Xe-XIIIe siècles)." *Le Moyen Age* 91 (1985): 6–32.

———. "La famille de Porcelet et l'aristocratie provençale (972-1320)." Thèse de 3ème cycle, Université de Provence, 1983.

———. *Une famille de la noblesse provençale au moyen âge: Les Porcelet.* Avignon: Aubanel, 1986.

Azzolina, Liborio. "La Compiuta Donzella di Firenze." *Antologia Siciliana* 9 (1902): 3–42.

Bergert, Fritz. *Die von den Troubadours genannten oder gefeierten Damen.* Beihefte zur Zeitschrift für romanische Philologie, 46. Halle: Niemeyer, 1913.

Bezzola, Reto R. "La transformation des mœurs et le rôle de la femme dans la classe féodale du XIe au XIIe siècle." *Les origines et la formation de la littérature courtoise en Occident (500-1200).* Paris: Champion, 1960. Part 2, vol. 2, pp. 461–85.

Biller, P. P. A. "Birth-control in the West in the Thirteenth and Early Fourteenth Centuries." *Past and Present* no. 94 (1982): 3–26.

Borgognoni, Adolfo. "La condanna capitale d'una bella signora." *Studi d'erudizione e d'arte* 2 (1878): 89–105.

———. "Rimatrici italiane dei primi tre secoli." In his *Studi di letteratura storica.* Bologna: Zanichelli, 1891. 161–202.

Burns, E. Jane. "The Man Behind the Lady in Troubadour Lyric." *Romance Notes* 25 (1985): 254–70.

Casey, Kathleen. "The Cheshire Cat: Reconstructing the Experience of Medieval Women." In *Liberating Women's History: Theoretical and Critical Essays.* Ed. Berenice A. Carroll. Urbana: University of Illinois Press, 1976. 224–49.

Chiari, A. "La Compiuta Donzella." In his *Indagini e letture* . Florence: Le Monnier, 1954. 1–7.

Dronke, Peter. *Women Writers of the Middle Ages: A Critical Study of Texts from Perpetua (†203) to Marguerite Porete (†1310).* Cambridge: Cambridge University Press, 1984.

Duby, Georges. *Le chevalier, la femme et le prêtre: Le mariage dans la France féodale.* Collection Pluriel. Paris: Hachette, 1981. Trans. Barbara Bray. *The Knight, the Lady and the Priest: The Making of Modern Marriage in Medieval France.* New York: Pantheon, 1983.

———. *Medieval Marriage: Two Models from Twelfth-Century France.* Trans. Elborg Forster. Baltimore: Johns Hopkins University Press, 1978.

Duhamel-Amado, Claudie. "Une forme historique de la domination masculine: Femme et mariage dans l'aristocratie languedocienne à la fin du XIIe siècle." *Cahiers d'histoire de l'Institut de Recherches Marxistes* 6 (1981): 125–39.

Egidi, F. "La Compiuta Donzella e i 'fedeli d'amore.'" *Rivista Letteraria* 10 (1938): 18–25.

Erickson, Carolly, and Kathleen Casey. "Women in the Middle Ages: A Working Bibliography." *Mediaeval Studies* 37 (1975): 340–59.

Farmer, Sharon. "Persuasive Voices: Clerical Images of Medieval Wives." *Speculum* 61 (1986): 517–43.

Ferrante, Joan M. "The Education of Women in the Middle Ages in Theory, Fact, and Fantasy." In *Beyond Their Sex: Learned Women of the European Past*. Ed. Patricia H. Labalme. New York: New York University Press, 1980. 9–42.

———. "Male Fantasy and Female Reality in Courtly Literature." *Women's Studies* 11 (1984): 67–97.

———. *Woman as Image in Medieval Literature From the Twelfth Century to Dante*. New York: Columbia University Press, 1975. Durham, North Carolina: Labyrinth Press, 1985.

Fossier, Robert. "La femme dans les sociétés occidentales." *Cahiers de civilisation médiévale* 20 (1977): 93–104.

Gold, Penny Schine. *The Lady and the Virgin: Image, Attitude and Experience in Twelfth-Century France*. Chicago: University of Chicago Press, 1985.

Gramain-Derruau, Monique. "Villages et communautés villageoises en Bas Languedoc occidental (vers 950—vers1350): l'exemple biterrois." Unpublished thesis for the Doctorat ès lettres, Université de Paris I, 1979. Report on the defence by Tricard, J. "Les villages du Biterrois au moyen âge." *Annales du Midi* 92 (1980): 120–26.

Gravdal, Kathryn. "Camouflaging Rape: The Rhetoric of Sexual Violence in the Medieval Pastourelle." *Romanic Review* 76 (1985): 361–73.

Herlihy, David. "Did Women Have a Renaissance? A Reconsideration." *Medievalia et Humanistica* 13 (1985): 1–22.

Kamuf, Peggy. "Marriage Contracts: The Letters of Heloise and Abelard." *Fictions of Feminine Desire: Disclosures of Heloise*. Lincoln: University of Nebraska Press, 1982. 1–43.

Kelly, Joan. "Did Women Have a Renaissance?" In *Becoming Visible: Women in European History*. Ed. Renate Bridenthal and Claudia Koonz. Boston: Houghton Mifflin, 1977. Reprt. in *Women, History and Theory: The Essays of Joan Kelly*. Chicago: University of Chicago Press, 1984. 19–50.

Kirshner, Julius, and Suzanne F. Wemple, eds. *Women of the Medieval World*. Oxford: Blackwell, 1985.

Krueger, Roberta L., and E. Jane Burns. "A Selective Bibliography of Criticism: Women in Medieval French Literature." *Romance Notes* 25 (1985): 375–90.

Leclercq, Jean. *La femme et les femmes dans l'oeuvre de Saint Bernard*. Paris: Téqui, 1983.

Lejeune, Rita. "La femme dans les littératures française et occitane du XIe au XIIIe siècle." *Cahiers de civilisation médiévale* 20 (1977): 201–17.

Leube-Fey, Christiane. *Bild und Funktion der dompna in der Lyrik der Trobadors*. Heidelberg: Winter, 1971.

Lucas, Angela M. *Women in the Middle Ages: Religion, Marriage, and Letters*. New York: St. Martin's Press, 1983.

McLaughlin, Mary Martin. "Survivors and Surrogates: Children and Parents from the Ninth to the Thirteenth Centuries." In *The History of Child-*

hood. Ed. Lloyd deMause. New York: Psychohistory Press, 1974. 101–81.

Mazzoni, Francesco. "I fedeli d'amore e la Compiuta Donzella." In *Almae luces, malae cruces*. Bologna: Zanichelli, 1941. 149–56.

Morewedge, Rosemarie Thee, ed. *The Role of Woman in the Middle Ages*. Albany: State University of New York Press, 1975.

Moroldo, Arnaldo. "Le portrait dans la poésie lyrique de langue d'oc, d'oïl, et de si, au XIIe et XIIIe siècle." *Cahiers de civilisation médiévale* 26 (1983): 147–67, 239–50.

Mundy, John H. "Le mariage et les femmes à Toulouse au temps des Cathares." *Annales: Economies, Sociétés, Civilisations* 42 (1987): 117–34.

Nelli, René, ed. *Ecrivains anticonformistes du moyen-âge occitan : I. La femme et l'amour*. Paris: Phébus, 1977.

Otis, Leah Lydia. *Prostitution in Medieval Society: The History of an Urban Institution in Languedoc*. Chicago: University of Chicago Press, 1985.

Paden, William D., with Mireille Bardin, Michèle Hall, Patricia Kelly, F. Gregg Ney, Simone Pavlovich, and Alice South. "The Troubadour's Lady: Her Marital Status and Social Rank." *Studies in Philology* 72 (1975): 28–50.

Pelaez, M. Review of Azzolina. *Kritischer Jahresbericht* 7.2 (1902–03): 248–50.

Power, Eileen. *Medieval Women*. Ed. M. M. Postan. Cambridge: Cambridge University Press, 1975.

Rajna, Pio. "Gaia da Camino." *Archivio Storico Italiano* Fifth series, 9 (1892): 284–96.

Shahar, Shulamith. *The Fourth Estate: A History of Women in the Middle Ages*. Trans. Chaya Galai. London: Methuen, 1983.

Stuard, Susan Mosher. *Women in Medieval Society*. Philadelphia: University of Pennsylvania Press, 1976.

———, ed. *Women in Medieval History and Historiography*. Philadelphia: University of Pennsylvania Press, 1987.

Switten, Margaret. "Marie de Montpellier: La femme et le pouvoir en Occitanie au douzième siècle." In *Actes du premier congrès international de l'Association Internationale d'Etudes Occitanes*. Ed. Peter T. Ricketts. London: A.I.E.O., 1987. 485–91.

Verdon, Jean. "Notes sur la femme en Limousin vers 1300." *Annales du Midi* 90 (1978): 319–29.

Wilson, Katharina M., ed. *Medieval Women Writers*. Athens: University of Georgia Press, 1984.

Zumthor, Paul. "Héloïse et Abelard." *Revue des Sciences Humaines* 91 (1958): 313–32.

Other Works Cited

Abel, Elizabeth. Preface. In *Writing and Sexual Difference*. Ed. E. Abel. Chicago: University of Chicago Press, 1980.

Alexandre, Pierre. "Les variations climatiques au Moyen Age (Belgique, Rhé-
nanie, Nord de la France)." *Annales: Economies, Sociétés, Civilisations* 32
(1977): 183–97.

Allacci, Leone. *Poeti antichi raccolti ai codici mss. della Biblioteca Vaticana e Barberi-
niana da Monsignor Leone Allacci e da lui dedicati alla Accademia della Fucina
della Nobile et esemplare città di Messina.* Naples: Sebastiano d'Alecci, 1661.

Almqvist, Kurt, ed. *Poésies du troubadour Guilhem Adémar.* Uppsala: Almqvist &
Wiksell, 1951.

Anglade, Joseph, ed. *Las Leys d'Amors: Manuscrit de l'Académie des Jeux Floraux.* 4
vols. Bibliothèque Méridionale, série 1, tomes 17–20. Toulouse: Privat,
1919–20.

————. "Les miniatures des chansonniers provençaux." *Romania* 50 (1924):
593–604.

————, ed. *Poésies de Peire Vidal.* 2d ed. Paris: Champion, 1923.

————. *Les troubadours: Leurs vies, leurs oeuvres, leur influence.* Paris: Colin, 1908.

Appel, Carl, ed. *Bernart von Ventadorn: Seine Lieder.* Halle: Niemeyer, 1915.

————, ed. *Provenzalische Chrestomathie.* 6th ed. Leipzig, 1930. Hildesheim:
Olms, 1971.

————. "Zu Marcabru." *Zeitschrift für romanische Philologie* 43 (1923): 403–69.

Audiau, Jean, ed. *Les poésies des quatre troubadours d'Ussel.* Paris, 1922. Genève:
Slatkine, 1973.

Avalle, D'Arco Silvio, ed. *Peire Vidal, Poesie.* 2 vols. Milano: Ricciardi, 1960.

Barbieri, Francesco Maria. *Dell'origine della poesia rimata.* Ed. Girolamo Tiraboschi. Modena: Società tipografica, 1790.

Bartsch, Karl, ed. *Chrestomathie Provençale.* 6th ed. entièrement refondue par
Eduard Koschwitz. Marburg, 1904. New York: AMS, 1973.

————. Review of Levy, *Guilhem Figueira. Zeitschrift für romanische Philologie* 4
(1880): 438–43.

Bec, Pierre, ed. *Burlesque et obscénité chez les troubadours: Pour une approche du
contre-texte médiéval.* Paris: Stock, 1984.

Bertacchi, G., ed. *Dante da Maiano: Rime.* Bergamo: Istituto Italiano d'Arti Grafiche, 1896.

Bertoni, Giulio. *Il Duecento.* Milan: Vallardi, 1910.

————. "Noterelle provenzali." *Revue des langues romanes* 55 (1912): 92–103.

————. *I trovatori d'Italia.* Modena: Orlandini, 1915. Roma: Società Multigrafica
Editrice, 1967.

Bettarini, R., ed. *Dante da Maiano: Rime.* Florence: Le Monnier, 1969.

Biagi, G., G. L. Passerini, and E. Rostagno, eds. *La Divina Commedia nella figu-
razione artistica e nel secolare commento: Purgatorio.* Turin: UTET, 1931.

Bloch, R. Howard. *Etymologies and Genealogies: A Literary Anthropology of the
French Middle Ages.* Chicago: University of Chicago Press, 1983.

Boase, Roger. *The Origin and Meaning of Courtly Love: A Critical Study of European Scholarship.* Manchester: Manchester University Press, 1977.

Boni, Marco, ed. *Sordello: le poesie.* Bologna: Palmaverde, 1954.

Bonnet, Marie-Jo. *Un choix sans équivoque: Recherches historiques sur les relations
amoureuses entre les femmes, XVIe–XXe siècle.* Paris: Denoël, 1981.

Boswell, J. *Christianity, Social Tolerance & Homosexuality. Gay People in Western Europe from the Beginning of the Christian Era to the Fourteenth Century.* Chicago: University of Chicago Press, 1980.

Boutière, Jean, ed. *Les poésies du troubadour Peire Bremon Ricas Novas.* Toulouse: Privat, 1930.

Boutière, Jean, and Alexander Herman Schutz, eds. *Biographies des troubadours.* 2d ed. Rev. by Jean Boutière and Irénée-Marcel Cluzel. Paris: Nizet, 1964. Rprt. 1973.

Bradley, Sister Ritamary. "Backgrounds of the Title *Speculum* in Mediaeval Literature." *Speculum* 29 (1954):100–15.

Branciforti, Francesco, ed. *Il canzoniere di Lanfranco Cigala.* Firenze: Olschki, 1954.

Brochier, Jacques-Elie. "Deux mille ans d'histoire du climat dans le Midi de la France: Etude sédimentologique." *Annales: Economies, Sociétés, Civilisations* 38 (1983): 425–38.

Brunel, Clovis. *Bibliographie des manuscrits littéraires en ancien provençal.* Paris: Droz, 1935.

Brunel-Lobrichon, Geneviève. "Le chansonnier provençal conservé à Béziers." In *Actes du premier congrès international de l'Association Internationale d'Etudes Occitanes.* Ed. Peter T. Ricketts. London: A.I.E.O., 1987. 139–47.

Bullough, Vern L. *Homosexuality: A History.* New York: New American Library, 1979.

Burckhardt, Jacob. *The Civilization of the Renaissance in Italy.* New York: Modern Library, 1954. First published in 1860.

Burrows, Toby. "Unmaking 'The Middle Ages.'" *Journal of Medieval History* 7 (1981): 127–34.

Camproux, Charles. *Le joy d'amor des troubadours.* Montpellier: Causse et Castelnau, 1965.

Cantù, Cesare. *Storia universale.* Turin: Unione tipografico-editrice, 1851.

Cathala-Coture, Antoine de. *Histoire politique, ecclésiastique et littéraire du Querci.* 3 vols. Montauban: Cazaméa, 1785.

Chabaneau, Camille. "Les biographies des troubadours en langue provençale." *Histoire générale de Languedoc.* Vol. 10. Toulouse: Privat, 1885. 209–412.

———. *Notes sur quelques manuscrits provençaux perdus ou égarés, suivis de deux lettres inédites de Pierre de Chasteuil-Gallaup.* Paris: Maisonneuve et frères et C. Leclerc, 1886. [= *Revue des langues romanes* 21 (1882): 209–17; 23 (1883): 5–22, 70–80, 115–29; 26 (1884): 209–18; 27 (1885): 43–46; 28 (1885): 72–88, 259–82.]

Chabaneau, Camille, and Joseph Anglade, eds. *Jehan de Nostredame: Les vies des plus célèbres et anciens poètes provençaux.* Paris: Champion, 1913. Rprt. Genève: Slatkine, 1970.

Chambers, Frank M. *Proper Names in the Lyrics of the Troubadours.* University of North Carolina Studies in the Romance Languages and Literatures, 113. Chapel Hill: University of North Carolina Press, 1971.

———. "Raimon de las Salas." In *Essays in Honor of Louis Francis Solano.* Ed.

Raymond J. Cormier and Urban T. Holmes. Studies in the Romance Languages and Literatures, 92. Chapel Hill: University of North Carolina Press, 1970. 29–51.

Chaytor, H.J. *The Troubadours of Dante*. Oxford: Clarendon Press, 1902.

Cluzel, Irénée-Marcel. "Le troubadour Montan." In *Mélanges d'histoire littéraire, de linguistique et de philologie romane offerts à Charles Rostaing*. Liège: Association des Romanistes, 1974. 153–64.

Contini, G. *Poeti del Duecento*. Milan-Naples: Ricciardi, 1960.

Crescimbeni, G. M. *Dell'historia della volgar poesia*. Venice: Lorenzo Baseggio, 1730. First edition 1698.

Croce, Benedetto. *Conversazioni critiche*. 3d series. Bari: Laterza, 1932.

Cropp, Glynnis M. *Le vocabulaire courtois des troubadours de l'époque classique*. Genève: Droz, 1975.

Curtius, E. R. *European Literature and the Latin Middle Ages*. Trans. Willard R. Trask. New York: Harper Torchbooks, 1953.

Davenson, Henri [pseudonym of Henri-Irénée Marrou]. *Les Troubadours*. Paris: Seuil, 1961.

De Bartholomaeis, Vincenzo, ed. *Poesie provenzali storiche relative all'Italia*. 2 vols. Roma: Istituto Storico Italiano, 1931.

De Lollis, Cesare. "Appunti dai MSS Provenzali Vaticani." *Revue des langues romanes* 33 (1889): 157–93.

———. "Di Bertran del Pojet trovatore dell'età angioina." In *Miscellanea di studi critici edita in onore di Arturo Graf*. Bergamo: Istituto Italiano d'arti grafiche, 1903. 691–710.

Del Monte, Alberto, ed. *Peire d'Alvernhe: Liriche*. Torino: Loescher-Chiantore, 1955.

Dejeanne, Jean-Marie-Lucien, ed. *Poésies complètes du troubadour Marcabru*. Toulouse: Privat, 1909. New York: Johnson, 1971.

Derrida, Jacques. *De la grammatologie*. Paris: Editions de Minuit, 1967. Trans. Gayatri Chakravorty Spivak. *Of Grammatology*. Baltimore: Johns Hopkins University Press, 1976.

De Sanctis, F. *Storia della letteratura italiana*. Bari: Laterza, 1925. First edition 1870–71.

Diez, Friedrich. *Leben und Werke der Troubadours*. 2. vermehrte Auflage von Karl Bartsch. Leipzig: Barth, 1882. Hildesheim: Olms, 1965.

Dragonetti, Roger. *La technique poétique des trouvères dans la chanson courtoise: Contribution a l'étude de la rhétorique médiévale*. Brugge: Tempel, 1960.

Dronke, Peter. *Medieval Latin and the Rise of European Love-Lyric*. 2d ed. 2 vols. Oxford: Clarendon Press, 1968.

Emiliani Giudici, Paolo. *Storia della letteratura italiana*. Florence: Le Monnier, 1853.

Enciclopedia biografica e bibliografica italiana. Series VI: *Poetesse e scrittrici*. Ed. Maria Bandini Buti. Rome: E.B.B.I., 1942.

Foster, Jeannette Howard. *Sex Variant Women in Literature*. New York: Vantage Press, 1956. Baltimore: Diana Press, 1975.

Frank, István. *Répertoire métrique de la poésie des troubadours.* 2 vols. Paris: Champion, 1953–57.

Gatien-Arnoult, Adolphe Félix, ed. *Monumens de la littérature romane.* 4 vols. Toulouse: Paya, 1841–49.

Gauchat, Louis, and H. Kehrli. "Il canzoniere provenzale H." *Studj di filologia romanza* 5 (1891): 341–568.

Giovanni da Seravalle. *Fratri Johannis de Serravalle . . . translatio et comentum totius libri Dantis Aldigheri.* Prato: Giacchetti, 1891.

Godefroy, Frédéric. *Dictionnaire de l'ancienne langue française et de tous ses dialectes du IXe au XVe siècle.* 10 vols. Paris: Vieweg, etc., 1881–1902.

Goldin, Frederick. *The Mirror of Narcissus in the Courtly Love Lyric.* Ithaca: Cornell University Press, 1967.

Gonfroy, Gérard. "Les grammairiens occitano-catalans du moyen âge et la dénomination de leur langue." *La Licorne* 1980 no. 4, 47–76.

Gouiran, Gérard, ed. *L'amour et la guerre: L'oeuvre de Bertran de Born.* 2 vols. Aix-en-Provence: Publications de l'Université de Provence, 1985.

Grabmann, M. *Die Geschichte der scholastischen Methode.* 2 vols. Freiburg, 1909–11. Rprt. Darmstadt: Wissenschaftliche Buchgesellschaft, 1961.

Grundmann, Herbert. "Litteratus-illiteratus: Der Wandel einer Bildungsnorm vom Altertum zum Mittelalter." *Archiv für Kulturgeschichte* 40 (1958): 1–65.

Gschwind, Ulrich, ed. *Le roman de Flamenca.* Romanica Helvetica, 86A-86B. Berne: Francke, 1976.

Guarnieri, Gino. *Da Porto Pisano a Livorno città.* Pisa: Giardini, 1967.

Gubar, Susan. "The Blank Page and Issues of Female Creativity." In *Writing and Sexual Difference.* Ed. E. Abel. Chicago: University of Chicago Press, 1980. 73–93.

Guida, Saverio, ed. *Il trovatore Gavaudan.* Modena: S.T.E.M.-Mucchi, 1979.

Hagan, P. "The Medieval Provençal 'Tenson': Contribution for the Study of the Dialogue Genre." Diss. Yale University, 1975.

Hamlin, Frank R., Peter T. Ricketts, and John Hathaway, eds. *Introduction à l'étude de l'ancien provençal.* Genève: Droz, 1967. 2d ed. 1985.

Higounet, Charles. "Le milieu social et économique languedocien vers 1200." *Vaudois languedociens et pauvres catholiques.* Cahiers de Fanjeaux, 2. Toulouse: Privat, 1967. 15–22.

Hill, R. T., and T. G. Bergin, eds. *Anthology of the Provençal Troubadours.* 2 vols. 2d ed. New Haven: Yale University Press, 1973.

Histoire littéraire de la France. Nouvelle édition. 39 vols. Paris, 1865–1962. Rprt. Nendeln, 1973–74.

Hoby, Otto, ed. *Die Lieder des Trobadors Guiraut d'Espanha.* Freiburg (Schweiz): St. Paulus, 1915.

Irigaray, Luce. *Speculum de l'autre femme.* Paris: Minuit, 1974.

Jauss, Hans Robert, and Erich Köhler, eds. *Grundriß der romanischen Literaturen des Mittelalters.* 13 vols. Heidelberg: Winter, 1968—.

Jeanroy, Alfred. *La poésie lyrique des troubadours.* 2 vols. Toulouse: Privat, 1934.

———. Review of Kjellman. *Romania* 50 (1924): 113–17.

———. "Sur la tençon *Car vei fenir a tot dia*" [P-C 112,1]. *Romania* 19 (1890): 394–402.

Jedin, Hubert, ed. *Handbuch der Kirchengeschichte*. Vol. 3, Part 2: *Die mittelalterliche Kirche: Vom kirchlichen Hochmittelalter bis zum Vorabend der Reformation*. 2d ed. Freiburg: Herder, 1973.

Jones, Ann Rosalind. "Writing the Body. Toward an Understanding of l'Ecriture féminine." In *The New Feminist Criticism*. Ed. Elaine Showalter. New York: Pantheon, 1985. 361–77.

Kay, Sarah. "Two Readings of the *Lai de l'Ombre*." *Modern Language Review* 75 (1980): 515–27.

Kjellman, Hilding, ed. *Le troubadour Raimon-Jordan vicomte de Saint-Antonin*. Uppsala: Almqvist & Wiksell, 1922.

Klein, Karen Wilk. *The Partisan Voice: A Study of the Political Lyric in France and Germany, 1180–1230*. The Hague: Mouton, 1971.

Köhler, Erich. "Zum Verhaltnis von *vers* und *canso*." *Études de philologie romane et d'histoire littéraire offertes à Jules Horrent*. Liège: n.p., 1980. 205–11.

Kolsen, Adolf, ed. *Dichtungen der Trobadors*. 3 vols. Halle: Niemeyer, 1916–19.

———, ed. "25 bisher unedierte provenzalische Anonyma." *Zeitschrift für romanische Philologie* 38 (1917): 281–310.

———, ed. *Sämtliche Lieder des Trobadors Giraut de Bornelh*. 2 vols. Halle: Niemeyer, 1910–35. Genève: Slatkine, 1976.

———, ed. *Trobadorgedichte*. Halle: Niemeyer, 1925.

———, ed. *Zwei provenzalische Sirventese nebst einer Anzahl Einzelstrophen*. Halle: Niemeyer, 1919.

Kuster, H. J., and R. J. Cormier. "Old Views and New Trends: Observations on the Problem of Homosexuality in the Middle Ages." *Studi medievali* 3rd ser. 25 (1984): 587–610.

Labande, Léon Honoré. *Avignon au XIIIe siècle*. Paris: Picard, 1908.

Lavaud, René, ed. *Poésies complètes du troubadour Peire Cardenal*. Toulouse: Privat, 1957.

Lavaud, René, and the Duc de la Salle de Rochemaure, eds. *Les troubadours cantaliens: XIIe-XXe siècles*. Aurillac: Imprimerie Moderne, 1910.

Lavaud, René, and René Nelli, trans. *Les troubadours: Jaufre, Flamenca, Barlaam et Josaphat*. N.p.: Desclée de Brouwer, 1960.

Lavis, Georges. *L'expression de l'affectivité dans la poésie lyrique du Moyen Age (XIIe et XIIIe siècle)*. Paris: Belles Lettres, 1972.

Lawner, Lynne. "Marcabru and the Origins of *Trobar Clus*." In *Literature and Western Civilisation*. Ed. D. Daiches and A. Thorlby. 2: *The Mediaeval World*. London: Aldus, 1973. 485–523.

Lazar, Moshé. *Amour courtois et fin'amors dans la littérature du XIIe siècle*. Paris: Klincksieck, 1964.

———, ed. *Bernard de Ventadour: Chansons d'amour*. Paris: Klincksieck, 1966.

Lejeune, Rita. "Les allusions à Merlin dans la littérature occitane (XIIe–XIIIe siècles)." *Bulletin bibliographique de la Société internationale arthurienne* 12 (1960): 128.

Levy, Emil, ed. *Guilhem Figueira, ein provenzalischer Troubadour*. Berlin: Lie-
    brecht, 1880.
Limentani, Alberto. *L'eccezione narrativa: La Provenza medievale e l'arte del racconto*.
    Torino: Einaudi, 1977.
Linskill, Joseph, ed. *The Poems of the Troubadour Raimbaut de Vaqueiras*. The
    Hague: Mouton, 1964.
Lipking, Lawrence. "Aristotle's Sister: A Poetics of Abandonment." *Critical In-
    quiry* 10 (1983): 61–81.
Lote, Georges. *Histoire du vers francais*. 3 vols. Paris: Boivin, 1949–55.
Mahn, Carl August Friedrich, ed. *Die Werke der Troubadours in provenzal-
    ischer Sprache*. 4 vols. Berlin: Duemmler, 1846–86. Genève: Slatkine,
    1977.
Mansi, Jean Dominique, et al., eds. *Sacrorum Conciliorum nova et amplissima collec-
    tio*. Editio novissima. 53 vols. Florence: Zatta, etc. 1758–1927.
Marchello-Nizia, Christiane. "Amour courtois, société masculine et figures du
    pouvoir." *Annales: Economies, Sociétés, Civilisations* 36 (1981): 969–82.
Marshall, J. H., ed. *The 'Razos de trobar' of Raimon Vidal and associated texts*. Ox-
    ford: Oxford University Press, 1972.
Martin-Chabot, E., ed. *La chanson de la croisade albigeoise*. 1: *La chanson de Guil-
    laume de Tudèle*. 3d ed. Paris: Belles Lettres, 1976.
Massi, Francesco. *Saggio di rime illustri inedite del secolo XIII scelte da un codice antico
    della Biblioteca Vaticana*. Rome: Tip. delle Belle arti, 1840.
Massó Torrents, Jaime. *Repertori de l'antiga literatura catalana: La poesia*. Barcelona:
    Alpha, 1932.
Meneghetti, Maria Luisa. *Il pubblico dei trovatori: ricezione e riuso dei testi lirici cortesi
    fino al XIV secolo*. Modena: Mucchi, 1984.
Menocal, María Rosa. "The Etymology of Old Provençal *trobar, trobador:* A Re-
    turn to the 'Third Solution.' " *Romance Philology* 36 (1982): 137–48.
Meyer, Paul, ed. *Les derniers troubadours de la Provence*. Paris: Franck, 1871. Rprt.
    Genève: Slatkine, 1973.
Mölk, Ulrich. *Trobar clus, trobar leu. Studien zur Dichtungstheorie der Trobadors*.
    München: Fink, 1968.
Mongitore, A. *Bibliotheca Sicula sive de scriptoribus siculis*. Palermo: A. Feli-
    cella, 1714.
Monson, Don Alfred. *Les Ensenhamens occitans: Essai de définition et de délimita-
    tion du genre*. Paris: Klincksieck, 1981.
Muller, Charles. *Initiation à la statistique linguistique*. Paris: Larousse, 1968.
Nichols, Stephen G., Jr. and John A. Galm, with A. Bartlett Giamatti, Roger J.
    Porter, Seth L. Wolitz, and Claudette M. Charbonneau, eds. *The Songs
    of Bernart de Ventadorn*. University of North Carolina Studies in the Ro-
    mance Languages and Literatures, 39. Chapel Hill: University of North
    Carolina Press, 1962.
Nicholson, Derek E. T., ed. *The Poems of the Troubadour Peire Rogier*. Manchester:
    Manchester University Press, 1976.
Niestroy, Erich, ed. *Der Trobador Pistoleta*. Beihefte zur Zeitschrift für ro-
    manische Philologie, 52. Halle: Niemeyer, 1914.

Nostredame, Jean de. *Les vies des plus célèbres et anciens poètes provençaux.* Lyon, 1575. Hildesheim: Olms, 1971.

Paden, William D., ed. *The Medieval Pastourelle.* 2 vols. Garland Library of Medieval Literature, 34A-35A. New York: Garland, 1987.

———. "The Role of the Joglar in Troubadour Lyric Poetry." In *Chrétien de Troyes and the Troubadours: Essays in Memory of the Late Leslie Topsfield.* Ed. Peter S. Noble and Linda M. Paterson. Cambridge: St. Catharine's College, 1984. 90–111.

Paden, William D., Tilde Sankovitch, and Patricia H. Stäblein, eds. *The Poems of the Troubadour Bertran de Born.* Berkeley: University of California Press, 1986.

Paris, Gaston. "Lancelot du Lac, II. *Le Conte de la Charrette.*" *Romania* 12 (1883): 459–534.

Paris, Louis, ed. *La chronique de Raims.* Paris: Techener, 1837.

Paterson, Linda M. *Troubadours and Eloquence.* Oxford: Clarendon Press, 1975.

Pattison, Walter T. *The Life and Works of the Troubadour Raimbaut d'Orange.* Minneapolis: University of Minnesota Press, 1952.

Pickens, Rupert T. "Jaufre Rudel et la poétique de la mouvance." *Cahiers de civilisation médiévale* 20 (1977): 323–37.

———. *The Songs of Jaufre Rudel.* Studies and Texts, 41. Toronto: Pontifical Institute of Medieval Studies, 1978.

Poe, Elizabeth Wilson. "The Lighter Side of the *Alba: Ab la genser que sia.*" *Romanistisches Jahrbuch* 36 (1985): 87–103.

———. "New Light on the Alba: A Genre Redefined." *Viator* 15 (1984): 139–50.

Pound, Ezra. *Personae.* New York: New Directions, 1926.

Quadrio, F. S. *Della storia e della ragione di ogni poesia.* Bologna: F. Pisarri, 1739–44.

Radcliff-Umstead, Douglas, ed. *Human Sexuality in the Middle Ages and Renaissance.* Pittsburgh: Center for Medieval and Renaissance Studies, 1978.

Rajna, Pio. "Un serventese contro Roma ed un canto alla vergine." *Giornale di filologia romanza* 1 (1878): 84–91.

Rand, E. K. Editor's Preface. *Speculum* 1 (1926): 3–4.

Raupach, Manfred, ed. "Elias Fonsalada: Kritische Ausgabe." *Zeitschrift für romanische Philologie* 90 (1974): 141–73.

Rigolot, François. *Poétique et onomastique.* Genève: Droz, 1977.

Riquer, Martin de. *Los trovadores: Historia literaria y textos.* 3 vols. Barcelona: Planeta, 1975.

Rochegude, Henri-Pascal, ed. *Le Parnasse occitanien.* Toulouse, 1819. Rprt. Genève: Slatkine, 1977.

Roscher, Helmut. *Papst Innocenz III. und die Kreuzzüge.* Göttingen: Vandenhoeck u. Ruprecht, 1969.

Roubaud, Jacques. *Les troubadours: Anthologie bilingue.* Paris: Seghers, 1971.

Rouillan-Castex, Sylvette. "L'amour et la société féodale." *Revue historique* 272 (1984): 295–329.

Sainte-Palaye, Jean Baptiste de la Curne de. *Histoire littéraire des troubadours.* 3 vols. Paris, 1774. Genève: Slatkine, 1967.

Sakari, Aimo. *Poésies du troubadour Guillem de Saint-Didier.* Mémoires de la Société Néophilologique de Helsinki, 19. Helsinki: Société Néophilologique, 1956.

Sansone, Giuseppe E., ed. *La poesia dell'antica Provensa: Testi e storia dei trovatori.* Biblioteca della Fenice, 50. Milano: Guanda, 1984.

———, ed. *Testi didattico-cortesi di Provenza.* Bari: Adriatica, 1977.

Santangelo, S. "Appunti sulle lettere di Guittone d'Arezzo." Reprinted in his *Saggi Critici.* Modena: STEM, 1959. 275–90. First published 1907.

Schutz, A. H., ed. *Poésies de Daude de Pradas.* Bibliothèque Méridionale, 1re série, 22. Toulouse: Privat, 1933.

Selbach, Ludwig. *Das Streitgedicht in der altprovenzalischen Lyrik.* Ausgaben und Abhandlungen, 57. Marburg: Elwert, 1886.

Serper, A. *Huon de Saint-Quentin, poète satirique et lyrique: Etude historique et édition de textes.* Studia humanitatis. Madrid: J. Porrúa Turanzas, 1983.

Shepard, William P., and Frank M. Chambers, eds. *The Poems of Aimeric de Peguilhan.* Evanston: Northwestern University Press, 1950.

Siberry, Elizabeth. *Criticism of Crusading 1095–1274.* Oxford: Clarendon Press, 1985.

Siegel, Sidney. *Nonparametric Statistics for the Behavioral Sciences.* New York: McGraw-Hill, 1956.

Smith, Nathaniel B. *Figures of Repetition in the Old Provençal Lyric.* North Carolina Studies in the Romance Languages and Literatures, 176. Chapel Hill: University of North Carolina Department of Romance Languages, 1976.

Smith, Nathaniel B., and Thomas G. Bergin. *An Old Provençal Primer.* New York: Garland, 1984.

Stehling, Thomas, trans. *Medieval Latin Poems of Male Love and Friendship.* New York: Garland, 1984.

Stengel, Edmund. *Die beiden ältesteten provenzalischen Grammatiken.* Marburg: Elwert, 1878.

———. "Die provenzalische Liederhandschrift Cod. 42 der Laurenzianischen Bibliothek in Florenz." *Archiv für das Studium der neueren Sprachen und Literaturen* 50 (1872): 241–84.

Sumption, Jonathan. *The Albigensian Crusade.* London: Faber, 1978.

Switten, Margaret L. "Raimon de Miraval's 'Be m'agrada' and the Unrhymed Refrain in Troubadour Poetry." *Romance Philology* 22 (1969): 432–48.

Thiolier-Méjean, Suzanne. *Les poésies satiriques et morales des troubadours du XIIe siècle à la fin du XIIIe siècle.* Paris: Nizet, 1978.

Thomas, Antoine. *Francesco da Barberino et la littérature provençale en Italie au moyen âge.* Paris: Thorin, 1883.

Throop, P. A. "Criticism of Papal Crusade Policy in Old French and Provençal." *Speculum* 13 (1938): 379–412.

———. *Criticism of the Crusade: A Study of Public Opinion and Crusade Propaganda.* Amsterdam: Swets & Zeitlinger, 1940.

Tiraboschi, Girolamo. *Storia della letteratura italiana.* Florence: Molini, Landini, 1807.

Toja, Gianluigi, ed. *Arnaut Daniel: Canzoni*. Firenze: Sansoni, 1960.

Topsfield, L.T., ed. *Les poésies du troubadour Raimon de Miraval*. Les Classiques d'Oc. Paris: Nizet, 1971.

Trucchi, F. *Poesie italiane inedite de dugento autori*. Prato: Raineri Guasti, 1846.

Valli, L. *Il linguaggio segreto di Dante e dei 'fedeli d'amore.'* Rome: Biblioteca di Filosofia e Scienza, 1928.

Van Vleck, Amelia E. "Style and Stability in Troubadour Lyric of the Classic Period (1160–1180)." *DAI* 44 (1983): 165A. University of California, Berkeley, 1983.

Walsh, P. G., ed. *Andreas Capellanus on Love*. London: Duckworth, 1982.

White, Lynn, Jr. *Medieval Technology and Social Change*. Oxford: Clarendon Press, 1962.

Wiacek, Wilhelmina M. *Lexique des noms géographiques et ethniques dans les poésies des troubadours des XIIe et XIIIe siècles*. Les Classiques d'Oc. Paris: Nizet, 1968.

Wilhelm, James J., ed. *The Poetry of Arnaut Daniel*. New York: Garland, 1981.

Woledge, B. "Old Provençal and Old French." In *Eos: An Enquiry into the Theme of Lovers' Meetings and Partings at Dawn in Poetry*. Ed. Arthur T. Hatto. The Hague: Mouton, 1965. 344–89.

Woolf, Virginia. *A Room of One's Own*. San Diego: Harcourt Brace Jovanovich, 1929.

Zink, Michel. "Musique et subjectivité: Le passage de la chanson d'amour à la poésie personnelle au XIIIe siècle." *Cahiers de civilisation médiévale* 25 (1982): 225–32.

Zufferey, François. *Bibliographie des poètes provençaux des XIVe et XVe siècles*. Publications Romanes et Françaises, 159. Genève: Droz, 1981.

Zumthor, Paul. "De la circularité du chant (à propos des trouvères des XIIᵉ et XIIIᵉ siècles)." *Poétique* 2 (1971): 129–40.

———. *Langue, texte, énigme*. Paris: Seuil, 1975.

———. *Merlin le prophète: Un thème de la littérature polémique de l'historiographie et des romans*. Lausanne, 1943. Rprt. Genève: Slatkine, 1973.

Index

Occitan poems are indexed under the name of the author or under "Anonymous" and the incipit. Information in the Checklist of Poems by the Trobairitz has not been indexed except for reference to the article on each poem.

Contributors

GENEVIÈVE BRUNEL-LOBRICHON, *Attachée à la Section Romane, Institut de Recherche et d'Histoire des Textes, Paris.*

FRANK M. CHAMBERS, *Professor Emeritus of French, University of Arizona.*

PAOLO CHERCHI, *Professor of Italian, University of Chicago.*

JOAN M. FERRANTE, *Professor of English and Comparative Literature, Columbia University.*

SARAH KAY, *Lecturer in French, Girton College, Cambridge University.*

WILLIAM D. PADEN, *Professor of French, Northwestern University.*

ANGELICA RIEGER, *Lecturer in German, University of Paris IV-Sorbonne.*

TILDE SANKOVITCH, *Professor of French, Northwestern University.*

H. JAY SISKIN, *Assistant Professor in French Linguistics, Northwestern University.*

KATHARINA STÄDTLER, *Lecturer in German, University of Abidjan (Ivory Coast).*

JULIE A. STORME, *Assistant Professor of French, Saint Mary's College, Notre Dame, Indiana.*

AMELIA E. VAN VLECK, Assistant Professor of French, University of Texas, Austin.

FRANÇOIS ZUFFEREY, *Professeur de français médiéval, University of Lausanne.*

UNIVERSITY OF PENNSYLVANIA PRESS
MIDDLE AGES SERIES
EDWARD PETERS, *General Editor*

Edward Peters, ed. *Christian Society and the Crusades, 1198–1229.* Sources in Translation, including The Capture of Damietta by Oliver of Paderborn. 1971

Edward Peters, ed. *The First Crusade: The Chronicle of Fulcher of Chartres and Other Source Materials.* 1971

Katherine Fischer Drew, trans. *The Burgundian Code: The Book of Constitutions or Law of Gundobad and Additional Enactments.* 1972

G. G. Coulton. *From St. Francis to Dante: Translations from the Chronicle of the Franciscan Salimbene (1221–1288).* 1972

Alan C. Kors and Edward Peters, eds. *Witchcraft in Europe, 1110–1700: A Documentary History.* 1972

Richard C. Dales. *The Scientific Achievement of the Middle Ages.* 1973

Katherine Fischer Drew, trans. *The Lombard Laws.* 1973

Henry Charles Lea. *The Ordeal.* Part III of Superstition and Force. 1973

Henry Charles Lea. *Torture.* Part IV of Superstition and Force. 1973

Henry Charles Lea (Edward Peters, ed.). *The Duel and the Oath.* Parts I and II of Superstition and Force. 1974

Edward Peters, ed. *Monks, Bishops, and Pagans: Christian Culture in Gaul and Italy, 500–700.* 1975

Jeanne Krochalis and Edward Peters, ed. and trans. *The World of Piers Plowman.* 1975

Julius Goebel, Jr. *Felony and Misdemeanor: A Study in the History of Criminal Law.* 1976

Susan Mosher Stuard, ed. *Women in Medieval Society.* 1976

James Muldoon, ed. *The Expansion of Europe: The First Phase.* 1977

Clifford Peterson. *Saint Erkenwald.* 1977

Robert Somerville and Kenneth Pennington, eds. *Law, Church, and Society: Essays in Honor of Stephan Kuttner.* 1977

Donald E. Queller. *The Fourth Crusade: The Conquest of Constantinople, 1201–1204.* 1977

Pierre Riché (Jo Ann McNamara, trans.). *Daily Life in the World of Charlemagne.* 1978

Charles R. Young. *The Royal Forests of Medieval England.* 1979

Edward Peters, ed. *Heresy and Authority in Medieval Europe.* 1980

Suzanne Fonay Wemple. *Women in Frankish Society: Marriage and the Cloister, 500–900.* 1981

R. G. Davies and J. H. Denton, eds. *The English Parliament in the Middle Ages.* 1981

Edward Peters. *The Magician, the Witch, and the Law.* 1982

Barbara H. Rosenwein. *Rhinoceros Bound: Cluny in the Tenth Century.* 1982

Steven D. Sargent, ed. and trans. *On the Threshold of Exact Science: Selected Writings of Anneliese Maier on Late Medieval Natural Philosophy.* 1982

Benedicta Ward. *Miracles and the Medieval Mind: Theory, Record, and Event, 1000–1215.* 1982

Harry Turtledove, trans. *The Chronicle of Theophanes: An English Translation of anni mundi 6095–6305 (A.D. 602–813).* 1982

Leonard Cantor, ed. *The English Medieval Landscape.* 1982

Charles T. Davis. *Dante's Italy and Other Essays.* 1984

George T. Dennis, trans. *Maurice's Strategikon: Handbook of Byzantine Military Strategy.* 1984

Thomas F. X. Noble. *The Republic of St. Peter: The Birth of the Papal State, 680–825.* 1984

Kenneth Pennington. *Pope and Bishops: The Papal Monarchy in the Twelfth and Thirteenth Centuries.* 1984

Patrick J. Geary. *Aristocracy in Provence: The Rhône Basin at the Dawn of the Carolingian Age.* 1985

C. Stephen Jaeger. *The Origins of Courtliness: Civilizing Trends and the Formation of Courtly Ideals, 939–1210.* 1985

J. N. Hillgarth, ed. *Christianity and Paganism, 350–750: The Conversion of Western Europe.* 1986

William Chester Jordan. *From Servitude to Freedom: Manumission in the Sénonais in the Thirteenth Century.* 1986

James William Brodman. *Ransoming Captives in Crusader Spain: The Order of Merced on the Christian-Islamic Frontier.* 1986

Frank Tobin. *Meister Eckhart: Thought and Language.* 1986

Daniel Bornstein, trans. *Dino Compagni's Chronicle of Florence.* 1986

James M. Powell. *Anatomy of a Crusade, 1213–1221.* 1986

Jonathan Riley-Smith. *The First Crusade and the Idea of Crusading.* 1986

Susan Mosher Stuard, ed. *Women in Medieval History and Historiography.* 1987

Avril Henry, ed. *The Mirour of Mans Saluacioune.* 1987

María Rosa Menocal. *The Arabic Role in Medieval Literary History.* 1987

Margaret J. Ehrhart. *The Judgment of the Trojan Prince Paris in Medieval Literature.* 1987

Betsy Bowden. *Chaucer Aloud: The Varieties of Textual Interpretation.* 1987

Felipe Fernández-Armesto. *Before Columbus: Exploration and Colonization from the Mediterranean to the Atlantic, 1229–1492.* 1987

Michael Resler, trans. *EREC by Hartmann von Aue*. 1987

A. J. Minnis. *Medieval Theory of Authorship*. 1987

Uta-Renate Blumenthal. *The Investiture Controversy: Church and Monarchy from the Ninth to the Twelfth Century*. 1988

Robert Hollander. *Boccaccio's Last Fiction: "Il Corbaccio."* 1988

Ralph Turner. *Men Raised from the Dust: Administrative Service and Upward Mobility in Angevin England*. 1988

David Anderson. *Before the Knight's Tale: Imitation of Classical Epic in Boccaccio's Teseida*. 1988

Charlotte A. Newman. *The Anglo-Norman Nobility in the Reign of Henry I: The Second Generation*. 1988

Joseph F. O'Callaghan. *The Cortes of Castile-León, 1188–1350*. 1989

William D. Paden. *The Voice of the Trobairitz: Essays on the Women Troubadours*. 1989

William Chester Jordan. *The French Monarchy and the Jews: From Philip Augustus to the Last Capetians*. 1989

Edward B. Irving, Jr. *Rereading* Beowulf. 1989

David Burr. *Olivi and Franciscan Poverty: The Origins of the* Usus Pauper *Controversy*. 1989

Willene B. Clark and Meradith McMunn, eds. *Beasts and Birds of the Middle Ages: The Bestiary and Its Legacy*. 1989

Richard C. Hoffmann. *Land, Liberties, and Lordship in a Late Medieval Countryside: Agrarian Structures and Change in the Duchy of Wrocław*. 1989

Robert I. Burns. *Emperor of Culture: Alfonso X the Learned and His Thirteenth-Century Renaissance*. 1989

Mary Frances Wack. *The Lover's Malady in the Middle Ages: The "Viaticum" and Its Commentaries*. 1989